SAS: The First Secret wars

The Unknown Years of Combat

& Counter-Insurgency

Tim Jones

I.B. TAURIS

LONDON · NEW YORK

Dedicated to: Pauline & Ray

& Howie & Ed

Tis strange - but true; for truth is always strange;

Stranger than fiction: if it could be told.

Byron - *Don Juan*

Paperback edition published in 2010 by I.B.Tauris & Co Ltd
6 Salem Road, London W2 4BU
175 Fifth Avenue, New York NY 10010
www.ibtauris.com

Distributed in the United States and Canada Exclusively by Palgrave Macmillan
175 Fifth Avenue, New York NY 10010

First published in 2005 by I.B.Tauris & Co Ltd

ISBN: 978 1 84885 566 3

A full CIP record for this book is available from the British Library
A full CIP record is available from the Library of Congress

Library of Congress Catalog Card Number: available

Printed and bound in India by Thomson Press India Ltd

Contents

Acknowledgements

I wish to thank the military historians and writer/researchers on the SAS, Tony Kemp, Gordon Stevens and Peter Darman - who pointed me in the right direction. Many thanks also to the staffs of various institutions who helped me, especially the Public Record Office of England & Wales, Kew, Middlesex; the Liddell Hart Centre for Military Archives, King's College, London; the British Library, London; the Ministry of Defence Old Whitehall Library, London; the Imperial War Museum, London; the India Office Library and Records, London; the Airborne Forces Museum, Southsea, Hampshire; the National Army Museum, London; Churchill College, Cambridge; and the National Library of Wales, Aberystwyth. Additionally, I was assisted by the staffs of the University of London Senate House Library, London; the British Library of Political and Economic Science, L.S.E., London; the University of Liverpool Library; the Liverpool Hope University College Library; and Flintshire County Reference Library, Mold.

I especially want to thank the Trustees of the Liddell Hart Centre for Military Archives, King's College, London; the Montgomery Collections Committee of the Trustees of the Imperial War Museum, London; and The Master, Fellows and Scholars of Churchill College in the University of Cambridge, for permission to utilise and/or quote from copyright papers in their ownership and care. Many thanks to the Trustees of the Imperial War Museum for their kind permission to reproduce all the photographs from their collection featured in the photo section of this book.

I received valuable assistance too from the late Lt.-Col. Ian F. 'Tanky' Smith, and Lt-Col. Keith Edlin and the SAS Regimental Association; the Adjutant, Ministry of Defence Garrison, Hereford; Jason Mavrikis of Total Defence and Security, Athens, Greece; H.W. Foot, the Honorary Archivist of the Museum of Army Flying, Middle Wallop; and Major D.A. Lewis, Regimental Archivist of the Grenadier Guards. I also received invaluable help from the late Brig. J. Mike Calvert; Lt.-Col. David G.C. 'Dinky' Sutherland; the Right Honourable the Earl Jellicoe; the late Maj. Alastair McGregor; Col. John Waddy; General Sir John 'Shan' Hackett; Maj. Michael Ward; Col. the Honourable C.M. Woodhouse; Sgt. Sid Dowland; and Philip Warner. Others who loaned a hand were John Thomas; Alastair Massie; the Ministry of

Defence, London, and Hayes, Middlesex; the *Daily Telegraph*; John Murray Publishers, London; Frank Cass Publishers, London; Kate and all at IB Tauris Publishers, London; Johnny Cooper of Lycabettus Press, Athens; Mr. W. Duggan, Curator of the Museum of Army Transport; Lt.-Gen. I. Kirochristos, and Maj.-Gen. D. Gedeon, the Director/Deputy Director of the Hellenic Army General Staff Army History Directorate, Athens, Greece; the Royal Artillery Historical Trust; Zeno's Books, London; Dr. Richard Aldrich; Mr. Alexander Zervoudakis; Dr. Tim Moreman; Mrs. R. Keep; Mrs. R. Bennett; Mrs. E. Martinage; and Ed, Ade, Mark, Bill, Og and Andy, who also gave me their views about the project, Dave, Jake, Steff, Miffy and Joel on the tech front, and especially Howy for helping to prepare the manuscript for publication.

Abbreviations

AAC	Army Air Corps
AATDC	Army Airborne Transport Development Centre
AG	War Office Adjutant-General
AMFOGE	Allied Mission For Observation Of the Greek Elections
ASC(G)	Allied Screening Commission (Greece)
BATT	British Army Training Team
BEF	British Expeditionary Force
BIT	British Instruction Team
BLO	British Liaison Officer
BLU	British Liaison Unit
BMA	British Military Administration
BMM(G)	British Military Mission (Greece)
BMRC	British Military Reparations Committee
BPPM	British Police and Prisons Mission, Greece
BTG	British Troops, Greece
CAT	Chinese Assault Team
CIA	Central Intelligence Agency
CID	Criminal Investigation Department, police
CIGS	Chief of the Imperial General Staff
CINC	Commander in Chief
CINCFELF	Commander in Chief, Far East Land Forces
CINCMELF	Commander in Chief, Middle East Land Forces
CMSWC	Commando, Mountain and Snow Warfare Centre
C.O.	Commanding Officer
CO	Colonial Office
COIN	Counter-insurgency
COS	Chiefs of Staff
CQB	Close-quarter battle
CTC	Combined Training Centre, Volos, Greece
DL/AW	War Office Directorate of Land/Air Warfare

DMI	WO Directorate of Military Intelligence
DMO	WO Directorate of Military Operations
DMT	WO Directorate of Military Training
DPA	WO Directorate of Personnel Administration
DSD	WO Directorate of Staff Duties
DSE	Democratic Army of Greece
DTI	WO Directorate of Tactical Investigation
EAM	National Liberation Front, Greece
EDES	National Democratic Greek League
ELAS	National Popular Liberation Army, Greece
FELF	Far East Land Forces
FO	Foreign Office
GOC	General Officer Commanding
GGS	Greek General Staff
GNA	Greek National Army
GRCC	Greek Reconstruction Claims Committee
GRF	Greek Raiding Forces
GSS	Greek Sacred Squadron
IRA	Irish Republican Army
I.S.	Internal Security
IZL	National Military Organisation, Palestine
JGF	Jungle Guerilla Force
JPS	Joint Planning Staff
JUSMAPG	Joint United States Military Advisory and Planning Group
KKE	Communist Party of Greece
LFG	Land Forces Greece
LHI	Fighters for the Freedom of Israel
LRDG	Long Range Desert Group
LRPG	Long Range Penetration Group/Chindits
MCP	Malayan Communist Party
MCU	Mobile Control Unit
MEBRM	Military Establishment, British Reparations Mission
MEF	Middle East Forces

MELF	Middle East Land Forces
MI9	Military Intelligence, section 9
MI(R)	WO Military Intelligence (Research)
MPABA	Malayan Peoples' Anti-British Army
MPAJA	Malayan Peoples' Anti-Japanese Army
MPF	Malayan Police Force
MRLA	Malayan Races Liberation Army
OC	Officer commanding/in-charge
PMF	Police Mobile Force, Palestine
PPF	Palestine Police Force
RAF	Royal Air Force
RAFDG	RAF Delegation to Greece
RAMC	Royal Army Medical Corps
RASC	Royal Army Service Corps
RE/ME	Royal Engineers/Electrical and Mechanical Engineers
RHAF	Royal Hellenic Air Force
RUC	Royal Ulster Constabulary
SAS	Special Air Service
SBS	Special Boat Section/Squadron/Service (as opposed to the Royal Marines Special Boat Sections)
SCAPP	WO Standing Committee on Army Post-war Problems
SEP	Surrendered Enemy Personnel
SHAEF	Supreme HQ, Allied Expeditionary Force
SIS	Secret Intelligence Service, or MI6
SNS	Special Night Squad
SOE	Special Operations Executive
SOP	Standard Operating Procedure
SRG	Special Recce Group
TA	Territorial Army
UN	United Nations
UNRRA	United Nations Relief and Rehabilitation Administration
URM	United Resistance Movement
WO	War Office

Preface

This study – the culmination of over 10 years of research – is not an 'official' history of the Special Air Service Regiment [SAS]. The classic accounts of the world's leading special forces unit are Philip Warner's official history, *The SAS*; Major-General John Strawson's officially-backed *The History Of The SAS Regiment*; and Tony Geraghty's approved text, *Who Dares Wins*. However, while conducting doctoral research on the British Army in the early post-war years - when it engaged in a dozen or so campaigns against rebels and insurgents across the globe - it became clear that there was a vital gap in the history of the SAS Regiment between 1945 and 1951. Other works have revealed the involvement of former SAS personnel in Palestine, and of serving SAS soldiers in Malaya. But next to nothing has been written about the Greek Civil War, nor about developments in the UK and Middle East at this time. Yet, they are critical to the overall history of the SAS, whose very existence and current role cannot be understood properly without reference to them. This book reveals what went on from the end of the Second World War up to the Establishment of the Malayan Scouts (SAS) - which laid the foundations for the modern SAS Regiment. The highly sensitive nature of these developments, coupled with the passage of time, means that a complete account cannot be written, but enough is now known to gain a new insight into the SAS's secret history.

I received considerable help in this project from the Regiment and numerous former members, as well as scrutiny of the draft text, for which I am most grateful. All those with whom I was in touch were as intrigued as me by the idea that, contrary to the received wisdom, the SAS was not killed off at the end of the War and then resurrected for counter-insurgency in Malaya, in 1950. Ventures involving very few people, who were instructed to neither discuss their work nor retain written records about it, means that fragmentary evidence has had to be pieced together. Nonetheless, sufficient has been uncovered to provide a revised SAS history, and this would not have been possible but for the help of the individuals and institutions listed on the following pages.

Introduction

Dare all to win all

I n the last decade, there has been an avalanche of books about the world's leading and most respected special force - the Special Air Service Regiment - and various associated 'elite forces'. These works range from reprints of classic memoirs about the exploits of David Stirling's men in World War Two to the role of the Regiment in recent conflicts, such as Bosnia and Sierra Leone. There have even been books about SAS wives and a lampoon of the whole genre, *Who Cares Who Wins?*. It seems that anything remotely or even purportedly connected with the soldiers who sport the Winged Dagger badge will sell, including Ranulph Fiennes' *The Feathermen* and Paul Bruce's fictional *The Nemesis File*.[1] It's become the norm that, whenever and wherever there's a news story in which the possibility of a special forces deployment is raised, the SAS are always the first to be mentioned, viz the 'War on Terrorism' and Iraq. Even Hollywood grants the Regiment a revered status above all others (except, perhaps, the SIS's James Bond). An almost insatiable appetite has developed among the public for anything connected with the SAS,[2] and sales have been fuelled by the fact that it is rightly a 'closed', secretive organisation.

Histories of the SAS

Any exposure or insight into the SAS's covert activities is greeted with great public interest, and its role in various post-war counter-terrorist incidents and counter-insurgency [COIN] campaigns has been well documented (see my *Postwar Counterinsurgency And The SAS*). There are numerous accounts of deployments to the jungles of Malaya, Borneo and Brunei, the deserts and mountains of Oman, the streets and hills of Northern Ireland, and dramatic hostage rescues like Mogadishu.[3] The ever watchful news media have reported about the actions of the SAS or its former members in places like Gambia, Colombia, Guatemala, Rwanda, Botswana, Kenya, the Seychelles, Namibia, Angola, Mozambique, Peru, Sri Lanka, Papua New Guinea, Yugoslavia, Albania, Sierra Leone and Equatorial Guinea, to name but a few. Some clandestine missions are touched upon in the official history by Philip Warner[4] and in approved texts like those by Major-General John Strawson and Tony Geraghty.[5] But, as Gen. Strawson points out, it is in the nature of things that "many of the SAS's activities are unofficial"; in other words, operations that are authorised but not acknowledged by the powers-that-be, to whom deniability of knowledge about them is a useful political tool.[6] Consequently, it is extremely difficult to uncover details about such ventures, and this applies equally to SAS activities during the early post-war years - when, by most accounts, the Regiment was not even supposed to exist.

When studying SAS endeavours after half a century and more, there is bound to be some difficulty unearthing undisclosed information. Still, in recent years, some gaps in the Regiment's early history, since its formation in 1941 by Lt. (later Col. Sir Angus) David Stirling and his colleagues (see my *SAS: Zero Hour*) have been filled, notably in studies by the former Royal Marine James D. Ladd, the journalist Jack Ramsay and, especially, by the military historian Anthony Kemp.[7] Yet, despite the growing number of popular histories of the SAS,[8] scant attention has been paid to the crucial period from 1945 to 1951, when the SAS is supposed to have been expunged, only to "miraculously" rise from the dead in order to fight 'Communist Terrorists' during the Malaya Emergency. There has been an almost universal, unquestioning acceptance of the historical 'facts' about the birth of the modern SAS during the early Cold War years, and a dearth of fresh critical historical analysis of it. This study will show that, in reality, it was not just a matter of 'luck' that the SAS survived the cull of the British Army's Corps and Regiments during the seminal years immediately after World War Two.[9] Rather, the SAS has an untold history only hinted at to date - one that shines a whole new light on the Regiment's founders and the way that they decided to "dare all to win all", to save the SAS.[10]

It is not surprising that there has been very little scrutiny of the SAS's pastimes in the years up to 1951 by either military historians and writers or by members of the Regiment itself. It has been assumed, understandably, that the Malayan Scouts were created simply to meet the need for a counter-guerilla special force, and that some of the SAS's old hands were best placed to do this. This legend has been repeated *ad infinitum* in the literature, most notably by Philip Warner, whose influential official history of 1971 glosses over the five years from October 1945. He merely asserts that, on 8th. October 1945, the 1st. and 2nd. (British) SAS Regiments disbanded and, in a nutshell, "that was that".[11] Given that Warner's book was proclaimed to be "the first complete official history of the SAS Regiment, 1941-1971", this version of events has been repeated umpteen times and is the established, accepted official version. Among the works that reiterated the story were those by Gen. Strawson, the authorised biography of David Stirling by Alan Hoe (himself an SAS soldier), a "definitive analysis of the elite regiment" by the historians Craig Philip (who worked with the SAS) and Alex Taylor, and "complete" histories by another SAS man, Keith Connor, and Adrian Weale.[12] Tony Kemp's version of events differs slightly, placing the British SAS Regiments' final parades on 5th. October, while Tony Geraghty and others date their disbandment to the end of November. But, as one other writer has pointed out (albeit within a footnote in a little known book about military medals and awards), the SAS was not entirely disbanded at the end of 1945.[13] There is far more to the phoenix-like reappearance of the SAS than has been appreciated, and its official disbandment lasted for only a few months (without hindering the SAS's continued operation in the shadows).

In addition, another incorrect but widely cherished myth ought to be dispelled: that "it took an unusual war to resurrect the SAS" - namely, the counter-insurgency in Malaya.[14] This episode undoubtedly played a critically important part in the SAS's history, allowing it to develop its counter-guerilla expertise and to demonstrate to the British Army 'establishment' (its upper echelons) the value of retaining special forces within the military.[15] But, to argue that Malaya alone was "the experience upon which the post-war SAS was built",[16] ignores several other crucial, though generally overlooked, factors. Philip Warner correctly notes that, "had there been no Malaya there could have been no Oman operation", hence no Borneo 'Claret' operations, and so on.[17] But, as will be seen, had there been no Greek Civil War in the late 1940s, and an SAS involvement there (as well as other crucial contemporary developments elsewhere), the formation of an SAS force for Malaya would have been far less likely, making the Regiment's long term future that more uncertain.

Putting two and two together

In 1991, I submitted my doctoral thesis on British counter-insurgency policies and doctrine between 1945 and 1952. This focused on Britain's campaigns in Palestine, Greece and Malaya. Soon after, a new paperback by Tony Kemp, *The SAS At War, 1941-45*, intrigued and excited me by revealing that some SAS soldiers went to Greece after the Second World War, and that a number became "tangled up in the Greek Civil War there".[18] This was the first reference to an SAS presence in Greece following its liberation, and the arrival of a British Expeditionary Force (which included some of the SAS's brothers-in-arms, the Special Boat Squadron [SBS]). It shone new light on my doctoral research, which had uncovered a British covert COIN assistance programme in Greece that, by 1946, actively assisted the Greek authorities against the Communist insurgents. By that autumn, a British Military Mission to Greece [BMM(G)] came up with the far-sighted and inventive idea of setting up a counter-guerilla special force, dubbed 'Commandos'.[19] In view of the prevailing thinking and attitudes of leading BMM(G) officers - who were traditionalists and cautious in their COIN approach - and also of the involvement of British Commandos and the SBS/SAS in Greece during the War, I had wondered whether such a ground-breaking concept was floated by British special forces operatives working in Greece in 1946. But I had found no evidence of this. Tony Kemp's work provided a fresh impetus to my ongoing enquiries and, although the SAS's presence in Greece may on the face of it appear puzzling, it made perfect sense in the light of my research.

The British government was determined to support the strategically important post-war Greek government, and clandestine military aid was one way to help it at a time of great instability and uncertainty for Greece. But, the British had to be extremely careful not to give Stalin or any of Greece's neighbouring Communist leaders an excuse to send 'volunteers' to assist their Greek comrades in the fight against 'capitalist imperialism', as per Spain in the 1930s. This meant that everything must be done to prevent any leaks about covert British activities, making it unlikely that any written records of such an enterprise would be extant - especially given past and present political sensitivities in Greece about this traumatic period of its history. The war between 1945 and 1949 raged with a savagery only matched since by the Bosnian conflict of 1992-95, claiming up to 150,000 lives. Hence, Britain's active involvement on the Hellenic 'Royalist' side could touch raw nerves among the Greek Left (and, in reaction to this, on the Right). The Greek Civil War is now long forgotten by most people outside the Balkans (including the news media, which referred to Bosnia as the first civil war in Europe since 1945), but memories in Greece are long and often bitter.

British public records for the Greek entanglement from 1945 have been heavily 'weeded' by the censors of the War Office and other involved Departments of State. Others remain closed till 2022 or later (a 75-year closure indicating documents of a particularly sensitive and potentially embarrassing nature). Greek accounts of this period are kept behind closed doors too and they shall remain so for the foreseeable future.

The available public record is, therefore, patchy, containing only scattered clues rather than an in-depth account of exactly what happened. Even so, many intriguing pieces of information can be drawn together to reveal the now-barely visible picture of events between 1945 and 1951, when the SAS fought its most important and difficult battle to date - that for survival.

The SAS's 'unofficial' (i.e. deniable, as opposed to unauthorised) activities are planned, supported and executed by a small number of people who are briefed on a 'need-to-know' basis. Orders are given verbally and records are kept to an absolute minimum, thereby optimising security and personnel safety. This would have been the case in the 1940s as well, and with perhaps only a few score people being involved in enterprises such as that in Greece, most of them have taken their secrets to the grave. Indeed, it appears that even some of the SAS's most illustrious senior officers were unaware of what went on prior to the Regiment's recognised renaissance in Malaya at the turn of 1950/51. This makes complete sense given the *modus operandi* of the post-war SAS up to that time.[20] Equally, and unsurprisingly, those who were 'in the loop' never revealed all that they knew (an impression confirmed by Brig. Calvert when I quizzed him about potential SAS activities in Greece during an afternoon of reminiscence over a lunch and a jar or two within the lofty surroundings of the Special Forces Club in London).

Still, when the late Major Clarence L.D. 'Dare' Newell - known by many as 'the Father of the Regiment' - and another legendary SAS figure, the wartime commander of the SBS in Greece and, subsequently, the C.O. of 21 SAS, Lt.-Col. D.G.C. 'Dinky' Sutherland, co-wrote a memo on the history of the SAS in 1987, they asked whether it had been "chance or destiny that guided the fledgling SAS through the anxious, formative years?". They posited that, in all probability, "we will never know".[21] In fact, a good deal is now known and, while the authorities have rightly clamped down on revelatory SAS literature, this tome seeks merely to set the record straight by presenting the 'facts' (with apologies to E.H. Carr) as they appear in the historical record.

The focus of this work is on material that has only now come to light, and from which it is clear that, as esteemed SAS old stagers Dare Newell and David Sutherland noted, the Regiment's "salvation depended on a few, a very few, dedicated visionaries and persistent champions in the right place at the right time".[22] To a large extent, it is their story that is central to understanding how the SAS avoided the axe at the end of the War. And it is necessary first to look at the Regiment's position by then, in order to determine how its few 'champions' proposed to save it from extinction.

Towards a new beginning

The SAS was created in the Middle East Theatre of war during 1941 as 'L' Detachment of the non-existent Special Air Service Brigade (so-called to deceive German Intelligence). It was developed by Scots Guardsman and Commando, David Stirling, and several of his colleagues, who saw that there was room for a special force tasked solely with strategic small unit operations behind-the-lines, focusing on raiding, sabotage and harassment of the enemy's military forces and infrastructure (see my *SAS: Zero Hour* for a full and revised account). In other words, regular soldiers would take on a role more normally associated with irregular (non-Army) fighters, operating as guerillas. This was carried on with considerable success by foot and motor patrols between 1942 and 1944 in the Middle East and other Theatres, to such an extent that, by January 1944, a real SAS Brigade was established with the approval of the British Chiefs of Staff [COS], led by the Chief of the Imperial General Staff [CIGS], Field-Marshal (later Lord) Alan Brooke.

The SAS Brigade's strength included a HQ staff, the 1st. and 2nd. British SAS Regiments, the 3rd. and 4th. French SAS Regiments, the 5th. Belgian SAS Regiment, and 'F' Squadron (HQ Liaison) of the 'Phantom' special signals organisation. All told, the SAS had about 2500 personnel at this point and was at the peak of its powers. Yet, because the SAS had not been granted its own Corps Warrant by the Army Council (under which new Regiments are raised), it "technically had no separate existence as regiments in the British Order of Battle [orbat] and, for administration [purposes, it] needed to be part of some established [or regular Army] force". In view of the SAS's familiarity with and expertise in parachuting, the HQ SAS Troops - formed in 1944, under Brigadier Roderick 'Roddy' W. McLeod - was attached to the 1st. Airborne Corps HQ. It was commanded by the highly regarded Lieutenant-General (later General Sir) Frederick A.M. 'Boy' Browning. As James Ladd points out, when it came to choosing a 'home' for the SAS in the Army, the Airborne Forces "was the obvious choice",[1] if not one that truly represented its particular function and broader talents.

Suitably impressed by the SAS's pedigree, Boy Browning took it upon himself to get it incorporated into the British orbat for the forthcoming D-day landings in France.[2] He approached members of the top brass who would be making the crucial decisions in this regard and, in anticipation of acquiring a place in the invasion forces, SAS staff working with Airborne Corps personnel at their Moor Park Golf Course HQ, in north-west London, started planning for these operations. The onus for "initial and strategic [SAS] planning, staff duties and training", fell on the Brigade's Liaison Officer to the Airborne Forces, Lieutenant-Colonel Ian G. Collins (a pre-war tennis champion), who worked in the Service's Tactical HQ.[3] While carrying out these duties - which in geographical terms spanned far more than just the upcoming return of British forces to France - Collins gained valuable experience that would prove crucial to the SAS after the War. Not only did he deal with the preparation of all SAS operations, he took part in the coordination of action with the Commandos and "the activities of special agents". This included members of the Secret Intelligence Service [SIS, or MI6] and the Special Operations Executive [SOE]. Among other things, they assisted partisan Resistance fighters and movements around the world, just as SAS personnel were doing in Europe and the Middle East.[4]

The knowledge of such enterprises that Lt.-Col. Collins and his colleagues acquired stood them in good stead when it came time to looking beyond immediate wartime requirements and plotting the SAS's course in the post-war world. Collins, in particular, gained considerable insight into the way that guerilla forces worked, including nationalist partisans, who were the military arm of underground movements. He additionally developed relationships with other British and Allied agencies that were dealing with secret clandestine operations. Furthermore, numerous SAS soldiers gained first-hand experience of unconventional combat, fighting both as guerillas and alongside those operating in the *Maquis* and other anti-Axis irregular forces. All this meant that a pool of knowledge about unconventional warfare methods, organisation and their practitioners' vulnerabilities was developing within the SAS, which boded well for a future in which the guerilla would play an increasing role on the international scene. Indeed, during their exploits in Alsace-Lorraine, in eastern France, during August 1944, the SAS and their French comrades-in-arms became the target of massive German counter-guerilla sweep operations, which featured a vanguard force of "special anti-partisan units". These '*Jagd-kommando*' ('Pursuit Commandos') conducted independent small unit patrols too, just as their quarry did, and the Allied forces had several brushes with these units.[5] It is quite likely that such episodes made an impression upon senior British SAS officers and that they drew upon this wartime experience in due course.

By the autumn of 1944, it appeared to most Allied observers that the Axis was crumbling and that the European War would end sooner rather than later - certainly by 1946. Faced with the prospect of reductions in the British Armed Forces' funding and manpower, the SAS had to think of ways to survive the axe and remain available for special operations during peacetime. Hence, it needed to demonstrate both that such commitments were likely to arise in the near future, and that it was best equipped to handle them - as opposed to any of the dozens of other wartime special forces.

Adaptability and flexibility would be the SAS's bywords and, by at least 2nd. September 1944, such virtues were being demonstrated by Lt.-Col. Collins. At that time, "both Airborne HQ Troops and the SAS Brigade .. had begun to consider .. future employments", and Collins floated the idea of using the SAS for counter-intelligence work in Germany. In addition, he pushed for the creation of Teams that could pursue and arrest suspected Nazi war criminals who had committed war crimes such as the execution of SAS personnel, and who would be trying to flee justice before the end of the War. Looking beyond that time, Collins thought that another commitment that the SAS could fulfil was the disarmament of Axis forces in Scandinavia. Finally, the war in the Far East looked like going on into 1946, so an SAS deployment in Asia was mooted. By 5th. October 1944, Lt.-Col. Collins produced "the first of a number of .. [written] appreciations that were designed to 'sell' the SAS to often sceptical higher headquarters" and, in this drive, he was backed up by several senior officers who were friends of the SAS, including Brig. McLeod and Lt.-Gen. Browning.

By 1945, the HQ SAS Troops was trying hard to find "a role - any role - for the SAS", and a place in "the order of battle for any operation that was going", whether in North-West or South-East Europe, the Middle East or the Far East. Every effort was made to lobby those in positions of authority, in the knowledge that unless the SAS Brigade was "in at the finish with a record of adaptability to current circumstances", then it would not be in a position to "claim exemption from .. post-war cuts in manpower".[6]

Above and beyond the roles and missions suggested by Collins *et al*, at the end of 1944, the War Office was preparing for the possibility of a long drawn-out German underground resistance to an Allied invasion. In doing so, the Service Department's Intelligence officers studied the potential problems posed by a determined, well-organised guerilla foe, and they produced reports recommending traditional-style large-scale counter-guerilla operations, such as area sweeps or drives. But, they also referred to the possibilities offered by experimental small unit forces with air support, including the use of pseudo-guerilla units that donned civilian clothing and feigned guerilla status.[7] Some SAS personnel may well have picked up on such ideas and proffered counter-guerilla action as a future SAS role that would be necessary in the post-war world and which the Regiment was well placed to undertake. Indeed, by the end of 1944, there was a precedent for this that was well known to the SAS.

In December 1944, the SAS's cousins in the SBS took a leading role in the suppression of Communist urban guerillas operating in Athens as part of a wider attempt to seize power there. As James Ladd indicates, Lt.-Col. Sutherland's SBS soldiers got embroiled in what "was the first brush for their SAS line of descendants with urban terrorists". Indeed, the SAS had at least one official observer on the spot, who was monitoring how the British forces tackled the Leftist gunmen - Major Roy Alexander Farran. Subsequently a legendary figure in the Regiment, at that point, he was the commander of third ('C') Squadron, 2nd. SAS Regiment. He already knew that part of the world and had propositioned the War Office Directorate of Military Intelligence [DMI] to send him to Greece, likely for the express purpose of assessing how counter/guerilla forces operated. Whatever the case, he was posted as the SAS's observer at the Land Forces Adriatic HQ. From there, he witnessed the fighting on the ground and, although Farran later described his Hellenic sojourn as "a bit of a holiday",[8] there was a serious side to his employment. Indeed, details of the operations there were reported to his superiors, notably 2 SAS's commanding officer, Lieutenant-Colonel Brian Morton Foster Franks.

Major Farran's views would have carried much weight with Franks and others, for, after fighting with 2 SAS in North Africa, Sicily and France during 1943/44 (including missions alongside SOE operatives), Farran had developed "a considerable reputation" in the Regiment. Hence, it is interesting to note that, by 1945, both he and Franks were enthusiastic advocates of a future counter-guerilla role for the SAS. As James Ladd notes, "although special forces of SAS or Commando units were not trained or equipped for anti-terrorist roles [in 1945], there was probably the notion in some quarters that they could be used for this purpose",[9] and this was nowhere more so than in 2 SAS. Another officer with an even more formidable record in unconventional fighting joined the SAS hierarchy at the turn of 1944/45.

Some historians have stated that, in December 1944, Brig. McLeod was replaced as commander of the SAS Brigade by Brigadier James Michael 'Mad Mike' Calvert. Others note that he took over command of the SAS in February or March 1945. But his biographer, David Rooney, states that Calvert arrived at its HQ near Halstead airfield in January 1945.[10]

Previously, Calvert had met the Stirling brothers (David and Bill) while instructing Commandos in 1940, before a posting with the War Office's Military Intelligence (Research) [MI(R)] section. There, he shared his thoughts about unconventional warfare with colleagues like General Sir Colin M. Gubbins (co-founder of the SOE) and Lieutenant (later Field-Marshal Sir) Gerald W.R. Templer (who went on to make his name as COIN supremo in Malaya). During his time at MI(R), Calvert wrote a booklet, *The operations of small forces behind the enemy lines*, in which he advocated the guerilla defence of Britain by regular Army and irregular forces, in the event of a Nazi invasion. Calvert was able to implement his theories in various territories, following Japan's conquest of South-East Asia and the Pacific. In 1941, he taught SOE and Commando leaders at the Burma Bush Warfare School and, in 1942, he organised 'V' (Viper) Force for guerilla operations on New Guinea. There, Australia's Independent Companies followed the example set by those that had raided Norway in 1940 (and which had included the core of many British Commando units). Thereafter, 'Mad Mike' served with General Orde Wingate and his special force of Chindits in Burma. They practised jungle warfare, including short guerilla patrols, "long-range penetration", and "strong-hold" tactics. Hence, on arrival at the SAS Brigade, he commanded great respect, both for his intellect and drive, fighting experience, and his will to see his new charge prosper.[11]

Towards a post-war vision

Brig. Calvert spearheaded the ongoing lobbying campaign and, on 21st. March 1945, a letter was sent to the War Office, enquiring about its future plans for the SAS. At that point, the 1st. and 2nd. SAS Regiments were engaged in northern Germany, and it has been said that, by this stage of the War, "any commander was pleased to have them under his Command, for their reputation was formidable". Indeed, by the time that the German authorities were surrendering, on 8th. May, the SAS's standing was considered "awesome", and one writer asserts that the SAS had already "become a legend".[12]

This may overstate things somewhat, but undoubtedly the SAS was held in great esteem in the British Army and Allied military forces in general. Thus, it was not too difficult for the SAS's leading lights to convince senior planners to pencil them in for the upcoming Far East campaign. By May 1945, the 1st. and 2nd. SAS Regiments, commanded by the revered Lieutenant-Colonel Robert Blair 'Paddy' Mayne and Lt.-Col. Franks, respectively, had returned to the UK following the Nazis' collapse and were busy training for action in Asia. However, before being committed there, the SAS had to supervise the disbandment of the Axis forces in Scandinavia. Hence, on 8th. May 1945, the two British Regiments were ordered with their Brigadier to carry out Operation Doomsday, along with other troops of the 1st. Airborne Division. The Special Air Service's specific remit was Norway, where Operation Apostle was carried out in just a few weeks.[13]

The day before the SAS received its Apostle instructions - 7th. May - Lt.-Col. Collins produced an "unofficial memo" at the 1st. Airborne HQ in Rickmansworth, Hertfordshire, for Calvert's approval. Entitled "Notes on [the] Future of [the] Special Air Service", it looked at the Brigade's possible future missions and deployments in war and peace. It proposed that wartime activities ought to consist of a number of familiar and well-practised tasks, executed by land, sea or air.

They were as follows:

1. Leading partisan Resistance forces in attacks on enemy Lines of Communication [LoC], possibly in cooperation with the SIS and the SOE (if it too survived after the War), as had been the case during the late hostilities.

2. Containing and diverting large enemy military forces by undertaking behind-the-lines operations, focusing on hitting LoCs.

3. Intelligence-gathering patrolling by foot and in vehicles (jeeps).

4. Demolitions work, with saboteurs concentrating on bridges, roads, stores, HQs and other vital points.

5. Operating in a strategic role to harass the enemy, and also conducting tactical operations as and when necessary.

This final proposal probably would have upset SAS purists who wished to hold to David Stirling's conception of a purely strategic force. But, in the circumstances that the Brigade was in in mid-1945, the principle was rightly adopted that beggars can't be choosers, as it was vital to demonstrate that the Regiments could carry out whatever special task was required of them, thereby strengthening the case for their survival in the post-war Army.

Further to this end, Lt.-Col. Collins' paper looked at the "role of SAS troops in peacetime", and it proposed their use in a variety of ways.

These were outlined as:

1. Exploratory survey expeditions in inhospitable regions to locate potentially lucrative oil fields and gold concessions. In addition, the SAS could boost national morale and prestige by undertaking polar explorations, and by becoming the conquerors of the world's highest peak, Mount Everest.

2. Testing out new equipment for the Armed Forces.

3. Most significantly, carrying out "observational or operational [missions] in civil wars such as [the one that raged between 1936 and 1939 in] SPAIN".

Lt.-Col. Collins and Brig. Calvert believed that there would be a particular need for the latter mission. This had already been demonstrated in Greece, and, Calvert asserted in later years, that he then perceived a Communist threat to various other states in Eastern Europe (like Bulgaria, Romania, Albania and Yugoslavia).

Finally, Collins proposed that, wherever SAS troops were deployed, the wartime practice of their founder should be followed, with the Special Air Service Regiment administered and commanded by the local General Officer Commanding [GOC], "depending on where they were based". This stipulation implies that the SAS hierarchy had in mind deployment to areas outside normal British military jurisdiction, with the example of Spain being used to make the point. He added that their sponsor agency or overseer should be the War Office Directorate of Air Warfare, and that, if and when the SAS were given the go-ahead to prepare for any post-war undertakings, they should have their own central Holding Depot (instead of sharing the Airborne Forces' Depot at Maida Barracks in Aldershot, Hampshire). The Depot would be used for planning, administration, mustering and the like, including devising arrangements to attach personnel from other arms or branches of the armed forces to the SAS, as and when required.[14] Presumably this would include specialists like signallers, medics, engineers and air-supply officers.

While the SAS top brass was looking to the future in May 1945, one of its previous proposals also bore fruit at that juncture, further boosting the post-war SAS case. Permission was given for Lt.-Col. Franks to pursue the mission of "hunting down war criminals responsible for the murder of captured SAS personnel". Although the War Office apparently was less than enthused about this and did not want major resources committed to it, Franks "was .. tasked with" organising groups of investigators from within the SAS's ranks to locate and arrest their enemies.[15] Lt.-Col. Franks put much time and effort into the project, both for its own merits and, possibly, with one eye on the future. For, by keeping in being part of the SAS structure, a foundation on which to build a broader special force capability would be laid. He and 2 SAS's intelligence officer, Major Eric 'Bill' Barkworth, "put together .. [a] special team" of SAS personnel and, by September 1945, at least two SAS War Crimes Investigations Unit Teams were ready to operate in France and Germany. The full story of their endeavours need not be repeated here.[16] But it's sufficient to note that these Teams figured in the SAS's development after the time of its supposed demise in the autumn of 1945, with Franks at the hub of all these activities.

The SAS lobby

Soon after the SAS Regiments went to Norway, Brig. Calvert broke his leg and, by June, was shipped back to the UK. He put his time to good use and immediately continued "lobby[ing] .. hard for the SAS to be employed in the Far East", possibly in China. He was backed by several notables such as Lt.-Col. David Stirling (who had returned from incarceration in Germany), his brother Lt.-Col. William 'Bill' Stirling (Franks' predecessor in charge of 2 SAS), General Browning, and the war hero MP, Fitzroy MacLean (who had fought alongside partisans in the Balkans with the SOE). Moreover, Calvert had the backing of the Prime Minister (later Sir) Winston Churchill, who had fought in the South African War of 1899-1902 against native 'Kommandos' of Boer guerillas, supported the formation of the British Commandos and many other special forces from 1940 onwards, and who was "always interested in SAS-type operations". Further, his son Randolph was a member of the 2nd. SAS Regiment, and so the P.M. was well disposed to the idea of post-war SAS deployments.[17] On the other hand, Churchill was to fall from office in July 1945, and it has been said that "the British General Staff could see no proper role for the SAS" after the War.[18] Therefore, it would not be an easy task for Calvert and other supporters of the SAS to sway the doubters to the Regiment's side, and it would take a concerted and determined effort to do so. This demanded the recruitment to the SAS cause of as much influential and weighty opinion as possible, both inside and outside the upper echelons of Whitehall. Hence, in June 1945, Brig. Calvert "wrote a paper [and sent it] to the CIGS, Field-Marshal [later] Lord Alanbrooke", outlining what he saw as potential roles for the SAS in the post-war world,[19] doubtless drawing on Lt.-Col. Collins' unofficial HQ memorandum.

Other historians have presumed that War Office studies of the SAS's wartime activities, undertaken as part of an effort to identify possible future missions for it, was initiated by the Directorate of Tactical Investigation, in October 1945.[20] In turn, this would imply that the Service Department was seriously thinking about retaining a special force capability and decided to look more deeply into its requirements. In fact, the War Office's actions stemmed not from any astute recognition of the potential value of special forces, but from Calvert's communications with the CIGS. Calvert specifically "asked [Brooke] for an investigation to be made of all special force operations" during the War, so that the usefulness of such units could be recognised and understood by the top brass.

The Brigadier requested that the enquiry ought to include not only all British special forces, but Allied units like the Australian Independent Companies that had operated on New Guinea and the various "German special forces". This would include the Reichswehr's counter-guerilla *jagd-kommando*, which had fulfilled a role that Calvert thought the SAS could adopt as its own in due course. Further, he asked that all captured German, Italian and Japanese commanders be "interrogated [and be obliged to complete] .. a special questionnaire on the efficacy or otherwise of our special forces", thereby contributing to the upcoming British deliberations about them.

Additionally, in his paper to Field-Marshal Brooke, Brig. Calvert posed several questions about the SAS Regiment's future, and he helpfully provided the answers "in order to stir people up"! The questions and answers that he presented were as follows:

" 1. Was there a role for the SAS in future wars?"

Unsurprisingly, his answer was affirmative. "There would be a role [both] before and at the beginning of a war, where the Special Air Service could be used to stir up trouble among .. dissidents [in enemy states] and also operate on [their] lines of communication etc", as Collins' paper espoused.

Brig. Calvert's second question was connected with his fourth (detailed below). He asked,

" 2. How should the elan and *esprit de corps* .. be preserved and form the basis of a new SAS?"

Calvert replied that, in all likelihood, after its initial post-war demobilisation and unit disbandments, the Army would set up a reserve force or "Territorial Army", under whatever title. (As it transpired, it was the Territorial Army - officially founded on 1st. January 1947). In view of the financial constraints that the weakened British economy would impose on the Armed Forces in the coming years, it would be politically difficult to justify the creation of new regiments, and so Calvert "recommended that a Territorial Army SAS Unit should be formed to keep the elan, *esprit de corps*, tradition and history of the SAS going, so that there was a[n SAS] centre of excellence and thought"[21] at all times.

From the available evidence, it appears that this scheme was discussed by leading SAS officers earlier on in 1945: Brig. McLeod and Brig. Calvert are said to have shared the view that a Territorial SAS Unit ought to be created. Furthermore, they agreed that "a small permanent cadre should be formed to keep the regiment alive, in addition to whatever Territorial or Yeomanry Unit was formed".[22] This is most significant, as they clearly felt that, whatever happened, there must be an SAS nucleus (even if it had to be an alternative or 'shadow' organisation), which could orchestrate the activities of any SAS units that managed to keep going after the War - such as the War Crimes Teams and any other bodies that might be created in the future.

This relates to Calvert's third and central question, which related to the Service's role in the medium to longer term.

" 3. What role would the SAS have in peacetime?"

Brig. Calvert has asserted that, he "forecast that there would be a tremendous amount of insurgency all over the world due to empires cracking up and nationalism prevailing". In order to deal with this threat, Calvert continued, "therefore, I said that [what was to become known as] counter-insurgency would be a worthwhile [and central] role in peacetime for the Special Air Service Regiment". He added both in an unpublished written memoir and an interview at the Special Forces Club in London that, "this is NOT being wise after the event".[23] (In fact, existing public records referred to subsequently show that this is indeed the case).

Finally, the SAS's commander asked,

" 4. What units should continue to exist after the [end of the Second World] War?"

The Brigadier recalled that his answer to this "was rather mixed". Besides the proposed auxiliary Army unit and the War Crimes Organisation, he suggested the establishment of an SAS force made up of men from the top British universities - namely, London, Oxford and Cambridge. He explained that he "wanted the SAS not only to be tough but [also] highly intelligent and good at languages", which would make it easier for the Regiment to send soldiers all over the world and mix with the locals (particularly Allied partisan forces). He thought that "three University SAS Squadrons should be formed" at Oxbridge and in the capital, and he decreed that all recruits should do at least six months linguistics training and be "experts in all technical subjects as well" (a philosophy that, in essence, was accepted by the Regiment in the following decades, and became a key factor in its operational successes).

If Brig. Calvert's recommendations had been accepted by the Whitehall decision-makers of the War Office and the Cabinet, then this could have resulted in the formation of an army 'elite'. But, in 1945, such a concept was generally frowned upon. (When Calvert returned to the SAS helm once more, in the early

1950s, and pushed the idea again, he believed "the authorities turned it down due to the rather left-wing atmosphere prevailing at the time").[24]

Hence, during 1945, no progress was made on this front. Even so, Calvert continued to try to build a head of steam behind the proposals that he had submitted to the CIGS. That summer, he sought to curry favour within the loftier heights of the Army, focusing on people with whom the SAS had good relations. He "wrote to as many Commanders-in-Chief and chiefs of staff in the British and Canadian" armed services as he could think of, including "Alexander, De Guingaud [and] Montgomery". General Sir Harold Alexander had backed the SAS's early exploits in the Middle East and knew Calvert from Burma. Field-Marshal (later Viscount) Bernard Law Montgomery was scathing about some special forces, which had a predisposition to act as "private armies" (like Popski's outfit in North Africa), operating independently of normal channels of command and setting a worrying example to the rank-and-file. He also believed that they posed major problems in terms of their administration, lax discipline, and difficulties in incorporating them into overall strategic plans, as well as having a debilitating tendency to "cream-off" the best soldiers from other units that needed them.

Despite such scepticism about special forces, Monty respected both Calvert and the SAS. He had dealt with the Regiment in North Africa during 1942 and, after an initial run-in with its founder, the Field-Marshal saw what the SAS could do and he became well disposed towards it. Thus, Calvert asked Monty and his other correspondents "to say what they thought of special forces and [to] send it to GENERAL ROWELL" as soon as possible. Major-General Rowell was a veteran of the Australian Independent Companies' operations in New Guinea during 1942 (and Calvert was a guerilla instructor in the Far East at this time), and, fortuitously for the SAS, Rowell was currently the War Office Director of Tactical Investigation. It was Rowell that the CIGS asked to "carry out the .. investigations and interrogations" requested by Calvert,[25] which appear to have got underway during the summer of 1945.

Brig. Calvert has written that, in 1972, he "sent copies of [his] report [to the CIGS] and [of the] letters [to his potential allies in the fight for the SAS's survival,] to [the] HQ SAS, Duke of York's HQ" in Chelsea. Indeed, around that time, the SAS reviewed its historical records for the early post-war years, and the file sent to the Regiment by Calvert reportedly "came back without the relevant report and letters", which Calvert never saw again.[26]

Nonetheless, his hitherto ignored version of events appears to reflect those that occurred. For the War Office's Standing Committee on Army Post-war Problems [SCAPP] wrote a report on the "Pros and Cons for having Special Air Service Troops in Peace[time]", probably in July-August 1945. This date can be determined from the fact that the report refers to "the value of work done by the S.A.S. Regiment in this [as opposed to 'the last'] war .. [which] has been recognised by commanders in the field and endorsed by [the War Office] DTI in his study of Special Air Service operations carried out under SHAEF" (the Supreme Headquarters, Allied Expeditionary Force in Europe).[27] This means that the War Office DTI undertook an initial study of SAS operations in the North-West of Europe that were carried out between June 1944 and May 1945, quite distinct from the War Office's subsequent scrutiny of all SAS ventures, which began in October 1945 (detailed later).[28] Indeed, Calvert pointed out that the interrogations of former enemy personnel that he desired and requested were "done, and our enemies said that our own special forces had had a great, and often decisive effect, on the enemy Commanders in Chief".[29] This must have boosted the pro-special forces lobby within the British Army in the autumn of 1945 and contributed to the CIGS's decision to organise another geographically broader and more in-depth DTI study of SAS wartime activities.

In the interim, the 1st. and 2nd. SAS Regiments had returned from Norway in August 1945 to their Eastern Command bases in the Chelmsford and Colchester areas, and an SAS team led by Major Rooney "toured the USA". Meantime, the SAS Regimental Liaison and Rear HQ staff at Sloe House, Halstead, Essex,[30] kept up the pressure for, at least in the first instance, a Far East Theatre commitment. Yet, despite a British tradition of unorthodox military units stretching back to at least the Seven Years' War, powerful elements within the British Army 'establishment', and throughout the institution as a whole, despised the concept of special forces and sought to kill them off now that the War was coming to an end.

The War Office, along with the CIGS, Field-Marshal Dill, and his successor, Brooke, had been reticent about the formation of the Commandos in 1940-41. Criticisms of special forces ranged from charges of elitism to the danger of private armies encouraging unacceptable methods and attitudes among soldiery in general. They were also said to be difficult to control and fit into operational and logistical plans, and sceptics could point to examples of this during the War, such as incidents within the 8th. Army in North Africa.

Unusual arrangements and problems arising from the use of special forces, such as the employment of civilians and foreigners, were also deemed by many commanding officers as making unwarranted demands on their valuable time.

Unit commanders also despised the fact that such forces were expensive to train, maintain and equip, while their own men were often woefully short on such back-up. Moreover, detractors argued that special forces were unnecessary unless the Army was on the strategic offensive, as behind-the-lines raiding and other activities in conjunction with Resistance forces failed to pay major dividends compared to the costs incurred. Further, special forces were accused of being unsuited to some terrain and climates, as well as being prone both to the duplication of effort and ill-coordination. The last charge could be levelled at, among others, the SAS, SIS and SOE, notably in regard to wartime intelligence-sharing arrangements in the Balkans. Finally, even broad-minded officers such as Field-Marshal (later Sir) William Slim and General Archibald Wavell shared some of the concerns about special forces of sceptics like Montgomery and Brooke, believing that, given the right training and support, regular soldiers could carry out most special missions just as well.

Notwithstanding this fact, while the GHQ in India and the War Office loathed the unorthodox Gen. Orde Wingate, he was backed by Brooke, Wavell and Slim. Further, while they all initially voiced doubts about various special forces, in time, they backed the Commandos, SAS, 'V' Force and others.[31] However, with Japan's eventual agreement on 14th. August 1945 to surrender, there seemed nowhere left for the SAS to go. Among other respected historians, Philip Warner asserts that, "with the end of all the fighting, it was clear that there was no further use for the SAS". Alan Hoe and Eric Morris go so far as to argue that "the War Office .. had decided that any future conflict would be .. controlled .. by those forces which held the atom bomb .. [while] smaller limited intensity campaigns would not require the use of forces such as the SAS".[32] Such assertions are not borne out by the historical record.

At the end of the Second World War, the War Office planners had not made any concrete decisions about future strategy based on the role of atomic weapons and, with regard to the use of special forces, the more forward-looking thinkers in the Service Department were vigorously presenting the case for retaining them by August 1945. Indeed, Brig. Calvert discerned that there was a body of favourable opinion large enough to make it worthwhile requesting the appointment of a Colonel Commandant to lead the post-war Special Air Service.

He favoured Lieutenant-General (later General Sir) Miles Christopher 'Bimbo' Dempsey, who was "one of the few senior officers at the time who really understood what SAS troops could do". As the Commander-in-Chief of 13 Corps in Italy during 1943, he had been extremely impressed by the daring antics of the Special Raiding Squadron [SRS] (as the 1st. SAS was called for a spell). He had let it be known that he "looked forward to further association with them in future" and had offered himself as Colonel Commandant of the SAS should the Regiments become an Established part of the Army.[33] However, on 23rd. July, Dempsey wrote from the 2nd. Army HQ to Brig. Calvert that "the question of my appointment .. should be held in abeyance" until the SAS's future was decided, though he hoped that "it may be possible for the formation to continue, even as a supplementary reserve, in peacetime", and he added that it would be a "great honour and I hope that one day it may come about". Calvert was informed that such a decision about the SAS would have to await a host of others, however, and these would be taken in due course at the highest level, "owing to [the] uncertainty as [to] the composition of the post-war Army".[34]

Brig. Calvert and his colleagues were unable to make any progress with regard to the SAS's status during August 1945, though, and they shared the feeling of uncertainty about their future with the other major elements of the Airborne Forces that made up the Army Air Corps [AAC] at that time - the Parachute Regiment and the Glider Pilot Regiment [GPR]. For, among the various policy matters being considered by the War Office's SCAPP was a review of the requirements for Airborne Forces in the peacetime Army. A few months before, in May 1945, Lt.-Col. Collins had suggested that, in future, the SAS could be placed under the War Office Directorate of Air Warfare (headed by Major-General K.N. Crawford, who would be involved with SAS activities in Greece in 1946) and, as will be recounted in due course, the pro-SAS lobby must have pushed from then on for the Directorate to make a favourable approach on the Brigade's behalf to the SCAPP.

On 13th. August 1945, the DAW produced a memorandum entitled "Postwar Airborne Forces" and, by September, this had been sent to the Standing Committee. Within the Directorate's submission was a paper on "The future of the Airborne Forces in the Post-war Army", and this argued (doubtless in the light of recent War Office DTI investigations into special forces and interrogations of concerned Axis parties), that "the Special Air Service Regiment has proved its value in the present war and it is considered that it should be retained in some form in the post-war Army". Hence, the DAW was open to Calvert's idea of creating an auxiliary or some other type of SAS Unit, if a place in the regular orbat could not be secured. It was not the only branch of the Service Department that viewed this concept with favour either. As mentioned before, "the value of the work done by the SAS Reg[imen]t in this war .. ha[d] been recognised by commanders .. and .. [the War Office] DTI". The Directorate of Air staff wrote that the SAS had contributed crucially to the disruption of enemy planning and operations and, over and above its successes in Europe and the Middle East Theatres, "in the Far East very valuable work was done in stimulating local resistance and in supplying information by small uniformed parties left behind in or subsequently sent to Malaya, Timor, New Guinea and other places". This was done by the SOE and other special forces (including Calvert's 'V' Force) during the War, but the SAS must have been viewed as an organisation that would be capable of such activities in the future, above and beyond its proven skills in other arenas. Undoubtedly, this view would have been pushed by the Chindit leader and jungle fighter extraordinaire, Brig. Calvert.

Further, in weighing up the "Pros and cons for having SAS Troops in Peace", the central argument presented by the DAW to the SCAPP was that, in another global war, the British armed forces, almost inevitably, would find themselves committed to a defensive holding action in a friendly nation-state that had been invaded. The report concluded that such "conditions will therefore be favourable to the use of SAS troops, provided [that] they are quickly [made] available". Thus, it was self-evident that there were "good reasons for maintaining a[n] SAS organisation in peace[time]", and the Directorate recommended that "the principles and practise of the SAS Reg[imen]t should be kept alive by [the] foundation of a nucleus organisation", as Brigadiers McLeod and Calvert desired. In keeping with the latter's proposals to the CIGS, War Office officials also urged the SCAPP to adopt the idea that "the auxiliary army should maintain one squadron of the SAS Reg[imen]t, formed initially from Officers and Other Ranks [OR] who have served in the SAS during the War, and subsequently maintained from volunteers from universities and other sources". The memo does not indicate what other sources may have been tapped by the Regiment, but presumably extra manpower could be drawn from other special forces and from units with expertise useful to the SAS, such as the Royal Army Service Corps [RASC], Royal Army Medical Corps [RAMC], Royal Electrical and Mechanical Engineers [REME], and the Royal Signals Corps [RSC].

From wherever new SAS recruits came, it was envisaged that the SAS nucleus would be rapidly expanded during a pre-war crisis, in order to be ready for immediate deployment prior to or just after the outbreak of hostilities. It was felt that the mechanics of all this "should be the responsibility of the GOC Airborne Division", who would oversee the SAS's administration, planning, training and operational matters.

In addition, and in contradiction to Lt.-Col. Collins' May 1945 proposals, the DAW stated that "the Airborne Forces Depot [in Aldershot] should be regarded as the home of the SAS Reg[imen]t and should keep up a[n] SAS museum and SAS records of historic or sentimental interests". This was probably predicated on the basis of cost and simplicity, with the Army Air Corps' HQs being amalgamated onto one site, thereby cutting out some duplication of effort and expense.

The War Office report also made the noteworthy recommendation that the GOC Airborne Division should institute a rolling review of SAS techniques and operations, which were understood to be different to those carried out by the infantry as a whole or by other airborne soldiers. To this end, a Training Formation was to be founded, consisting of "a squadron of the [Airborne] Divisional Reconnaissance Regiment (or other sub-unit of the Division) .. [which would] be nominated to practise and develop SAS methods, but would not itself belong to the SAS Reg[imen]t". Again this proposal is likely to have sprung from the need to maximise resources in view of impending financial cuts affecting the whole Armed Forces. In the short term, the SAS would have grudgingly accepted this (while trying to take on this work themselves when they had become Established in the post-war Army).

While the fiscal logic was self-evident, the War Office staff recognised that there would need to be "practise [in] and study" of the type of operations that SAS personnel would be called upon to do, and that they would need to undertake "practical exercises". Indeed, the Directorate accepted that the SAS itself would have to be at the hub of all its specific preparations because of the unique characteristics of its men. It grasped that, in particular, "the leaders of SAS parties, if they are to be really successful, must possess a special flair for this type of work, and, to some extent, a special mentality. They are individualists, who are at their best when working on their own, and are not necessarily men who [would] do well in normal units".

In order to ensure that the SAS and its training unit were up to date with the latest technology and kit of both friendly and potential enemy armed forces, another perceptive suggestion was for the Army Airborne Transport Development Centre [AATDC] to "undertake [the] development of special equipment for SAS troops". Additionally, they would need to train with and be comfortable in the use of all "weapons and equipment of foreign powers", thereby allowing them to use any and all weaponries on the battlefield as circumstances dictated. This included every type of motor vehicle, explosive and munition, parachute, small boat, fire-arm and close-quarter combat weapon.

Furthermore, the War Office paper pushed for the AATDC to "deal with any special equipment required for [a post-war] SOE and other clandestine organisations", the likes of which included the SIS, Phantom and the SBS. Evidently, the Directorate assumed that the links forged between such organisations during the War - especially between the SAS and SOE - would continue, so that they would be able swiftly to resume their partnership in coordinating and assisting partisan guerilla forces. In readiness for the next war, the SAS additionally was to follow Calvert's dictum with regard to the "study of certain [unnamed] foreign countries and languages", probably centred on South-Eastern Europe. Other preparations for the Regiment's proposed strategic role of "operating for extended periods at a distance from their base" included instruction in the use of "long-range wireless sets and practising the technique of air supply". Finally, the War Office outline envisaged that Special Air Service Regiment peacetime training would involve "numbers .. so small that they can be assumed to be covered by the allowance of 2000 per year for Regulars not in the airborne forces".[35]

Disbandment looms

In spite of the fact that the War Office Air Directorate's report contained more pluses than minuses about the SAS, traditionalists who feared the consequences of being seen to give succour to "private armies" - and, as a result, encouraging soldiers to question authority or act as they wished - seem to have convinced others that the concerns being raised had some validity. Hence, the War Office SCAPP shied away from making any recommendation to retain the SAS or other Airborne Forces. Instead, while the pro-SAS lobby continued to work behind the scenes to keep the SAS flame alive, in September 1945, permission was granted by the authorities to return the 3rd., 4th. and 5th. SAS Regiments to their home armies in France and Belgium. Further, the British SAS Regiments were told to make ready for their own upcoming dissolution and, by

4th October 1945, "authority for [the] disbandment of 1 & 2 B[attalio]n [sic.] SAS Reg[imen]ts" was received by the SAS Brigade HQ. On the following day, 5th. October 1945, passing-out parades were staged at the 1st. SAS's HQ near Chelmsford, Gloucestershire, and at the 2nd. SAS HQ near Colchester, Essex.

Many SAS officers and ORs were packed off to other army units (often their original 'home' regiments in which they had served prior to their transfer to the Brigade earlier in the War). Others left the Army altogether and returned to civvy street, or joined like-minded organisations such as the SIS. (Indeed, the Secret Intelligence Service became a home for numerous personnel who'd fought in or alongside British military special forces and other unorthodox units during the War, recruiting personnel from the SAS, SBS, Commandos, the Special Operations Executive in its various guises and forms, and other specialised bodies. This meant that the SIS retained a repository of wisdom on unconventional warfare that could be drawn upon in the future by the powers-that-be as the Cold War emerged, and Calvert did his best to nurture a relationship with the SIS in order to further boost the Regiment's base of support among the special operations fraternity. As will be seen, in time he emphasised that cooperation between the SIS and SAS would be mutually beneficial, thereby trying to head off SIS opposition to a would-be competitor for tasks and resources). The SAS's winding-down process was scheduled to last until 16th. November 1945.

On the face of it, it seemed that the SAS's HQ staffs were simply left to tie up any loose ends in terms of administration, paperwork and remaining stores, with the Regiment "officially in 'suspended animation' " prior to its final shutdown.[36] Yet, in the absence of an Army Order from the Army Secretariat to officially rescind the SAS's licence to operate, its champions exerted as much pressure as they could in the corridors of power in a last-ditch attempt to save the Service in some form.

By October 1945, they were pushing for another and far more wide-ranging DTI review of the SAS's activities and roles, looking not only at SHAEF operations but those done in all Theatres of war. This could provide it with the time and opportunity that it needed to convince the powers-that-be not to liquidate the Service completely and, evidently, those in key senior positions were convinced of the value of such an exercise. The CIGS gave the SAS the benefit of the doubt, instructing Major-General Rowell and his staff to study all of the SAS's wartime endeavours in various Theatres and to report their findings to him as soon as possible.

Fighting back

On 12th. October 1945, Brig. Calvert wrote from SAS Troops HQ at Halstead, Essex, to many of his fellow senior officers, including such luminaries as Lt.-Col. David Stirling, Lt.-Col. Brian Franks, Lt.-Col. Ian Collins, Lt.-Col. the Earl Jellicoe, Lt.-Col. David Sutherland and Major Roy Farran. He informed them of General Rowell's upcoming in-depth study of the Regiments, and he urged them to write to the DTI with their views about past and future SAS activities, along with any supporting materials, such as official reports, letters, commendations or other documents. He explained that "the officer immediately concerned" was Lieutenant-Colonel C.A. Wigham, who had already in his possession "reports on SAS operations in W. EUROPE", which would have been passed on to him in connection with the Directorate's earlier analysis of the SAS's activities under the auspices of SHAEF. Calvert added that, "reports of SAS operations in ITALY and the MEDITERRANEAN Theatre [were currently] .. being obtained and forwarded" to Wigham, and presumably those for the Middle East, Northern and South-Eastern Europe would follow them.

As the Brigadier further related in his circular letter to his colleagues, "the object of this investigation is to decide whether the principles of operating in the SAS manner are correct" and, therefore, whether a strategic behind-the-lines capability was a necessary and worthwhile one to have in the post-war Army. If the answer to this question was positive, then the DTI team were to look at whether, in the light of its findings, SAS units should "be trained and maintained in peace[time]". Lastly, Brig. Calvert enlightened his comrades about "the actual terms of reference [given to the DTI team, which] were: 'An investigation of SAS techniques, tactics and organisation, without prejudice to a later examination of all organisations of a similar nature which were formed and operated in various theatres of this last war' ".[37] The importance of this stipulation about the possibility of a future study of other special forces will become apparent later, and the SOE and Phantom, to name but two, were also lobbying the authorities for their continued existence at this juncture.

In his letter of 12th. October 1945, the SAS commander refuted "the usual criticisms of the SAS type of force" that were levelled at them by their opponents. Calvert listed these in quotation marks, and noted that they were "the most normal ones" used against them. Hence, it is quite likely that these had been used by the SAS's critics during August and September 1945, when they tried to sway the key decision-makers away from approving the retention of the SAS in the Army, thereby contributing to its planned dismantling by the middle of November 1945.

The anti-special forces lobby's arguments were familiar ones that were deployed *ad infinitum* to slay the hydra of "private armies". Special forces were charged with incommensurately "taking up .. Commanders' valuable time", both with regard to fitting them into top level planning, and in dealing with problems that allegedly arose from their usage (notably the charges of indiscipline and prosecution of unsanctioned operations). It also was argued that army special forces had no immediately obvious function unless the armed forces were engaged in a fighting retreat or "fall-back" operations following an invasion, and even then there was "overlap .. with SOE and other clandestine organisations", such as the SIS. Another brick-bat used to beat the SAS was the supposed fact that it was "not adaptable to all countries". This criticism was not made of the other organisations mentioned and may have arisen due to the SAS's lack of jungle warfare experience. Yet, there was no evidence that the Regiment was simply incapable of combat in this environment (as it would prove later in Malaya, Brunei, Borneo and elsewhere). Moreover, these types of special units were condemned for "skim[ming] the regular [i.e. more 'normal' Army] units of their best officers and men", and levying an unwarranted and unworthwhile "expense per man". At the same time, in somewhat contradictory fashion, it was asserted that "any normal battalion could do the same job" just as effectively.

While some special forces were guilty of certain charges, and the SAS was by no means perfect (facing problems with, for example, parachute insertion, intelligence-work and other matters), Brig. Calvert addressed each point and demolished every argument laid against the SAS, drawing on wartime examples to make his points. He stressed its strategic capabilities, adaptability and flexibility, complementary and particular fighting skills, and its overall economy of force, manpower and resources. In looking ahead to the new world order, Calvert stated that if the SAS could carve out a niche for itself, it must cooperate with whatever other "types of units [were established by their political masters to] .. undertake operations". The Brigadier believed that among these would be his old associate Gubbins' SOE, and he hoped that it would retain "a world-wide organisation with an organisation in every .. country .. [in which conflict was] likely" to occur. This would be of great advantage to the SAS, because "when necessary, [the] SAS can [then] operate on [the basis of] this [SOE] organisation". It would have ready-made links to Resistance networks and agents, communications and other back-up facilities, as well as expert knowledge of the area at the SAS's disposal. Indeed, Calvert had started to make active preparations for post-war special forces cooperation and coordination, having presented his proposal for SAS/SOE partnership to leading members of the SOE, including General Gubbins. The SAS commander noted that, "all senior officers of [the] SOE with whom I have discussed" the plan agreed that it offered a way forward for both organisations. Indeed, on 14th. September 1945, the SOE's chief recommended the creation of a post-war global SOE network and, among the places that already figured in SOE planning for this, was Greece - the significance of which will become clear in due course.[38]

Champions of the SAS cause

Brig. Calvert received strong support for his campaign to save the SAS from his colleagues, notably Lt.-Col. David Stirling, and the commander of the 1st. SAS at the end of the War, Lt.-Col. 'Paddy' Mayne. But, over and above the wartime type of activities that Calvert envisaged for the future SAS, he wanted a peacetime Internal Security [I.S.] role for the Regiments - and not all of his comrades were as keen on this idea. Still, a number of them backed the concept, including Lt.-Col. Collins, who had incorporated the idea into his May 1945 memorandum. Moreover, Calvert received enthusiastic approbation for it from both Major Farran and the commander of the 2nd. SAS, Lt.-Col. Franks.[39]

Major Farran led one of 2 SAS's squadrons in 1945, having fought with it gallantly between 1943 and 1945 in N. Africa, Italy and France. During this time, he had acquired substantial guerilla fighting experience, as well as seeing things from the other side of the fence in Athens. General Strawson notes that, in response to Calvert's letter, "the legendary Roy Farran .. made a number of suggestions remarkable for their prescience". In fact, these were shared by the Brigade's C.O. and other colleagues, and included suggestions for behind-the-lines action in any Third World War with Russia, and peacetime deployment of the SAS for the purpose of "quelling [up]risings in various parts of the Empire", where the Regiments could offer "the immense advantage of economy of force .. in such affairs".[40] Similar views were held by Farran's immediate superior, Lt.-Col. Franks, who had fought alongside him in Italy during the 'Termoli' operations of October 1943 (following spells with other special forces such as the Commandos' 'Layforce', and Phantom, of which more in the next chapter). Farran and Franks were in constant touch during 1945, with Franks overseeing SAS operations in Western Europe, and they doubtless discussed the idea of an SAS I.S. role after the 2nd. SAS had returned to the UK in the summer of 1945.

Franks' opinions would have carried considerable weight, for he was "held in the highest esteem by all under his command", being as he was full of "understanding, initiative and brave[ry]". He was, according to Tony Kemp, "an inspiring leader [and,] .. after David Stirling, probably the most original thinker produced by the SAS during the War".[41] This accolade should perhaps be shared by Brig. Calvert, but it is true to say that, when Calvert received orders for a posting to the Indian Army (and thence the Army Staff College at Camberley), it was upon Brian Franks that the mantle of responsibility fell with regard to the fight for the SAS's survival - and the establishment of both wartime and peacetime roles for it.

Lt.-Col. Mayne had decided not to remain in the armed services, and so Franks became the main driving force in the campaign to save the SAS from mid-October 1945 on. Indeed, on 12th. October - the day that Brig. Calvert wrote to his senior colleagues about the future of the SAS - the first meeting of the Special Air Service Regimental Association was held at Wyvenhoe Park, the HQ of Franks' 2nd. SAS.

The Association was set up (like the SOE Comrades organisation) "to provide a means by which the Regiment can keep in touch with one another and maintain the *esprit de corps*". Franks was nominated as its Chairman, with Lt.-Col. David Stirling as President, while the Vice-Presidents were Calvert, Mayne, Collins and Bill Stirling. Among the dozen officers and men attending the first meeting were Association Secretary, Sergeant C. Gleed (2 SAS), SAS 'Original', Regimental Sergeant-Major Graham Rose (1 SAS), Lt.-Col. E.C. Baring (HQ SAS Troops), and Major J.J. Astor of SAS Phantom. But it was Franks who was acknowledged as the "key figure" in organising the SAS at this time and, subsequently, Lt.-Col. David Stirling went so far as to say that "had it not been for Brian Franks we would have been consigned to oblivion". Therefore, along with Mike Calvert, Brian Franks can be considered to be a true "founding father of the post-war .. SAS".[42] Yet, while this fact has been broadly acknowledged by senior members of the SAS and historians alike, the precise reasons for such an accolade have not been fully explained before, nor presented in any detail. (A similar state of affairs has pertained with regard to the founding of the Regiment in 1941, though my *SAS: Zero Hour* elaborates for the first time about how it really came into being). The following chapters will remedy the situation and plug a crucial gap in the history of the Regiment and some of its leading personalities.

2

A life-line: Greece

Brian Franks had been in the Guards Brigade Number 8 Commando in 1940 and served under Colonel Robert E. Laycock in his Layforce, as its signals officer. Franks then took command of the first ('H') Squadron of the Phantom special signals organisation, which concentrated on battlefield intelligence ('F' Squadron was later attached to the SAS Brigade). He was based with Phantom in the Middle East, before going on to fight with Brigadier T.B.L. Churchill's 2nd. Special Service Brigade [SSB] as its Brigade-Major. (The 2nd. SSB consisted of Army and Royal Marine Commandos, including one Commando led by Col. Ronald J.F. Tod, whose name will crop up here again). Franks served in Italy in 1943 and, nearing the end of that year, he transferred to 2nd. Special Air Service Regiment. While there, he worked in conjunction with the SRS [1st. SAS] and, by May 1944, he was chosen as 2 SAS's new commander, succeeding its founder, Lt.-Col. Bill Stirling. Thereafter, Franks led the 2nd. SAS in its victorious campaigns in France, where he fought alongside men from the SOE, SIS and partisan forces, gaining considerable experience of guerilla warfare along the way, before fighting in northern Germany during spring 1945.[1]

Once the Nazis were defeated, Lt.-Col. Franks seems to have fixed upon the idea then being floated in the SAS of getting involved in future "civil wars". The guerilla experience that he shared with numerous other SAS soldiers must have heightened his interest in SAS counter-guerilla action as a way of prolonging the Regiments' existence, and foremost among the supporters of this idea was his right-hand man, Major Roy Farran. He had had recent personal experience of counter-guerilla operations in Greece, where he undertook the sort of "observational" role expounded in May 1945 by the SAS HQ as a mainstay of post-war SAS activities. Farran witnessed an attempt by Left-wing Greek irregulars in December 1944 and January 1945 to seize Athens and establish a Socialist state in Greece. However, this was forestalled by British military forces, including a contingent of the technically separate but nonetheless closely linked brother unit of the SAS, the Special Boat Squadron. It was an off-shoot of the SAS and it included in its ranks many "SAS old hands", under the command until mid-December 1944 of Lt.-Col. George (The Earl) Jellicoe, and then Lt.-Col. David Sutherland. With prior knowledge of Greece, Major Farran convinced Land Forces Adriatic - under which the SBS operated - to allow him to observe the fighting. While he was in the capital, the Major met many old friends, such as SOE agent (and, from autumn 1945, SIS operative, then "soldier of fortune") Xan Fielding, as well as other members of the special forces fraternity, including the leader of No. 9 Commando, Col. Ronnie Tod. In the summer of 1944, Tod had fought through the Greek islands in 'Foxforce' alongside the SBS and 350 men of the Greek Sacred Squadron [GSS] (or *Heros Lokos*), which had been grafted onto the SAS in the autumn of 1942, in anticipation of operations in the Balkans (and subsequently, in North Africa). The GSS was then attached to the SBS prior to action in the Aegean Sea in 1944, but the links between the GSS and SAS remained strong, and the *Heros Lokos* wore SAS badges and insignia until their official disbandment on 21st. July 1945. While Farran was in Greece at the turn of 1944/45, he met up with some of Colonel Kristodoulos Tsigantes' GSS fighters, before returning to the UK early in 1945.[2] Hence, when Farran and Lt.-Col. Franks were seeking to establish the SAS's credentials as an I.S. force later on that year, the disturbed domestic situation in Greece would have been both well known to them (as it was to key supporters of the SAS cause, such as Churchill and Dempsey, who had recently visited Greece and been briefed about I.S. there), and an ideal location in which to try to put their theory into practise.

As was mentioned previously, the orders for the dissolution of the British SAS came through early in October 1945 and, at that point, Brig. Calvert was preparing to hand the Sloe House HQ over to his second-in-command, ex-Rifle Brigade officer and SAS Brigade-Major (since 1944), Major Lemon Evelyn Oliver Turton 'Pat' Hart. Indeed, Pat Hart was the last SAS officer to leave the SAS Brigade HQ at the end of the year, but those best placed to breathe life back in to the 1st. and 2nd. SAS Regiments during this critical period were their respective commanding officers. It has been assumed by all historians of the SAS that they were Lt.-Col. Paddy Mayne and Lt.-Col. Brian Franks. But this 'fact', reiterated by none other than David Stirling in 1984,[3] is, like numerous others about the early post-war SAS, actually incorrect. In reality, "at the end of the war, Mayne had no desire to stay on in the peacetime army", and he and several SAS pals decided to set off on an Antarctic survey expedition (putting into practise another of the post-war roles proposed in Lt.-Col. Collins' May 1945 memorandum). Mayne later returned to his job as a solicitor in the UK, where he kept in touch with SAS affairs as a Vice-President of the SAS Regimental Association.[4] But he was not the last commander of the 1st. SAS in 1945.

In October 1945, Lt.-Col. Mayne's deputy in the 1st. SAS was Major Harry Wall Poat. He had fought with the Regiment in Tunisia and Sicily during 1943, before taking up his post as Mayne's aide in 1944. Poat went on to fight along the Rhine in Operation Archway during March and April 1945. There, he was commander of 'A' and 'D' Squadrons of 1 SAS, which was part of 'Frankforce', under Lt.-Col. Franks. Before returning to civilian life "growing tomatoes in Guernsey",[5] Harry Poat was drawn into Calvert and Franks' scheme to keep at least part of the SAS going. By November 1945, Poat was commanding officer of the 1st. SAS and, as such, he was roped into their plans to maintain an SAS nucleus and to deploy personnel to a place where there was a good chance that, in due course, they could "observe" and learn about guerillas, and even develop counter-guerilla techniques and tactics. The most obvious choice to implement this scheme at the end of 1945, and a land with which the SAS stalwarts were most familiar, was Greece.

Greece in 1945

Prior to the attempted *coup de main* of December 1944/January 1945, there was internecine conflict among the Greek Resistance, the nature of which is still the subject of heated debate among historians. Without delving into the controversy over various players' aims, methods and policies at particular moments (see my *Postwar Counterinsurgency And The SAS* for a fuller discussion of the emergence of the Communist insurgency in Greece), it is reasonable to summarise that, following the invasion of Greece in 1941, the British - traditional friends and allies of the Greeks - tried to support numerous Greek partisan groups of different political hues, while favouring those of the Right more than those of the Left. Foremost among the Greek guerilla organisations that were meant to fight the Axis was the National Liberation Front (EAM - *Ethniko Apeleftherotiko Metepo*), which was a Leftist agglomeration of socialists and communists. By September 1941, it had organised a military arm, the irregular Popular National Liberation Army, or ELAS (*Ethnikos Laikos Apeleftherosis Stratos*). In addition, the Greek Communist Party (KKE - *Kommounistiko Komma Elladas*), led by Nikos Zachariades, created bands of *andarte* guerillas that operated mainly in the mountains that cover much of Greece and rise up to 9000 feet. They were commanded from April 1942 onwards by the formidable Ares Velouchiotes. To the right of the political spectrum there were several politico/military organs too, arguably the most notable of which was the National Democratic Greek League (EDES - *Ethnikos Demokratikos Ellinikos Syndesmos*), led by the charismatic Napoleon

Zervas. It was his group that received most support from the British government during the War.

By 1943, the clashes between the various partisan factions escalated, and EAM/ELAS were attempting to set up a parallel government-in-waiting that could take power when the invaders withdrew. Indeed, it declared that it was the provisional national authority when Axis forces began to leave Greece during March 1944. The blood-letting between the Left and Right intensified henceforth, though ELAS had eliminated most of its organised opposition other than EDES and one other right-wing group by this time. The British tried to deflect the Greeks away from factional fighting into a coordinated offensive against the occupiers, but tension continued to rise steadily throughout the summer. Colonel George Grivas' 'X' organisation of former Greek Army officers prepared for the worst, along with the remnants of the regular Army, such as the Sacred Brigade and the Field Artillery Regiment. In September 1944, a large British Expeditionary Force [BEF] under General Sir Ronald M. Scobie landed in Greece and sought to keep the sides apart. The British government hoped that a pro-British Western-style democracy could be established in the longer term, which was not what EAM/ELAS and the KKE wanted. Still, they appear to have preferred to avoid a head-on clash with the British forces at this juncture.

Following the BEF's arrival, popular opinion swung to the centre-right, and when the Greek Mountain Brigade, led by General Thrasyvoulos Tsokalotos, entered Athens in November, the chances of the Greek Left taking power waned. General Scobie called for the various resistance bodies to demobilise and disarm. This was vehemently opposed by ELAS and KKE forces in the light of recent clashes with the Right, and with tension in the air in December 1944, EAM organ-ised demonstrations in the capital against any hand-over of weapons. This proved to be the spark that set off an explosion of violence, as ELAS and the Communists attempted to seize the capital. Whether this was part of a calculat-ed plan is the subject of much debate and besides the point in this context. What is important is that it led to the deployment of 75,000 British troops, including the SBS, who crushed the urban guerillas by 9th. January 1945. Thereafter, the British retained their own occupying forces to try to oversee the restoration of normality in Greece, which patently would not occur overnight. The British forces (later totalling over 95,000, and in a strong parallel to Iraq from 2003 onwards) were committed to a potentially lengthy stay in Greece, while the economy, administration and government of the state were reconstructed.

British intervention

The British Army was required to monitor the demobilisation of ELAS and other armed organisations, and the participants agreed to this in principle, on 15th. February 1945, at Varkiza. But, although many weapons were handed in during the following months in accordance with the Agreement, clashes between paramilitary bands of the Left and Right continued unabated, Ares Velouchiotes for one conducting extensive guerilla operations until his death in spring 1945. Indeed, over the course of the year, the scale of the attacks and tit-for-tat murders increased, with many mountain villages and towns subject to banditry while the Greek security forces were in relative disarray. Houses were raided and burned by armed gangs, inhabitants abducted, beaten, tortured, mutilated, raped and murdered on both sides, and vendetta killings between families spiralled out of control. (At a time of grave poverty, this was often over issues like the stealing of a pig or roof tiles).

The prospects of a stable Greek political administration seemed to be slipping ever further away as lawlessness and disorder became endemic across much of the country, and "during 1945 there were frequent rumours that a military coup was imminent". This was forestalled largely by the stabilising presence of the British military and,[6] in April 1945, Prime Minister Churchill noted that "we have had to take all the risk, do all the work, shed all the blood and bear all the abuse. Poor old England".[7]

Within this cauldron, the British attempted to rebuild Greece's financial, social, military and political structures. From January 1945, a British Military Mission to Greece worked on re-creating a professional Greek National Army [GNA], while, by mid-1945, a British Police and Prisons Mission [BPPM] concentrated on reconstituting the Greek police and National Guard gendarmerie. "The British wanted to withdraw their troops at the earliest opportunity", so as to reduce the financial cost to Britain at a time when its economy was severely weakened, and they "therefore needed conditions orderly enough for parliamentary elections to take place that could produce a government with independent authority" and legitimacy, thereby allowing more British troops to withdraw. However, by the time that Nikos Zachariades returned from incarceration in a German concentration camp, in July 1945, independently-acting Communist cells and ELAS bands were engaged with 'X'-ites and the right-wing supporters of National Action in an ever more bitter struggle, so that the Internal Security situation deteriorated from bad to worse. Although historians still debate the KKE's intentions at this point, it did retain its underground *aftoamyna* self-defence organisation and, by the late autumn of 1945, Leftist armed "gangs .. were increasingly aggressive", especially in mountainous northern Greece. British troops were being called on to intercede between the factions more and more between July and December 1945. And from October onwards, British civil and military authorities on the ground perceived a sharp rise in the number of politically motivated irregular attacks and acts of violence, which caused them grave concern.[8]

Lt.-Col. Franks and his colleagues, particularly Major Farran and Brig. Calvert, would have been aware of the overall picture in Greece (which the SOE had singled out for post-war attention). In fact, the SAS is said to have had a Spanish-born Intelligence Officer on the ground at this juncture, who acted as an information conduit for the home Regiments.[9] Although British armed forces were not engaged in systematic counter-guerilla clearance operations in Greece in 1945, the rapidly deteriorating I.S. conditions, caused in the main by the activities of ex-partisan guerillas (alongside whom the SBS had fought the Germans), offered a timely and unmissable opportunity for SAS personnel to be deployed to a familiar and easily reached territory, where they could be ideally placed to demonstrate their potential for counter-guerilla operations, if and when they were called upon for this. In doing so, the Regiments could prove their worth as a peacetime I.S. force to the Army top brass in Britain and, even if events conspired so that this did not come about, the deployment of SAS soldiers to Greece on whatever pretext would give the SAS nucleus back in the UK another mast on which to fly the SAS flag while the War Office's DTI team reviewed its future.

Defying death - delaying disbandment

By the start of November 1945 - a month after the British SAS's supposed final passing-out parades - Brig. Calvert and Lt.-Col. Franks were busy putting their plans to prolong the life of the SAS Regiments into practice. Franks wrote from the 2nd. SAS's HQ near Colchester to the War Office Directorate that was invested with the power to raise or disband Army Units: the Directorate of Organisation. Acting through the Office of the Adjutant-General [AG], it had approved the formation of many new units during the War, including the SAS, often raising forces in the strictest secrecy and without retaining any documentation about its action. This makes it difficult to determine exactly what went on inside the AG sections during 1945, but it is known that, on 6th. November, Lt.-Col. Franks wrote to AG Section 2(B) about the "disbandment [procedures for the SAS, and that he] .. requested that [the] disbandment [completion] date [of 16th. November] for this Regiment be retarded until 30th Nov[ember] 1945".

Lt.-Col. Franks stated that there were several reasons for this delay, notably "outstanding questions which will have to be sorted out in the Orderly Room"; the need to arrange for "a small Rear Party .. to hand over the camp" to its owners; and the problem "of a few outstanding .. vouchers" that had to be cleared up in connection with the SAS's campaign in Italy. Additionally, there was the fact that "the Director of Tactical Research [sic.] at the War Office requires as much information as possible on SAS methods, [and] records [for this purpose] are being compiled" at present. He emphasised that he needed to retain "key personnel" who could remain in place to tie up all the loose ends, one of which was the "disposal of foreign-born personnel" (who, incidentally, included Spaniards among their number).

Furthermore, the first thing on the list of Franks' "reasons for this request[ed delay, was that] .. most men will have been posted to their new Units but there will inevitably be some exceptional cases".[10] At first sight, this comment doesn't appear to have any particular significance, for the War Office envisaged an ongoing process of interviews and transfers of SAS officers and men to the Parachute Regiment, and of ORs to the rest of the AAC or other Army regiments or Corps. Indeed, it was not until 28th. November that a Second-Lieutenant K. Preedy was transferred to 2 Para. from the SAS,[11] and there were doubtless others like him. However, Franks' statement can be seen in a wholly different and much more telling light when it is taken in conjunction with a similar request to the War Office Adjutant-General by Major Harry Poat, commander of 1 SAS, who wanted to delay its disbandment as well.

On 13th. November 1945, Major Poat wrote from his Regimental HQ at Highlands Hall, Chelmsford, Gloucestershire, seeking "application .. by this unit for an extension of the time allowed [by the War Office for disbandment] until 30th. November". He noted that this had been granted for 2 SAS, so he was clearly aware of Franks' activities. Likewise, the Major gave several reasons for his request, some of which were identical to Lt.-Col. Franks'. Poat repeated that there was a need "to leave a Rear Party in the Unit location, in order to clear the area thoroughly [before they relinquished it,] as the Camp is unlikely to be occupied again". There was a similar "appearance of several [outstanding] claims and accounts", as well as "a hitch .. in the return of [some] ordnance stores". Moreover, the foremost reason that 1 SAS's C.O. put forward for deferring its disbandment was "the fact that personnel have been called on [undoubtedly by Franks, the SAS's most senior officer,] to volunteer for special jobs, [and] the posting of officers, in particular, are not yet complete".[12]

As had been the case for 2 SAS, Major Poat was granted permission by the War Office to tackle its "unit problems" by 30th. November 1945. Despite the fact that the nature of the "special jobs" that both SAS commanders listed as their first and primary reason for delaying the Regiments' disbandment is not specified, Poat's request and Franks' previous reference to personnel transfers are highly significant when weighing up the overall picture of the SAS's activities during this period. The SAS undeniably was engaged by mid-November 1945 in actively preparing some of its officers and men from both Regiments for specific, unusual tasks and, soon afterwards, Maj. Poat thanked Brig. Calvert "for your great efforts in seeing that SAS men got .. a good job after the disbandment".[13] Arrangements were in hand but not yet completed and, therefore, the SAS HQs needed to continue to function for a while longer as the transfers of personnel for the "special job" were undertaken.

The key issue is the nature of the SAS's "special jobs". To determine this, it is worth recalling that Lt.-Col. David Stirling reminisced about the SAS War Crimes Organisation and how "Brian [Franks] set up a London HQ" for it, so as to ensure "that the operation went [on] unhindered" in the face of War Office apathy about it. He did this with the assistance of Randolph Churchill, son of the former premier and Franks' brother-in-arms in Layforce and 2 SAS. Further, in spite of his fall from office, Winston Churchill retained a great deal of political clout both in Britain and overseas, and, in addition to agreeing to become the Patron of the SAS Regimental Assocation, he gave "a lot of direct help" in establishing and supporting the SAS's new 'shadow' HQ,[14] from which its nucleus could operate. It oversaw the work of the War Crimes Teams in Germany who were busy tracking down those responsible for atrocities committed against fellow SAS troops and other military personnel. But it is not the case that "apart from [them] .. there were no British soldiers wearing the Winged Dagger [at the end of 1945 - following the supposed final disbandment - and that] Stirling's creation appeared to have had its day".[15]

Rather, as will be seen, SAS officers and men were being sent off by Brian Franks to Greece during November 1945, following in the tradition of similar wartime SAS "volunteer" missions, like those planned in 1942 for action in Persia and Iraq, in 1944 for the Netherlands, and in 1945 for Germany.[16] Further, David Stirling himself had set an example and precedent during the War by carrying out more than one "private enterprise job" irrespective of authorised planning arrangements (leading to charges of "private armies"), and this determination to do what was right whatever the "fossilised layers of shit" - as Stirling called them - at higher levels thought, was part of the SAS's ethos (for other examples see my *SAS: Zero Hour*).[17] In the face of the greatest danger ever to confront the Service - its impending extinction - Lt.-Col. Franks (assisted by Calvert and Poat) did whatever was necessary to get his Greek project off the ground, thereby providing the Regiments with a life-line.

Establishing a foothold

Lt.-Col. Franks set about attaching an SAS force to one of the many and unusual para/military organisations operating in Greece - the Allied Screening Commission, Greece, [ASC(G)]. It had been conceived in July 1945 by MI9, the agency responsible for directing and supporting efforts at escape and evasion from the enemy by Allied personnel who had been captured or found themselves stranded involuntarily behind the enemy's lines. The ASC(G) was tasked with "gathering and screening claims for reward or recognition [from] .. GREEK civilians who assisted Allied Escapers and Evaders during the War", especially during 1943. The Commission functioned with a staff of about 10 officers and 16 ORs during July and August 1945, with offices in Athens and Salonika (Thessaloniki). They dealt with claims from numerous locals with whom they were in touch, and their work-load increased in September and October as more people came forward for much-needed monetary redress at a time of great social distress in Greece. The ASC(G) consequently grew to more than a dozen officers and about 40 ORs, and two new Sub-Centre offices were opened to deal with Crete and the Aegean Islands (Cyclades), with the biggest Commission contingent based in the capital under the command of Lieutenant-Colonel H.J. Rydon.

From the few remaining records of the ASC(G), it can be discerned that Lt.-Col. Rydon and his staff were gearing up for a major effort to trace as many genuine claimants as they could over the next few months, before the Screening Commission was wound down (thereby further saving scarce British financial resources). Indeed, on 19th. October 1945, the ASC(G)'s Operational Order Number 1 directed its personnel, henceforth, to be pro-active in investigating Greek claims for reparation, which would entail their leaving the cities and visiting numerous locales in the countryside according to a timetable that should be publicised prior their arrival. In order to carry out this task effectively, British soldiers would be required to venture out into remote, difficult and dangerous terrain, in which irregular bands of both the Right and Left were active, and be self-contained and self-assured enough to complete their mission within a tight and politically pressured time-frame.

Although there was a large pool of manpower in Greece from which the ASC(G)'s new recruits could have been drawn, most would have been angling to get home after the end of the War, and Lt.-Col. Franks could have argued that highly motivated SAS soldiers with unequalled experience both of guerillas and of operating independently in isolated and highly exposed environments (and, incidentally, boasting possession of driving/mechanical and, in some cases, linguistic skills), were ideal for this time-pressured "special job". They could carry it out more efficiently and expeditiously than any other readily available service-men, and active preparations were in hand for them to do so by November 1945.

At the beginning of that month, the ASC(G) had "17 officers and 33 ORs" available for duty (13 officers and 30 ORs in Athens, one officer and two ORs in Salonika, one officer and one OR in Crete, and an officer on Rhodes). But, by 1st. December 1945, its actual strength had risen to 26 officers and 63 ORs, and most if not all of this one-off major increase in the Commission's manpower was due to reinforcement by officers and men from the 1st. and 2nd. SAS Regiments. Judging by remaining public records about the ASC(G), this taskforce must have been sent to Greece in November 1945 by Poat and Franks during their HQs' extended period of operation. According to the Commission's War Diary for the week ending 1st. December 1945, SAS soldiers had already arrived in Greece, where they would have settled in and prepared themselves for their unusual work. In a Commission Field Return of Officers for this period, there are references to the attachment to the ASC(G) of "10 S.A.S. officers", who were officially desig-nated as "I.O.s", or Intelligence Officers. For administrative purposes, this was to be both their given function and the Intelligence Corps their "Parent Corps or Regiment". The Commission's War Diary added that, "Posting Orders [were] Awaited" for the 10 SAS officers and, while the identity of all these SAS personnel is not clear, it is worth noting that the Allied Screening Commission's weekly Field Returns of Officers throughout December 1945 list "Officers attached in excess of W[ar] E[stablishment], less First Reinforcements", who were distinguished by the fact that "Posting Orders [were] Awaited" for them. Further illuminating details about them include dates denoting the time of their attachment to the Commission, their parent units, and the "Nature of [their] Attachment".

The table for the last week of December 1945 features the following information:

A[cting]Major P.A.T. Pinder	R[oyal] A[rtillery]	10/11/45	GSO II
A/Major G.K. Stuart	K[ing's] D[ragoon] G[uards]	21/12/45	IO
T/[emporary] Captain A. Protopapas	General List	17/11/45	IO
T/Captain E.P. Gibbs	R[oyal] A[rtillery]	14/12/45	IO
T/Captain R.T.C. Harrap	Intelligence Corps	01/12/45	IO
T/Captain G.R. Wiley	General List	21/12/45	IO

A large number of the tens of thousands of British soldiers in Greece were members of infantry and artillery regiments, and, as will be shown, there is evidence that the Royal Artillery was used as an administrative cover for some of the SAS contingent in the ASC(G) (as had been the case in the War). Whether any of the officers listed above came from the SAS is not known for certain, but the chances are that such "IO"s worked on tasks given to the 1st. and 2nd. SAS.

Over and above the SAS officers attached to the Commission in November and December 1945 who had "Posting Orders Awaited", an ASC(G) Field Return of Other Ranks for the week ending on 1st. December 1945, as well as those for the rest of the month, incorporate a separate list of men with an identical distinction that "Posting Orders [were] Awaited" for them. They were four "Serjeants", two Lance-Serjeants, two Lance-Corporals, and one Private, all of whose function was listed simply as "Clerk", along with another six Privates who were classed as "Driver/Batman". This gives a total of 15 ORs, and these reinforcements were unmistakeably identified in the ASC(G) documentation as "S.A.S." troopers.

Thus, by December 1945, there were about 25 SAS personnel attached to the ASC(G) and, although surviving records do not reveal the dispositions of all of them for the rest of their stint with the Commission, it is known that that organ had 18 officers and 59 ORs in Athens during December, compared to 13 officers and 30 men in November. In addition, a Sub-Centre at Volos was opened during December, with 2 officers and 10 ORs. And taking into account other transfers in and out of the ASC(G), it seems reasonable to assume that the bulk of the SAS mission was stationed in the Greek capital at the outset, and, once it was organised and acclimatised, some of its manpower was farmed out to other Sub-Centres, ready to travel into the Greek countryside.

Indeed, on 12th. December, the Commission's officers received new instructions in a "Directive on the Operation of Mobile Teams". These were to be formed to carry out enquiries in Greek rural areas and to make on-the-spot payments of up to £50 for valid reparation claims. The Teams were to consist of one officer, one OR driver, and one "Interpreter/Clerk", as "the bare minimum". These designations imply that the SAS's nine "Clerks" were to be used as interpreters in the Mobile Teams, along with the six SAS drivers and their officers. Indeed, the Directive stated that the minimum number of Mobile Teams operating at any one time in any given Sub-Area "should always be two" and, in view of the fact that, at this point, there were five Sub-Centres - at Athens, Salonika, Volos, Crete and in the Aegean Islands - up to 10 Mobile Teams could have been formed in December 1945. This would tally with the request for 10 SAS officers, while the 12th. December Directive argued that, "it is desirable that at least one B[ritish] OR should accompany the officer i[n] c[harge], preferably a Clerk", again tying in with the nine SAS "Clerks". However, with only six SAS drivers, it seems that there were either only half-a-dozen SAS Mobile Teams, or alternately, that the SAS "Batmen" were restricted to mainland driving operations (from the three Sub-Centres there), while other personnel were drafted in as drivers for Teams active on the Greek islands.

Whatever their number (probably between six and ten in all), the ASC(G)'s SAS Mobile Teams were urged to make up to 75% of their assessments and payments of claims in the field, in order to cut down the amount of time and effort that would be required to complete the Commission's work. In any case, this was due to come to an end by 31st. May 1946, the deadline set by the Attlee Cabinet (albeit later extended) for the withdrawal of all British armed forces from Greece. It was assumed that, by then, the Commission would have paid out considerably more than it had done to date, which was a total of £57,019 8/- 8d. from 1042 claims up to December 1945.

The Sub-Centre Mobile Teams were to travel in 15-cwt. trucks across physically treacherous and potentially bandit-infested mountains and, in view of this danger, "as far as possible, teams w[ere to] .. be self-contained and independent and .. carry:- small arms and ammunition; bedding; stationery etc.; [a] supply of rations; [and a] supply of petrol and oil". Each Team was to "follow carefully planned itineraries covering all areas through which Escapers and Evaders have passed", and they were to "halt at pre-determined collection points" in towns and villages designated by Allied Screening Commission (Greece) Command personnel who had traversed "the route [already and arranged] for due notice to be given to [Greek] helpers of the arrival of the team, for example, by contacting the Priest, Mayor or Chief of Police of the community", and by placing notices in the local press. Each Mobile Team's officer was meant to have made prior "contact [with] Presidents of Villages where it is intended that his team should halt, and make necessary arrangements for reception, accommodation, etc.". The Teams were to stop off every 15-20 miles in the more densely populated areas, less frequently where the population was sparser and, once a Mobile Team had arrived in its target locale, the officer was to "call all helpers together and announce [through an intepreter, if necessary,] the object of the team's visit with a few well chosen words".

The December 1945 War Office Directive laid down too that Greek "helpers will be interrogated and Claim forms will be completed" promptly. Interrogations would be undertaken after the officer had asked the "Mayor, President or other reputable persons" to identify "possible Black List personalities amongst claimants". All *bona fide* "helpers" would then be rewarded for their past assistance and paid from Sub-Centre "strong-boxes .. issued to Mobile Teams for safe-guarding .. money .. under the personal supervision of the officer-i[n]-c[harge]".

Meantime, with success dependent upon advance warning of a Team's impending arrival in the next locale, "during the interrogation, the truck will be despatched to warn [of] future stops", making use of "local .. telephones" and radio links to maintain contact and report progress back to the Team. Following the completion of their interrogations and payments, the Directive instructed that all written records relating to these activities should be destroyed, as "these are Top Secret documents". On completing their tours, the Mobile Teams would return to their Sub-Centres. Although the actual make-up of all the Teams is unknown, one that was ordered on 28th. December to make for Tripolis on the Peloponnese on 7th. January 1946 was a five-man unit led by Lieutenant C. Button, a veteran of World War 1 who had operated with the SAS in Persia during 1942; Lieutenant P.N.H. Poole, who led an SAS team in Normandy during 1944 and patrolled with *Maquis* resistance fighters; Lieutenant K.V. Lilley; SAS Sgt. Langton; and a Trooper Rees. This SAS Mobile Team set up their sub-HQ at Tripolis and, from 11th January, Lilley, Poole and two ORs undertook their duties, collecting and verifying claims made to the ASC(G) in their locality.

By this time, the rest of the British Army in Greece was withdrawing from the Greek countryside to its garrisons, so as not to be pulled into the spiralling violence between armed bands of the Right and Left that were clashing in the run up to the 31st. March 1946 Greek parliamentary elections. But while the Cabinet had directed in mid-December 1945 that British soldiers were to avoid becoming embroiled in 'peace-keeping' at this politically sensitive moment, in contrast, the Mobile Teams were instructed to take all "precautions .. to protect any sums of money carried .. from bands of brigands operating in the mountainous region" of Northern and Central Greece. Hence, the War Office clearly envisaged that the SAS may be drawn into armed confrontations with Greek irregulars and, although it's not possible to say whether, in his communications with the War Office at the end of 1945, Franks floated the idea that, if needs be, the SAS could develop counter-guerilla techniques and expertise that would be of value to the hard-pressed Greek security forces, the Service Department must have been at least aware of the possibilities that the deployment of the SAS force offered - even if officials were initially sceptical about such a role.

Indeed, in mid-January 1946, the War Office's Scientific Advisor was direct-ed by the Army Council to organise operational research in India into the develop-ment of new counter-guerilla methods and forces,[18] indicating Whitehall's interest in such matters at this juncture. The SAS's Greek commitment gave the

Regiments a breathing space in which to pursue their lobbying campaign back in Britain, as well as to demonstrate their flexibility and effectiveness, while additionally being ideally placed to at least "observe" and learn, and perhaps take on an "operational" (as per Collins' memo) role should the need and opportunity arise. The situation in Greece offered the Service a chance to prove itself again, this time in the post-war world, and Lt.-Col. Franks seized it, doing his utmost from then on to haul the SAS back from the brink.

Confirmation of the despatch of an SAS group to Greece in November 1945 was provided by another SAS legend and one of the 'Originals' of David Stirling's 'L' Detachment, Sergeant-Major Robert 'Bob' Bennett. One of the most respected figures in the Regiment's history, 'Benny' Bennett "set standards that today's SAS men still aspire to", and he was, by 1945, already "renowned in the early history of the SAS".[19] More importantly in this context, from his parent regiment the Grenadier Guards, he went on in 1940 to the Guards' Commando (Layforce). He served in it with Brian Franks and, during the war years, Bennett "volunteered for anything that was going". Hence, he would have been an ideal candidate for the post-war "special job" in Greece and, after initially leaving 1 SAS (in which he had served heroically in North Africa, Sicily, mainland Italy, France and Germany), he "had found little to interest him" on civvy street. Therefore, he was eager to get back into 'the action', and Brian Franks was able to offer his old comrade-in-arms (actually aged only 26) the chance to do that. Undoubtedly backed by the likes of Lt.-Col. Collins and Brig. Calvert at the Regimental Association (who themselves had pressed the Army higher-ups persistently for an SAS COIN role), Lt.-Col. Franks utilised the Association apparatus with its invaluable database of SAS "old boys" to contact men like Bennett who had left the Regiment and draw them into the Greek mission.

According to Bennett's account of proceedings at the end of 1945, an SAS HQ for the Greek operation was located secretly within the unlikely setting of the prestigious and palatial Hyde Park Hotel in Knightsbridge, west London. Brian Franks was the General Manager of the Hotel Group before the War and, on returning to the Hotel by December 1945 - following the closure of 2 SAS's official HQ - he utilised some of its rooms to organise the enterprise and to put up Bennett and other SAS men, who could scarcely have afforded to stay in such grand surroundings under normal circumstances. Indeed, the Hotel's bar reportedly "became a sort of unofficial meeting place cum employment exchange for SAS personnel who were in the London area". From the Hyde Park's portals, at least "one group was sent off to Greece" by Lt.-Col. Franks. Confirming what is known from ASC(G) records, Bob Bennett recalled that he and 20 or so other SAS soldiers went to Greece "on a strictly unofficial basis";[20] that is, without any public acknowledgement of the venture from Whitehall. This is hardly surprising in view of both the official closure of the SAS's HQs and the current political climate of fiscal retrenchment in which such a scheme could lead to difficult questions being asked about its financing and its remit.

The existence of this SAS contingent only came to light in the early 1990s, with the publication of a few lines of an interview with Bob Bennett in two books by Tony Kemp. (He and his fellow researcher Gordon Stevens were involved in the late 1980s in the production of an unbroadcast television series about the Regiment). But while Tony Kemp wrote that, "in theory the SAS ceased to exist .. [yet] in practice odd little pockets of it survived for quite some time in strange places .. [like] Greece",[21] my research into the British military's involvement in the Greek I.S. situation from 1945 onwards shows that the SAS's presence in the Balkans is far less bizarre than it at first appears. Public records about the Allied Screening Commission to Greece, combined with Bob Bennett's recollections about his "job .. to investigate claims from Greeks who had helped forces personnel during the War and to arrange [the] payment of outstanding debts",[22] confirm that Lt.-Col. Franks arranged for the SAS's attachment to the Commission, and that he subsequently supported its activities through the Regimental Association and his 'shadow' HQ at the Hyde Park Hotel.

The remaining evidence suggests that the SAS mission was backed up by at least some officials in the War Office and, of all its various branches, it is most likely that the Directorates of Intelligence, and of Military Operations [DMO], were involved. The DMO had supervised the Regiment's operations during the War, including those in the Middle East Theatre. (This included Greece during 1945, and thereafter). It oversaw SAS activities through the wartime Raiding Forces HQ and then, after the end of the War in 1945, the Directorate remained clued-in to post-war developments in Greece. Further, while Bob Bennett initially had to take the rank of Bombardier to serve as a "Batman" (or driver) there, he "insisted [that he was] .. in the pay of the British Army" throughout his Greek tour of duty, indicating that the SAS's 'directing staff' in the Hyde Park Hotel was allowed by the military authorities to "set up the administration of salaries etc.", as was the case in numerous subsequent 'non-attributable' (i.e. deniable) post-war SAS operations.[23]

In order both to boost *esprit de corps*, and to reinforce the inherent political statement that was being made by the very existence of the SAS's shadow HQ and the operation of SAS Mobile and War Crimes Teams in south-eastern and northern Europe - that the SAS was still around and had a role to play in the new international order - Lt.-Col. Franks additionally insisted that the SAS must retain their distinctive Winged Dagger badges and regimental identification markings. He apparently acquired the War Office's approval to make this a matter of policy, for the post-war SAS units (with their common nomenclature of "Teams") continued to don their distinguishing apparel. The SAS War Crimes Investigation Teams were allowed "to wear [SAS] regimental insignia and berets" in the course of their work in Allied Occupied Europe and in the UK, and they did so until "as late as 1949". Similarly, the SAS group in Greece "continued to wear full SAS insignia" during their time there.[24]

Over and above these concessions to the supposedly defunct 1st. and 2nd. SAS Regiments and their covert London HQ, the commander of the SAS's War Crimes Organisation, Major 'Bill' Barkworth, "was officially listed under his parent regiment", thereby making it less likely that unwanted questions would arise about the continued existence of the SAS from curious Whitehall officials, politicians, the press, or parliament. Likewise, this arrangement was made with regard to Greece, with Bob Bennett, for one, being required to officially "enlist in the Royal Artillery as a bombardier",[25] once more indicating that the organisation of cover arrangements for the SAS was a matter of high-level policy.

Wining and dining - the culinary offensive

Unfortunately, there are very few further snippets of written information about the crucial period at the turn of 1945/46, and the "unofficial" status of the SAS taskforce means that there probably would have been little, if anything, written down by those involved in the first place.[26] Nevertheless, it is known that Lt.-Col. Franks "used his considerable political connections" to keep the SAS Mobile Teams going during 1946, as was the case with the War Crimes Teams. Like David Stirling before him, the *de facto* leader of the new SAS was "not entirely above using politics to serve his own long term aims" with regard to the Regiments, and Franks particularly used his affiliation with Randolph Churchill (formerly of 2 SAS) to ensure that his 'babies' prospered. Sir Winston Churchill was the most perceptive Western politician of his day in terms of the growing

Soviet threat to Europe, and he was warning of its dangers by 1945. Not long before his famous Fulton, Missouri, "Iron Curtain" speech, of 5 March 1946, he became the SAS Regimental Association's Patron, and doubtless he would have been most interested in the SAS's activities in a country that he knew from personal experience early in 1945 could be endangered by the KKE's forces. Further, Franks continued networking behind the scenes, with the Hyde Park Hotel and several Pall Mall clubs (such as White's, in which David Stirling was a resident in 1946), becoming the battle-ground of what, in retrospect, was the SAS's most crucial campaign: that for the hearts and minds of key "politicians and senior military officers". They were "wined and dined" by Franks as part of a "tireless effort" to sell the SAS to the Whitehall players (including Boy Browning, who was currently dealing with guerillas in the Dutch East Indies),[27] at a time when the War Office was considering what future, if any, there was for the Regiments. In addition, the DTI was bombarded with pro-SAS submissions, and from the few available surviving records it seems that the Service Department was at least aware of what the SAS group was up to in Greece.

By the start of 1946, British military and political intelligence sources in Greece were reporting back to London on the reorganisation of the KKE's military units and an upsurge in Communist irregular attacks. Although the Party's leader, Zachariades, appears to have preferred a classic Leninist urban coup should other paths to power fail, the emergent Communist insurgency gravely undermined internal security in Greece and even threatened to disrupt or delay the scheduled 31st. March government elections. The British set great store by these, hoping that, once they were held and a legitimised administration was in office, things would improve and the expensive British military presence in Greece could be scaled down forthwith. This prospect now appeared to be in real jeopardy, and the worsening situation must have both concerned and excited the SAS HQ in London, as the possibility of some sort of I.S. role for its troops loomed larger.

In fact, as has been mentioned, on 15th. December 1945, the British Land Forces Greece [LFG] HQ and British Troops Greece [BTG] had been ordered to keep out of active I.S. operations in the run up to the national elections. The British government did not want to give various neighbouring Communist states any grounds for arguing that the result of the vote would be affected by pressure from the British military, and that this should be balanced by the despatch of armed 'volunteers' to back the KKE. Consequently, I.S. lay in the hands of the Greek security forces - the paramilitary National Guard and police forces, supported by a fledgling and weak GNA. It was made equally responsible for retaining I.S. by the Greek government, but it had little in the way of training or preparation for this prior to 1946.[28]

At about the same time that these developments were occurring, on 5th. January 1946, the ASC(G)'s Mobile Teams were urged to act with the "utmost rapidity" and pay all valid claims to "helpers", so that the organisation's work could be wrapped up before the May 1946 deadline. On that day in January, one more "S[taff] Serjeant" with "Posting Orders Awaited" was added to the ASC(G)'s Field Return of Other Ranks. It is unclear where he was assigned to, but, at that time, there were Mobile Teams operating out of bases in Athens (18 officers and 48 ORs), Salonika (5 officers and 5 ORs), Crete (4 officers and 4 ORs), Volos (5 officers and 4 ORs), the Peloponnese (2 officers and 2 ORs), and the Cyclades (one officer). There are few further details about the Teams' work, though it is known that Captain G.W. Saunders led a three-man unit that was active in the Athens district, and the SAS contingent in Greece included Captain T. Bryce, Sgt. Allen and Sgt. James McDiarmid (from Perth, and formerly of the Black Watch), who had fought with the SAS in North Africa during 1943 and was currently in contact with the SAS Regimental Association through one of its superiors, Regimental Sgt.-Major Rose.[29]

From early 1946, the Teams concentrated on clearing up claims made for assistance given by locals to SOE Force 133 (which should have been relatively easy to verify, given that there were at least 20 former SOE operatives attached to various British security bodies in Greece, including the BMM(G), from 1945, while the British Ambassador, Rex Leeper, had headed an SOE section in 1941). By the end of January 1946, the Commission had paid out £65,628 16/- 2d., but, on 7th. February, its 39 officers and 63 ORs were instructed to stop taking any more claims at the end of that month, with the War Office refusing to make any more payments after 28th. February (by which time the total given out by the ASC(G) reached £82,638 16/- 2d.).[30] Thus, by early February 1946, it would have been abundantly clear to Lt.-Col. Franks and his colleagues that the ASC(G) 'home' for the SAS was soon to be taken away, and that, if the Service's presence was to continue and burgeon in Greece, fresh arrangements would have to be made.

A changing role, spring 1946

Furthermore, in view of the downwards spiral on the I.S. front in Greece, and the British government's earnest wish to see the Greek elections staged on time and without any major hindrances, it is likely that Lt.-Col. Franks turned this tricky situation to his and the SAS's advantage and firmly pushed the idea of an SAS counter-guerilla mission. The embryonic Greek National Army was in dire need of help in this respect and, while the Attlee government could not afford to take the risk of authorising its occupying forces to assist in I.S. action at this point, a small, covert and deniable SAS unit could have offered some valuable assistance, as well as fresh insights into counter-guerilla warfare, as the Communist military menace grew.

An SAS COIN commitment may have been favoured by the Greeks themselves, especially by the likes of Colonels Roussos, Tsigantes and Kalinski Andrews, who, until a few months before, were senior members of the SAS's cousins, the Greek Sacred Squadron. It is worth recalling too that Calvert had countenanced and begun to actively seek post-war cooperation with the SOE. Its top officers agreed with his vision and, after the War, no less than half a dozen SOE personnel were transferred to the BMM(G), and they could have helped the SAS at this time.[31] Indeed, Richard Aldrich has asserted that there is "some evidence .. [albeit publically unavailable] .. that SOE [personnel] .. assist[ed] in the fight] .. against [the Communist] guerillas in Greece [until] as late as 1948".[32]

The lack of public records means that it is hard to say what exactly was going in Greece during the first months of 1946, and so it is necessary to introduce an element of speculation about events. And it is what the released records do not say that is sometimes most revealing. By 21st. February 1946, the War Office's Deputy Assistant Adjutant-General [DAAG] informed the SAS's sponsor Directorate - Air - that, after a three months (unexplained) delay since the supposed dissolution of the SAS, "we are now in a position to cancel the Royal Warrant that authorised the f[or]m[atio]n of the SAS Regiment". The timing of this decision is not as arbitrary as might be presumed, for it seems to have arisen as a result of the impending curtailment of the SAS's "special job" with the ASC(G), and it came a day after the Chiefs of Staff, unusually, approved of training for the GNA in "modern methods of guerilla warfare". Indeed, with Brian Franks' culinary offensive in full swing, he would have been lobbying hard for the Greece-based SAS group to remain in place in some shape or form and, in fact, there was a further delay in the cancelling of the Royal Warrant for the SAS. The DAAG explained that, "we think it might be advisable to defer .. until the future of other regiments of the AAC (Glider P[ilot]) Regiment and Parachute Regiment are settled".[33] (As will be seen, this took longer than expected).

Further, it seems more than mere coincidence that, on 8th. February 1946 - the day after the Allied Screening Commission (Greece) was directed to cut short its operations - the War Office Adjutant-General contacted the Officer-in-Charge of Army Air Corps Records (which included the SAS) in Edinburgh, "in order that action may be taken to effect the [delayed] formal disbandment of the Special Air Service Regiment, AAC". To this end, the Directorate of Organisation stated that it "desired to ascertain whether any OR[s] are still borne on the str[ength] of that regiment and, if so, how they are situated".[34] This could indicate that some War Office staff were uncertain about the current position in Greece, or alternately, that they were double-checking that there were no administrative loose ends left to tie up before taking action to formally wind up the SAS Regiment.

Whatever the case, Major B.K. Smith of AAC Records wrote back to the War Office on 13th. February 1946, "that there are no personnel borne on the strength of the Special Air Service Regiment, all personnel having been either transferred from the AAC or posted to the Parachute Regiment". But, he added a crucial caveat to this, that "it is possible that there are a few personnel serving in Greece [with the ASC(G)] and [in] North West Europe [in the War Crimes Organisation] which may still be wearing S.A.S. shoulder flashes". The AAC administration may not have been informed about precisely what it was that they were doing or for how long these missions would last. But the Major must have been included 'in the loop' so far as their existence for official administrative purposes was concerned, in order to keep the books straight and to deflect any unwanted attention from these SAS personnel. The Major elaborated that some time before (probably on 1st. December 1945, when the SAS HQs were closed down), "these men were posted *on paper only* [emphasis added] to the Army Air Corps H[igh]l[an]d B[attalio]n and Army Air Corps Depot [Aldershot], on disbandment of the SAS Regiment".

It is therefore quite clear that, after departing from Eastern Command on 30th. November 1945, the 1st. and 2nd. SAS Regiments were transferred on paper to their old wartime heartland (the Stirlings having been two of many SAS men who came from Scotland, while the Brigade's training area was at Prestwick Aerodrome in Ayrshire).[35] The retention of the SAS by the Army Air Corps served as another cover to conceal the operation of the shadow HQ run by the SAS nucleus in London, from which the activities of the Greek Mobile and War Crimes Teams were orchestrated.

Judging by the evidence, it's a distinct possibility that, around the end of February 1946 (just as Churchill planned to warn of a Communist 'Iron Curtain' in Eastern Europe), Brian Franks' charm offensive with the Whitehall power-brokers won the SAS another stay of execution, the War Office being persuaded to allow its Greek unit to acquire a new status and cover. Bob Bennett recalled that he had served "for four years .. in Greece with [what he referred to as] the British Military Reparations Committee" [BMRC] and that he and other SAS soldiers "became entangled in the Greek Civil War" from 1946 onwards.[36]

Such a cover name would have attracted little attention in Greece or Britain. In the unlikely event that its presence became the subject of public interest, it would have been seen to address the concurrent calls coming from the Greek Centre and Right, via the media, for the British government to back the campaign of the Athens-based non-governmental organisation styled as the "Greek Reconstruction Claims Committee" [GRCC], which was busy pressing the case for international recognition of Greece's "right to reparations".[37]

In the middle of March 1946, Captain (later Major) Michael Ward arrived in the Greek capital as GSO II, to help Major P.A.T. Pinder at the ASC(G)'s HQ, to wind down the Commission. Public records show that Ward was doing this from April onwards. He had fought in wartime Greece as a member of the SOE, alongside the Greek partisans, as well as SBS/SAS soldiers. Yet, he could not recall that there was any group of SAS men working in or alongside the Allied Screening Commission during the time that it finished its work up to the middle of 1946.[38] The ASC(G)'s strength in April 1946 appears little different to that in March, when its 39 officers and 69 ORs were stationed more broadly in geographical terms than ever before, as shown below:

Athens	16 officers 40 ORs	Salonika	5 officers 7 ORS
Thebes	3 officers 2 ORs	Crete	4 officers 4 ORs
Volos	4 officers 5 ORs	Peloponnese	4 officers 4 ORs
Corinth	2 officers 1 ORs	Cyclades	1 officer

However, while the ASC(G)'s staffing figures for April 1946 show little apparent change, with the Commission having 37 officers and 60 ORs (only two officers and nine men less than in March), it seems that the SAS contingent was in the process of leaving the ASC(G) by April, and most of this loss was made up before Major Ward took over the main responsibility for it. This would explain why he was unaware of the presence of a specific SAS group at this stage. ASC(G) files show that, by April, there were departures from the organisation other than those that were part of the Army's ongoing demobilisation - codenamed 'PYTHON' - which saw the bulk of the British armed forces stationed in Greece return to the UK over the course of the next couple of years. In the ASC(G)'s "Release Returns" for April 1946, there is an interesting "Release" list for the week ending 6th. April, which may provide evidence of the transfer of SAS personnel from the Commission to a new home.

This listing gives the following information:

"Release"	"By Ranks"	"By Trades"	TOTAL
A/S Group 29	1 Private	2 Serjeants, 2 Privates	4 Clerks
A/S Group 30	1 Serjeant, 4 Privates	5 Privates	5 Batmen/Drivers
A/S Group 31	3 Privates	1 Private	1 Orderly
A/S Group 32	1 Serjeant, 1 Private		

In the following week, there were further releases from the four Groups, which were presumably Sub-Area Groups (or "A[rea]/S[ub] Groups"), and although concrete conclusions cannot be drawn from this documentation,[39] it is feasible that some SAS Clerk interpreters and Batmen drivers were being transferred out of the ASC(G) ready to carry out other duties. If this is indeed the case, then the next question that requires addressing relates to the nature of their new role and disposition. The lack of available data means that it is innately difficult to determine this. But, in a secret War Office Organisation Table for "Paramilitary Establishments", amended on 16th. March 1946, there is a mysterious unit listed next to the "Greek Election Observation Mission" (itself actually designated as the Allied Mission for Observation of the Greek Elections, or AMFOGE, which was based in Athens). This unusual unit was dubbed the "Mil. Est. Brit. Res. Min." [MEBRM], which consisted, on paper at any rate, of 2 officers and 13 ORs.[40] Although only speculation, it is not unreasonable to suggest that this was the "Mil[itary] Est[ablishment], Brit[ish] Re[paration]s Mi[ssio]n", a title that closely resembles Bob Bennett's recollections about a "British Military Reparations Committee" (and, as demonstrated by the alternate title given to AMFOGE, one possible permutation of the MEBRM). The MEBRM's complement may well have come from the ASC(G) some time between mid-March and mid-April 1946, and the number of officers and men lost by the Commission and listed in the British Reparations Mission tallies very closely (and is exact for officers).

Whether this was the case or not, it would have been relatively easy for the small 'BMRC' of Bombardier Bennett *et al* to go about its business surreptitiously without attracting undue scrutiny. During 1946, Greece was awash with unusual Greek, Allied and British "Paramilitary" and "Special and Secret Establishments". In addition to the dozens of units making up the British Troops Greece, the LFG, and the BMM(G), there were numerous transient and more durable organisations involved in the security field. Among these were several military assistance groups attached to the United Nations' Relief and Rehabilitation Administration [UNRRA], 100 small British Army Teams attached to the AMFOGE, the RAF Delegation to Greece [RAFDG] and its associated units, the British Naval Mission to Greece, the BPPM, SIS front organisations (such as the Inter-Service Liaison Department, Middle East), and a 48-man British Army contingent linked for an undisclosed purpose to the Athens Embassy's Information Department.[41]

The BMM(G) reflected during 1949 that, at that juncture, there were dozens of unofficial Greek security force units operating along with established agencies, though there were "probably fewer unofficial units than in the past".[42] Hence, the deployment of "unofficial" or at least non-established forces was part and parcel of the Greek conflict, and the SAS/BMRC would have fitted into this cauldron without difficulty. Presuming that the British Military Reparations Committee was active by April 1946, there still remains the crucial question of the SAS's designated role in Greece from then on. Although the GNA was not handed joint responsibility along with the police and gendarmerie for counter-guerilla operational planning by the Greek government until July 1946 (by which time the KKE's insurgency had kicked into gear), from March of that year, the GNA became more and more involved in I.S. operations. The Greek parliamentary elections proceeded in that month, in the face of considerable unrest (and a KKE boycott), and the new Centre-Right administration returned by the people sought to consolidate its position. Backed by its British sponsors, it planned to hold a national referendum on a new Greek Constitution, thereby undermining the KKE's claims that the new administration did not fully represent the people's views on the political future of the country. This was to be held on 1st. September 1946 and, once that question was settled, the British hoped that the Greek government could assert its authority (thereby affording further reductions in the costly British military presence, at a time of growing economic difficulties for the UK). In the face of the mounting threat from thousands of ex-ELAS and Communist irregulars in Greece (as well as the many right-wing armed bands in existence), it is more than likely that British and Greek officials gave the go-ahead to the SAS rump to retain a deniable force in Greece that could provide much-needed I.S. assistance, if only as a stop-gap measure while other options were considered and arranged.[43]

It seems reasonable to assume that, from April 1946, the small SAS force offered counter-guerilla training advice to various GNA units in the light of their knowledge and experience of guerilla fighting. This would have focused on patrolling, ambushing, weapons-handling and close-quarter battle techniques, and Bob Bennett for one is known to have operated "in a training role". But, in addition, it is likely that some SAS soldiers showed their Greek trainees how things should be done in practice, by taking part in battlefield operations against the Communist insurgents. Indeed, as the KKE's military forces became better coordinated and their area of operations spread across Greece, by May 1946, the Foreign Office backed the idea of British troops lending active combat support to the GNA in the field. As Sir David Stirling and others have averred, Bob "Bennett was a good man to have alongside [one] in a fire-fight", and should the opportunity to engage the enemy have presented itself, he would not have been the type to pass it up and sit on the sidelines while his wards fended for themselves. He would have revelled in the chance to get to grips with the enemy and, in fact, it is on record that 'Benno' "serve[d] in Greece on anti-terrorist duties". Some of his SAS colleagues were engaged in similar clandestine activities and at least a few were "actively fighting on the Royalist [anti-KKE] side", possibly along with ex-members of the Greek Sacred Squadron.

The 'Olympus incident'

Indeed, while SAS activities at this time have gone largely unrecorded, it's worth mentioning an intriguing incident that might have involved Bennett, though this cannot be categorically verified. On 10th. October 1946, a Corporal and a Signalman from a Mobile Control Unit [MCU] left Larissa, in the mountains north-west of Volos, where the ASC(G) had had a Sub-Centre and Mobile Teams operating a few months before. MCUs were *ad hoc* units formed from various formations, due to a shortage of RASC personnel, and this MCU's vehicle broke down, requiring the men to arrange for another party to drive out and assist them. Another Signaller was despatched with "Private Jones of MCU Larissa", and they were accompanied by one "D[ri]v[e]r Bennett". Although the Curator of the Museum of Army Transport has averred that there were no dedicated SAS MCUs in Greece, he agreed that some SAS personnel were active on "anti-terrorist duties". And it is at least possible that Bennett was called upon to help with this distress call in the potentially hostile Thessaly mountains, south of Mount Olympus. As it happened, the rescue unit itself acquired a puncture en route to the stranded MCU vehicle, and so the group decided to call back to base via a local telephone. However, they were accosted by a band of 40-50 "Greek partisans", who reportedly questioned the Britons for about half an hour, before releasing them. The trio then returned to Larissa, presumably joined by their comrades some time afterwards. Whether this incident records a brush between SAS and guerilla fighters cannot be known for sure, but it at least illustrates the type of dangers faced by British soldiers at the time, and none more so than the operators of the BMRC.[44]

As indicated already, it is unfortunate that, from the time that the Foreign Office supported British military participation in counter-guerilla operations - in May 1946 - until that October (a date whose significance will become apparent in due course), there is a relative void in the British public record, with many key files destroyed, weeded or closed due to their sensitive contents.[45] Still, one fact that is known, is that, on 18th. June 1946, the Deputy Assistant Adjutant-General at the War Office informed the SAS's sponsor Directorate - Air - that, "all officers have now been removed from the Special Air Service Regiment".

On the face of it, it is something of a mystery as to why it took until this particular moment to effect this change, and uncertainty also clouds the question of how many officers and men the SAS retained, and until when. It is possible that new administrative arrangements for the two MEBRM/BMRC officers were only finalised within the 'back channels' of Whitehall in mid-June 1946, (or that the delay was caused by further changes either in the status of the SAS's home-based HQ directing staff, or with regard to the SAS War Crimes Organisation). Whatever the reason, the War Office DAAG continued that, in the light of the official removal of serving officers from the SAS, "the Reg[imen]t can, therefore, be formally disbanded, and we enclose a draft A[rmy] O[rder] for the July 1946 issue".[46] Hence, despite War Office statements made during February 1946, the Adjutant-General did not wait for the final settlement of new bureaucratic arrangements for the Army Air Corps and its constituent regiments (Glider Pilot and Parachute), before taking action with regard to the SAS. Rather, it went ahead with the disbandment of the Regiment after resolving its particular personnel matters and, apparently, after setting up a new organisation within which the SAS Greek contingent could work - the BMRC.

By virtue of Army Order Number 128 of the Army Council Secretariat, the SAS name was at last officially expunged from the Army lists, and it was noted that "the effective date of disbandment is 30th. June 1946". It appears that only two other, underused published sources have recorded this fact, that "almost a year after its sub-units had ceased to exist [although this is not wholly true] or disappeared into the ranks of other armies, Army Order 128 of August [sic.] 1946 tardily tidied up and officially disbanded the SAS as whole".[47] At the same time, the Whitehall authorities took the opportunity to officially wind up the SOE (even though it too was supposed to have ceased functioning but would survive beyond the grave under the auspices of the SIS).[48] Even when the War Office finally decided to hoist down the SAS colours (if not to make all its personnel redundant entirely), the Army Order was not acted upon on 30th. June. On 29th. July 1946, the Directorate of Air informed the Adjutant-General that it had been "passed for action", and the Directorate added that, "we are sorry for the delay which we cannot properly explain" - not an uncommon occurrence in this saga! The Order was finally filed in August 1946, declaring the SAS, at least in name, to be officially dead.[49] However, its resurrection (if indeed it can be called that) would not be long in coming.

As has been elaborated, despite these developments in mid-1946, the War Crimes Teams and the BMRC continued to function, and although it is not known precisely who at the highest levels of British officialdom was 'up to speed' with these arrangements, by the spring of 1946, Field-Marshal Montgomery was the CIGS-designate, and he took over from Field-Marshal Brooke in June 1946. In that month, Monty's friend and confidante, Major-General Sir Miles Dempsey, was appointed (fortuitously for the SAS) as the new Commander-in-Chief of the Middle East Land Forces [CINCMELF], (replacing Major-General Bernard Paget). While Montgomery was consistently ambivalent about special forces and worried about maintaining control over "private armies", and both men were tradition-alists with regard to the type of I.S. procedures that they preferred,[50] they shared an admiration for the SAS. Dempsey, in particular, supported the idea of a post-war SAS, was familiar with the I.S. position in Greece, and harboured the desire to become the SAS's Colonel Commandant. He would have been regularly in touch with Brian Franks and other senior SAS personalities as well, in his capacity as a senior figure in the SAS Regimental Association during this period. Additionally, Franks was using the new London Special Forces Club of old com-rades as a back channel of contact and was in touch with key SIS figures who had Balkans connections, such as David Smiley and Harold Perkins. Indeed, Stephen Dorril states that Franks was actually working for the SIS's War Planning Department in 1946, and in addition, the Regiment's reputation at the Middle East Forces [MEF] HQ was "very high".[51] Thus, if the Theatre Command was aware of the SAS's activities at this stage (which seems to have been the case, as will be shown), then it would have viewed these in a favourable or at least tolerant light. This helped the supporters of the SAS ideal to proceed with their counter-gueril-la experiment in the Balkans and, while the fight for the SAS's survival (albeit in another guise) continued on the battlefield, it was also played out in the Whitehall corridors of power.

Fighting for survival on two fronts

From October 1945 onwards, the War Office DTI was busy studying the past activities of the SAS and, bearing in mind what Brig. Calvert had requested that June, its investigation was expressly one undertaken "without prejudice to a later examination of all organisations of a similar nature". Hence, the pro-SAS lobby pressed its case and, by February 1946, Lt.-Col. Franks seems to have got backing in some parts of the War Office (such as the DAW) for the continuation of the SAS's Greek mission, albeit in another guise. Of all the Department's Branches and Directorates, though, the DMO was traditionally the most supportive of the SAS, and its chief during 1945/46, Major-General C.H. Sugden, may well have given Franks his support for the BMRC's work. Indeed, not long after it was constituted, it appears that the DMO was in touch with the DTI about extending the scope of its ongoing investigation into special forces. Also, in April 1946, a War Office Inter-Service Working Party enquiring into the worth of an auxiliary Army force recommended the establishment of a Territorial Army, opening up the possibility of a Territorial SAS Unit, as proposed by Brig. Calvert. It seems more than mere coincidence that, at this time, the DMO adopted another of Calvert's recommendations and called for a wide-ranging study of British and Allied special forces, with a view to pinpointing the Army's future requirements in this regard. By 17th. April 1946, the DMO officially asked the DTI to undertake a full-scale enquiry into the subject and, on the following day, a four-man Working Party under Major-General L.C. Manners-Smith began its work.[1]

It's unsurprising that the War Office DTI was asked to concentrate its attentions on wartime special forces yet not expressly consider the possibilities of a role for them in I.S. duties, which was a novel and unproven concept. Nonetheless, while the British had not had happy experiences with I.S. special forces when they were deployed in Palestine during the 1930s (as will be seen), in May 1946, an Indian Army Infantry Brigade was directed to investigate potential adaptations to counter-guerilla forces and techniques that may be required in the light of recent wartime experience, and to report on these to the War Office. The brief was to include "the use of ambushes" by "lightly equipped forces" with air support, and to assess the potential worth of "commando-paratroop type" troops, which was a very progressive development in historical terms.

Lt.-Col. Franks and his clique would have been pleased to gain approval for any type of SAS Unit, and a Territorial Army outfit trained for special operations offered the prospect of becoming the basis for a larger body in due course. In assessing the Army's future requirements for "special units and organisations" in a "General War", the DTI analysts scrutinised the records of a host of 'funnies' that operated during the War, including the SAS and SBS, the Commandos, the Long Range Desert Group [LRDG], Long Range Penetration Groups [LRPG], the Small Operations Group, various Land Forces Adriatic units, the Raiding Support Regiment, Combined Operations Pilotage Parties, 'V' Force, and many less well-known units. The DTI staff were directed to determine what type of units/organisations would be needed, if any, and how they should be organised, controlled and coordinated with other agencies, such as the SIS.[2]

Although most of the Working Party's time was spent collecting, collating, analysing and assessing a mass of written and oral information about special forces, Maj.-Gen. Manners-Smith also received some food for thought from practical demonstrations of such units' capabilities during the course of the Party's study. He was invited to exercises held on 26-27th. June 1946 at the Commando, Mountain and Snow Warfare Centre [CMSWC] at St. Ives, Cornwall (which was itself subject to review and had an uncertain future, due to the Admiralty's decision to disband the Navy's remaining Royal Marines Commandos - which was reversed by early 1947).

The two-day showcase included a demonstration of Commando Training methods and equipment, and prominent among the guests who were invited to see the review were representatives of the Combined Operations HQ. The most notable of these visitors were its chief, Major-General Robert E. Laycock (ex-commander of, among other special units, the Commandos' Layforce, as well as Chief of Combined Operations in October 1945, when the SAS was lobbying for its survival), who was intimately involved with the SAS Regimental Association; and another officer (who crops up repeatedly, henceforth) with links to the Regiment, Brigadier Bernard E. Fergusson. He had fought in pre-war Palestine, then alongside Calvert in wartime Burma, drawing on his close-quarter battle experience when training troops as a jungle warfare instructor in India.[3] Such contacts between supporters of the SAS and the War Office DTI boosted its cause, and the SAS's former C.O., Brig. McLeod - currently stationed at GHQ New Delhi - kept his successor, Brig. Calvert - a fulcrum for the SAS Association and its back channels to the powers-that-be - informed of relevant developments in India.

On 10th. June 1946, McLeod reported to Calvert that an Indian Long Range Squadron was to be retained "to operate in small parties or patrols" for "deep recce .. raids against communications, HQs or installations .. guerilla warfare [and] .. to raise, arm and train local irregular troops for 'partisan' warfare against enemy LoC", along the lines of the wartime SAS, SOE Force 136 (in Malaya) and Long Range Desert Group, utilising parachute insertion and motor patrol vehicles. By 9th. July, the Working Party had drafted its own "Paper on the Control of Special Units and Organisations, Parts 1 & 2", although the records show that it received further submissions until at least 22nd. August, and its final "Report on Special Units" was completed on 20th. September 1946.

The DTI Report concluded that, "there is a requirement for special units in modern war", and that these should be organised for "deep penetration behind the lines .. [the] collection and immediate reporting of information .. demolitions, and harassing activity". This proposal brought together the functions of the SAS and other specialised organisations in a more financially viable form, which was a necessary and central consideration over and above the military aspects of the matter, given the economic circumstances in which the British Armed Forces and the government found themselves. This would not have gone down well with some of the men who had fought in a variety of units with their own distinct purview, but the new realities had to be accepted if there was to be any special force capability in the future. The new units would execute "special operations .. in close cooperation with normal forces", and it was envisaged that these "may take the form of Commando operations .. special airborne operations ahead of the main assault .. special raids .. or long range recce into enemy-held territory for a specific object [that was] required by .. the main forces". In other words, the new Army special units would have to be prepared to carry out any and all special tasks required of them, with the main ones being strategic deep penetration, tactical vanguard operations, and intelligence-gathering. Flexibility would be the forté of the new forces, which must be capable of deploying men for any mission thrown up during another War, much in the same way as the SAS had done in 1944/45. Further, it was noted that the special forces may need to act in unison with partisan/guerilla forces, and the Report recommended that "the technique of this type of warfare should be included, in some degree, in the training of special units". Indeed, coordination of efforts with the SIS was regarded as essential in the context of Resistance support activities, as well as with the Combined Operations Small Raiding Unit being set up by the Admiralty, and any other similar bodies, such as the SBS, Small Operations Group and Royal Marines Commandos.

As a logical consequence of the Report's findings (and in keeping with Brig. Calvert's thinking), its authors proposed peacetime preparations of special units and the production of an "organisation in peace which can be readily expanded in war". In addition, the new groups would need to learn "lessons gained by the SAS in France", so that "the technique of secret maintenance of small forces by air [supplying] can be developed". The necessary skills were to be honed at dedicated training school facilities. However, the DTI officials did not argue that the recently disbanded SAS should be the core of any new special force. Rather, they put forward the idea of "Special Recce Groups" [SRG] (a neutral nomenclature probably devised to avoid any friction between former members of various defunct special forces who might want to enlist in them). They would be maintained "in Theatres overseas" where threats were deemed likely to appear. But, despite the likely creation of a Territorial Army - in which the SAS hoped to gain a foothold - the Report considered that "only Regular army personnel .. are suitable for posting to the S.R.G. on account of [the] terms of service". Soldiers would be attached for two-year tours of duty overseas (although some officers and instructors could serve for up to five years). The DTI staff thought that the total SRG manpower should be around 2200 - a figure close to the SAS's peak strength during 1945 - with "a Unit of between 200 and 300 [personnel] in each overseas Theatre", made up of Troops of about 50 men. A "Middle East Group" was given as the exemplar for other SRGs, with long-range patrolling pinpointed as its *modus operandi*. The significance of these recommendations will become clearer in due course. For now, it is ironic simply to note that, while the Report warned against allowing the formation of "private armies",[4] in the very Theatre that it focused its attention - the Middle East - the SAS's own "Paramilitary Establishment" - the MEBRM, or BMRC - was actively assisting the Greek security forces.

The Balkan front

More details about the SAS's activities in Greece during the spring and summer of 1946 have yet to emerge, but it is known that other British forces in the BTG were authorised to engage Greek irregulars should they or the villages that they patrolled come under attack and the local security forces prove unable to cope with these.[5] Further, the new British Ambassador to Greece, Sir Clifford Norton, noted early in October 1946, that there were "semi-official and independent forces" operating across the country, and that the British Army was providing at least some of these. In August 1946, BTG prepared numerous Teams for the "unofficial supervision" of both the vital Greek Constitutional plebiscite on 1st. September, and of newly-forming Greek counter-terrorist 'Home Guard' self-protection forces.[6] Moreover, there is evidence strongly suggesting that the SAS had sustained casualties during COIN operations in Greece by this time. From the Regimental Association's third *Newsletter* of November 1946, it can be surmised that, along with other wartime special forces personnel, Captain D.J. 'Stud' Stellin - a New Zealander who had fought in Greece in the SBS under Lt.-Col. David 'Dinky' Sutherland - returned there after the War, along with E.J. 'Manolli' Kanakakis, who had acted as an interpreter for the SBS on Crete during 1944. Other veterans operating during 1946, such as 2 SAS's Alan Cooper, were attached to what was called the 'International Squadron' of the SAS, which was evidently the Regiment's appellation for its Greece contingent (and reminiscent of the 'International Brigade' in Spain's civil war).[7] Consequently, for the purposes of simplification, the MEBRM/BMRC will be referred to hereafter as the SAS International Squadron.

Unsurprisingly, other indications of the SAS's covert presence in Greece are difficult to find in available public records. But, on 4th. October 1946, the GOC LFG, General Keith N. Crawford (who had had dealings with the SAS while leading the War Office Directorate of Air Warfare in 1945), intriguingly informed the Foreign Office's Southern Department (whose remit covered the Balkans, including Greece), that "no request has been made [by the Greek authorities] to British Troops to assist by *direct* intervention" (emphasis added). This could be interpreted as implying that some indirect British military assistance had been given to the GNA, and this could help to explain why the commander of the BMM(G), Major-General Stuart B. Rawlins, suddenly and puzzlingly stopped pressing the Greek General Staff to reinvigorate their security forces' efforts in November 1946. He may well have feared that the Greeks could gain the impression that the British were willing to take up more of the burden of the campaign themselves if local forces did not improve - a course of action that Rawlins deemed it necessary to inform Ambassador Norton would be "contrary to his instructions".[8]

Regarding pointers to an SAS presence in Greece, it is also notable that the British military in Greece asserted that the GNA needed to implement changes in tactics and organisation that had been developed "since .. [the] summer", when it became clear that large scale offensives like those done "by highly equipped and trained German formations" against Greek partisans during the War were making little impression on the Communist insurgents. Therefore, new techniques were required,[9] and among those that the British championed were the use of air support (particularly the air-supplying of ground units), and the employment of counter-guerilla special forces. This idea was being sponsored by forward-looking members of the BMM(G) by October 1946, and this major departure in British military thought on I.S. undoubtedly was inspired by British forces such as the Commandos, SOE and, especially, the SAS.[10]

Some writers have stated that this "British thinking [was] based on the .. experience of World War Two",[11] but the BMM(G) had a more recent example to follow as well. Indeed, its staff noted that, by November 1946, "valuable training experience has been gained in the field", and that the Greek General Staff had "put forward a proposal t[o] .. call up reservist .. ex-ANDARTES to form 40 mob[ile] col[umn]s, each of 75 men *under their own officers* to act against bandits" (emphasis added), in northern and central Greece.[12] This stipulation once more raises the question of who else could possibly have been made responsible for leading the Greeks' new special forces - and the finger again points to members of the 1st. and 2nd. SAS working with the Regiment's International Squadron.

The BMM(G) apparently "sponsored the organisation of [what were later called the [Greek] Commandoes [sic.], to speed [up] training and to provide small units [that had been] specially trained to combat guerillas". On 6th. November, the Joint Planning Staff [JPS] of the British Chiefs of Staff considered a report on the re-equipment and retraining of the GNA (of which there are no extant details). Montgomery and the Chiefs approved its recommendations, and it is likely that it advocated the creation of a GNA Commando force.[13] Then, on 19th. November 1946, Maj.-Gen. Rawlins and the Greek Chief of Staff, the staunch anti-Communist, General Panagiotes Spiliotopoulos, visited the War Office in Great Scotland Yard to discuss in some depth the Greek I.S. situation and the possibility of the British lending greater COIN assistance to Greece (including advisors). They also bore detailed plans for the formation of a special force of around 3000 air-supplied "Commandos", a label that would not arouse any particular suspicion about the force's genesis or indicate the presence of a clandestine SAS Squadron in Greece. It is evident that the Service Department accepted the idea of experimentation with this novel counter-guerilla concept, which, regardless, neither heralded a wholesale shift in counter-guerilla tactics in Greece nor involved major new risks to BTG manpower. On 28th. November, the Chiefs of Staff authorised the preparation of up to 4000 Commandos,[14] and 'Allied' plans for them were soon effected.

On 1st. December 1946, the GNA started to form its new Commando Companies. They were designed for offensive and intelligence-gathering patrolling, as well as to spearhead large-scale operations. On this matter, the Greek military "copied the British", and the GNA Commandos' dual tactical roles were similar to those undertaken by unorthodox forces like the early British Commandos and, in particular, the SAS. On 2nd. December, the CIGS arrived in Athens to oversee both the GNA's restructuring scheme, and its retraining programme for "operations in mountain country against an irregular enemy". The Athens Embassy marked the Greeks' enthusiasm for the establishment of 50-man "Chaser Companies" and, by the end of December 1946, "40 small independent Mountain Commando Companies .. specially trained for recce and long-range patrolling .. deep" into Communist-dominated territory were being readied for a major New Year offensive.[15] As will be seen, the SAS International Squadron was at the forefront of preparations for these too.

An "unusually imaginative decision"

Meantime, during November 1946, in the light of its Inter-Service Working Party's report on an auxiliary Army, "the War Office came to the conclusion that there was a place for a Territorial Army" in the post-war orbat, and it implemented its plans for this from 1st. January 1947. This once again opened up the possibility of an SAS Territorial Unit, and pressure for this was exerted behind closed doors by the SAS lobby, led by Lt.-Col. Franks. Despite "some formidable opposition from senior elements of the Regular Army", by November 1946, the Service Department came to the "unusually imaginative decision [that] .. there was room for an SAS type unit within the scope of the Territorial Army",[16] thereby fulfilling Calvert's vision. The SAS Unit was formed, neither in 1945 nor in 1949, as some authors assert, but in 1947.[17] Not long before the decision was taken to nurture another branch of the SAS family, on 14th. October 1946, the War Office SCAPP reported on the "Future of the Airborne Forces". It noted that, if the Army Air Corps was abolished at some point in the future, then the Parachute and Glider Pilot Regiments would have to be associated with another Corps (in order to meet the legal requirements of the Army Acts). "The same would apply to the S.A.S. Regiment if at any time it should be necessary to revive it".[18] There was no intimation that this was to happen soon, and the question arises as to why the War Office agreed to create an SAS TA Unit. James Adams argues that it was merely "a sop to its supporters", while Philip Warner and other historians have focused on the War Office DTI's support for the development of a "behind-the-lines" capability, while at the same time recognising that Britain's ongoing demobilisation and current financial hardship meant that it was "politically impossible [to form] .. a new regular regiment".[19] But, while this interpretation is valid as far as it goes, it's not the whole story.

The Directorate of Tactical Investigation's report on special units recommended the gradual deployment of regular SRGs in overseas Theatres, and the role and training of the new SAS TA Unit was to be similar to that envisaged for an SRG, being oriented as it was towards a "future [conventional] Middle Eastern conflict".[20] But, Philip Warner notes, rather obliquely, that "when the SAS was re-created and found a new role, it was due to its earlier [wartime] history rather than *its later activities*" (emphasis added). Although he didn't elaborate what the latter might have been, this points to the SAS Regiment's International Squadron in Greece.

In spite of what Warner wrote about the importance of the SAS's wartime operations in influencing the War Office and Cabinet decision-makers, he also implied that the Greek endeavour was a major influence on them. Referring to the Land Forces Adriatic HQ (which had overseen wartime SBS and GSS operations in the Balkans), he indicated that, under its auspices, there were "many nebulous and secret formations whose real point and purpose is to this day shrouded in obscurity". The same could certainly be said about the MEBRM/BMRC, which functioned within the ambit of the Land Forces Adriatic's successor HQ, the Land Forces Greece. The SAS's official historian continued, rather cryptically, that "not least compelling of the arguments for reviving the SAS from its post-war disbandment [of mid-1946] was that all these mysterious units could be better and more efficiently run if they came under one [Special Air Service] umbrella in peacetime".[21]

It is therefore quite feasible that the War Office's "unusually imaginative decision" owed as much to developments in Greece instigated by Lt.-Col. Franks, as to the Department's own study and assessment of special forces requirements. In fact, Franks was to become the Territorial Army Unit's first commander (adding to his responsibilities for the War Crimes Organisation and the International Squadron), with a new London HQ that would supervise all SAS activities.

Preparing the Greek Commandos in 1946

Back in Greece, on 2nd. December 1946, Field-Marshal Montgomery rubber-stamped the BMM(G)'s training plans for the Greek Commandos, while making it clear that normal "British Troops [Greece units] were not to become involved with the bandits".[22] On 3rd. December, Maj.-Gen. Rawlins asked for the secondment of 30 extra men to the Mission so that it could undertake its new tasks more easily,[23] and it was stated that they should operate in British Instruction Teams [BIT] attached to the GNA's Mountain Divisions. They would supplement the work of British Liaison Officers [BLO] who visited them "from time to time", some of whom may have come from the SAS International Squadron. Indeed, it could have provided the core of the additional manpower requested for the BITs, along with reinforcements either from the UK and/or elsewhere in the Middle East Theatre. It is worth noting too that the BMM(G) was given permission for two Majors to begin training courses for the Greek National Army in "Irregular Warfare" - which must have been formulated some time in advance - and, in the spring of 1946, the establishment of the MEBRM/BMRC was 15 personnel, including *two officers*.[24]

Even more enlightening are the minutes of a meeting held in Athens on 4th. December 1946, with Maj.-Gen. Rawlins and the rest of the local British army top brass in attendance. At this conference, General Crawford "stressed the need for [GNA] training in any new equipment and tactics", and it was recorded that, to this end, Field-Marshal Montgomery had agreed to meet their request for more British manpower. Further, it was suggested that "the provision of a RASC air supply officer and of SAS personnel should be considered".[25] This is an extremely significant reference, as, not only is this document one of the few from the 1945/46 period that was missed by the War Office's normally thorough 'weeders', there is no equivocation in it at all with regard to key issues about the SAS: Firstly, whether the SAS Regiment in fact existed (at a time that it was not supposed to); whether its personnel were suited to undertake counter-guerilla action (which was not something that they had done during the War); whether its personnel could be utilised for this purpose and, for that matter, how long they could be employed; how long it would take to get hold of them; and under what terms and conditions they would operate. Instead, it was apparently assumed by senior

British army officers in Greece that the SAS existed (and they referred to it as such), that its personnel were readily available for deployment in Greece, that they were suited to the type of work envisaged, and that they could quickly undertake an open-ended commitment. This implies that Crawford, Rawlins and their closest colleagues had known about the SAS International Squadron's presence in Greece for some time (albeit that it may have been outside their direct auspices); that the SAS had demonstrated their worth to date; and that the War Office (which helped to organise reinforcements for Greece) was *au fait* with what was going on.

On 9th. December 1946, the Land Forces Greece HQ asked the Middle East Forces Command to meet its "urgent [personnel] requirements" with all due haste. But, on 29th. December, it was obliged to contact the War Office directly about this.[26] This could mean that the personnel required were not currently available in the Theatre, so the LFG sought reinforcements from Britain. It is known that, before the new year, the War Office managed to procure for the BMM(G) the services of "a special British team" of "Commando" advisors/ trainers. And it has been averred by informed sources that "a team of three [SAS] officers [was] .. sent to Greece in 1946".[27] By the end of the year, the British Military Mission could report that "much hard work has been given to the preparation of training of [the Greek] Commando Companies", under the direction of the BMM(G)'s Head of Operations and Training, Lt.-Col. G.A. Fitzgerald (Royal Artillery).[28] The SAS team was charged with helping to ready the Commandos for the upcoming counter-guerilla offensive of spring 1947, which the authorities over-optimistically hoped could be decisive. The expanding role of the SAS in COIN was not confined solely to Greece either.

Fighting insurgency on two fronts
Greece and Palestine, 1947

By the middle of January 1947, the British government had authorised the BMM(G) to despatch its COIN operations advisors to GNA units "in the field" and to give clandestine assistance to them.[1] By 20th. January, the British army additionally had formulated six-week tactical training courses (later extended by a week) for the 2000 or so Greek Commando trainees who had been mustered by the GNA High Command for Mountain Warfare operations. Some of these men already had "commenced elementary training" and they were "being equipped for long-range mountain recce and patrolling" with other units' 'borrowed' equipment. Henceforth, British instructors oversaw their tuition at various Greek Army formation locations within the GNA's 'A', 'B' and 'C' Corps areas.

In 'C' Corps, for instance, some courses were run by soldiers from the 4th. British Infantry Division - which was a major component of the remaining BTG - and many came from infantry and RA units.[2] Thereafter, the Greek Commandos based at Liti received some "hard training under a Major" whose name has been blanked out of the British public record, and who was in all probability an SAS officer. In addition, there were "four young officers lent by 4 Brit[ish] Inf[antry] Div[ision]". Another Commando Company at Komitini received similarly tough tutoring from another unidentified Major, along with a Captain from the same Division. A short time afterwards, supplementary training in air support techniques was provided for the recruits. Although the identity of Britain's GNA Commando instructors has been purposely kept secret for several decades, it is evident that at least some of them came from the SAS.

A few days after the main Commando training programme got underway, on 28th. January, the BMM(G) alluded to the fact that "the services of a British Army officer qualified in Combined Operations Training has been promised by GHQ MELF and [that] this officer will be attached to the CTC [Combined Operations Training Centre, at] Volos", when he became available. One of his responsibilities as BLO (Combined Operations) would be to contribute to the training of GNA Commandos in the 'B' and 'C' Corps areas, where the bulk of the fighting between the security forces and the Communist insurgents was going on. He would be required, in addition, to make regular front-line visits to them and to advise them on operational matters.[3] Shortly after that, it was noted that Major Raymond Walter Keep had joined the BMM(G) as G2 (Combined Operations) and, although it is not known exactly how or when the GHQMELF went about acquiring his services, he was another old comrade who had fought in 2 SAS under Lt.-Col. Franks and who had attended the Regimental Association's first meeting. Thus, it is feasible that the commander-designate of the SAS Territorial Unit had a hand in Ray Keep's secondment from the Sudan Defence Force to Greece (as well as in that of other SAS veterans). There is another significant reference too in a "Table of Appointments" to the BMM(G) made during the quarter up to 31st. March 1947 that was missed by War Office weeders. Among the names of several new officers attached to the Mission is "Major R.W. Keep" and, alongside it, in the "Parent Regiment" column of the Table, is the supposedly non-existent "2nd. S.A.S.".[4] The BMM(G) and those involved in its reinforcement undoubtedly recognised the existence of the 2nd. SAS's International Squadron in Greece in 1947 (over and above the new TA Unit that would be recruited later on that year by Lt.-Col. Franks).[5]

Cloak and winged dagger in Palestine

Not long after the official attachment of SAS personnel to the BMM(G), their expertise was called upon once more, to assist in COIN operations elsewhere in the Middle East Theatre, in the United Nations Mandate of Palestine. It was administered by Britain, and it may well be that the Mandatory authorities were influenced, at least in part, by COIN tactical developments being made in their Mediterranean neighbour. This certainly cannot be discounted, for, as will be recounted, there were high-level contacts between key British COIN agents in Palestine and Greece during this period.

The Palestine insurgency had emerged a few months before that in Greece, when attacks on the British presence began in earnest in October 1945. Conflict in the territory was nothing new to the British, who had been trying to reconcile the competing claims of the Palestinian Arabs and the Jewish minority since taking up the League of Nations' Mandate in 1920. (This followed the Balfour Declaration of 1917 that promised the Jews British assistance in "the establishment of a national home for the Jewish people", while ensuring that this would not "prejudice the civil and religious rights of existing non-Jewish communities"). Ever-growing legal and illegal Jewish immigration during the 1930s had contributed to the eruption of an Arab Revolt between 1936 and 1939, which was suppressed by the British armed forces using traditional 'Imperial-policing' techniques (although Orde Wingate's 'Special Night Squads' experimented with short-duration undercover counter-guerilla patrolling and ambushing).

During the War, Zionist terrorist groups were subjugated and, on the election of a Labour government in July 1945, many Zionists hoped that there would be a shift in policy that would favour their cause and afford the creation of a Jewish national home. However, perceived British strategic and economic interests prevented an immediate partition of Palestine and subsequent British withdrawal. Instead, Britain remained in the Holy Land and, after months of delay in deciding its future policy, an insurgency movement led by the Jewish Agency became active. The Agency was the official voice of the 'yishuv' - the Jewish community - and it could call on its Haganah paramilitary forces, consisting of Palmach 'Striking Companies' (initially totalling 1500) and the Hish 'Field Force' (another 5000), to carry out operations against their former British allies. In addition, the Haganah units were joined by the IZL [Irgun Zvai Leumi, or National Military Organisation] and LHI [or Lehi, from Lochmei Herut Israel, or Fighters for the Freedom of Israel]. The IZL (who included the likes of Menachem Begin) had around 1500 members at first, and the LHI around 300 (about the size of the Active Service element of the post-1970s Provisional IRA).

These Jewish insurgent groups acted cohesively from autumn 1945 to summer 1946 in the United Resistance Movement [URM, or Tenuat Hameri Haivri], undertaking coordinated operations [Mavaak Tzamud, or Linked Struggle], and concentrating on urban guerilla warfare and terrorist attacks.[6] Their actions destabilised and outwitted the British security forces which, on the whole, were unfamiliar with such an I.S. threat. Although the Jewish Agency pulled the Haganah out of the URM after terrorist bombings that led to a repressive British response in mid-1946, by that time, the British were becoming concerned about the course of the COIN campaign. The British High Commissioner - the senior civil official in the territory - General Sir Alan Cunningham, was convinced that changes needed to be made to the security forces' approach, and he took action to this end.

On 1st. August 1946, the High Commissioner informed the Secretary of State for the Colonies that he was "anxious to be assured that our police methods are the best that can be devised, and [so] I should welcome a visit from some expert .. to advise me whether our police methods could in any way be improved".

He sought "a man of eminence in character [and] work [and who, in particular,] had experience of terrorist activities, in an unfriendly population. The only name which comes to my mind as suitable, [Cunningham added,] is that of Sir Charles [E.] Wickham".

Major-General Wickham was the current Head of the British Police and Prisons Mission to Greece that was reorganising and retraining the Greek police and National Guard gendarmerie for civic policing and I.S. duties. General Cunningham noted that, "I know Wickham and [I] would greatly welcome a short visit from him", in order to gain any "new ideas" that he may have, especially in connection with the CID and its intelligence work.[7] Sir Charles soon accepted the offer from his old acquaintance, and he travelled from Athens to Jerusalem, where he studied the Palestine Police Force [PPF] between 16th. November and 16th. December 1946.

Following his investigations, Wickham made several recommendations on how to improve the PPF's organisation and performance, one of which was that it should be reoriented towards 'normal' policing and, hand in hand with this, that the paramilitary Police Mobile Force [PMF] ought to be disbanded. This specialised reactionary force had been used for years to crush civil disturbances as and when they occurred, and Wickham felt that the ethos of a heavy-handed anti-riot squad was not one that was conducive to police COIN success.[8] Although there are no detailed records of the conversations held between some of the top British counter-insurgents in Palestine and Sir Charles about COIN methods, the authorities in Jerusalem started to implement his report soon afterwards and, within a couple of months of it, they were organising a police special force. It is certainly within the realms of possibility that special force developments made in Greece were discussed in the upper echelons of the Mandatory power, and that these sowed the seed from which a Palestine Police experiment grew, early in 1947.

The originator of the Palestine Police special force concept is not certain, but the historian Charles Smith asserts that it was the PPF's commanding officer, the Inspector-General, Colonel William Nicol Gray. However, a leading authority on the Palestine conflict, David A. Charters, argues that it was "the brain-child of Colonel Bernard E. Fergusson", who was one of Gray's three Assistant Inspector-Generals [AIG] during 1946. Nicol Gray had been "a wartime [Royal Marines] Commando and [a] protegé of Bob Laycock" (a leading light of the SAS Regimental Association).[9] Gray was appointed to replace Captain John Murray

Rymer-Jones, who had become ill during January 1946. But since taking up his post, that March, Gray had not implemented any major tactical changes. Yet, when Col. Fergusson (who was working with Laycock at the UK Combined Operations HQ earlier in 1946) arrived in Palestine, on 10th. December 1946, he found that the PMF (which he was due to command) was in the process of disbandment, at Sir Charles' behest. Therefore, Fergusson was made AIG (Operations and Training) of the PPF and, he later recalled, he was "directed .. to study the problem of terrorism in the urban areas of Palestine" and to look at ways of improving police counter-terrorist methods.[10] This new-found willingness to innovate indicates that Gray and his leading supporter, the High Commissioner, may well have been inspired by what had been going on in Greece, and that Wickham's visit to Palestine was not only rather fortunate, but also central to subsequent COIN changes that were made there.

Whatever the case, Fergusson pondered how to devise a fresh tactical approach and he drew on his knowledge of SAS training and his own special forces experience. (He was touted for the PPF Inspector-Generalship in March 1946, but the War Office had vetoed his appointment. Fergusson then went on to work with Gray's mentor, Laycock, while the Colonial Office accepted the Admiralty's preferred candidate as Inspector-General, despite opposition from within the ranks of the PPF over the selection of a military man rather than a Colonial policeman, as was the usual practice).[11]

Fergusson had served during 1943 and 1944 with General Orde Wingate in Burma and, along with Brig. Calvert, he was one of six Chindit Brigade leaders there. In 1945, Fergusson went on to India, where he taught jungle warfare techniques with the help of an agent called 'Tac-Tac', who was well known to both the Palestine Police and to the SAS, not least from his tuition of many of the Regiment's top soldiers in close-quarter combat, including 'taking out' opponents with 'double-tap' gun shots during room-to-room house clearance and other CQB drills. Other potentially useful knowledge that Fergusson possessed included a spell "in Palestine during the Arab rebellion" of the 1930s, so that he would have been aware of Wingate's undercover Special Night Squad units and their methods.[12] Yet, in spite of all of this pool of wisdom, Fergusson confessed that he felt desperately unsure of how to proceed, for when he "tried to translate [this] into the urban and suburban [environment of post-war Palestine, it] .. seemed to [him to] have no relevance". Fergusson found himself "destitute of ideas".

But, he later reminisced, "it seemed to me, baffled as I was, that we needed people with experience of terrorism or something closely allied to it" who could help in the development of fresh COIN tactics. He recognised that the PPF needed to "foresee [and] .. anticipate" insurgent operations and "give would-be raiders a bloody nose as they came in to raid". The police were not "to terrorise or .. repay in kind" by countenancing terrorist actions against the Jewish opposition or the *yishuv*, but instead, they would concentrate on dealing with activists implicated in attacks on the State.[13]

Fergusson must have been mulling over such thoughts by the start of 1947, but even if he could gain the additional assistance that he desired, there was another hurdle to overcome: approval at the highest level would be vital if the police were to undertake activities of a potentially sensitive political nature. Luckily for the Palestine authorities, in the light of continued Zionist terrorist incidents, on 15th. January 1947, the Attlee Cabinet informed Sir Alan Cunningham that it would support any "such action as you may take" to combat the insurgency.[14] This gave the High Commissioner and his top policemen the authority that they needed to go about acquiring individuals who may produce a workable alternative to traditionalist I.S. practices, and the search was soon underway.

In the latter half of January 1947, Fergusson was given permission to recruit up to four officers with experience of fighting "behind the lines .. during the War" to assist him, and he contacted friends from the SAS, such as his erstwhile comrade-in-arms, Mike Calvert, with whom he had recently been in touch on the subject of Combined Operations. As will be seen, Calvert spread the word about the likely formation of a COIN special force and surreptitiously prepared the ground for Fergusson, who travelled to London and, by 5th. February 1947, was in talks with the Military Secretary at the War Office, General F.A.M. 'Boy' Browning - an old friend of the SAS and a keen supporter of the idea of a post-war Regiment.

Fergusson used his SAS contacts to locate suitable candidates for the new force and, on 11th. February, Fergusson asked that, initially, three officers be posted to the PPF as Deputy-Superintendants, answerable directly to himself. They would be responsible for the command of 10-man undercover police squads, while a staff officer would be added once things had started to take shape. He emphasised that the squad leaders "should have experience and knowledge of terrorist methods" and, in view of the fact that Scotland Yard could not find anybody that fitted the bill, Fergusson looked to other sources for his new undercover squad subordinates. He knew that there were "in the Army a small number of officers who have both [a] technical and [a] psychological knowledge of terrorism, having themselves been engaged in similar operations on what may be termed the terrorist side in countries occupied by the enemy in the late War". Col. Fergusson would have known that such men could be obtained from the SIS and through contacts in the SAS (such as his friends and Regimental Association Vice-Presidents, Brig. Calvert and Maj.-Gen. Laycock). Hence, Fergusson drew up a list of potential volunteers, which he presented to the War Office and other London-based agencies during his February sojourn.

A week after beginning his consultations with the War Office and other agencies, he "submitted his plan for a new type of police activity" that would be unusual, but not unprecedented or illegal. The special squads would be ordered to "provoke contact [with the Jewish paramilitaries], to look for confrontation", and to apprehend them. However, his proposal to support the squads with three aircraft (in the manner of the SNS, the Chindits and the Greek Commandos) was rejected by the Service Department, presumably because this was seen as impractical in a suburban setting. Still, on 12th. February, the War Office DMO, Major-General A.D. Ward, enthusiastically agreed to help in the execution of the plan, by locating the personnel required to lead 'Fergusson Force' on the ground.[15]

Indeed, although the CIGS, Field-Marshal Montgomery, was an I.S. traditionalist and he consistently believed that the key to success lay in more repressive, large-scale offensive I.S. operations, the late John Rymer-Jones asserted that Col. Fergusson told him that the CIGS was "very keen on the idea" of a police special force.[16] Whether this was the case or not, General Cunningham was the driving force behind the scheme, while pointing out that Sir Charles Wickham had expressly warned against developing a wholly paramilitary police force (again indicating Wickham's influence on the PPF).[17] Fergusson then returned to Palestine to prepare for the formation of a new unorthodox Middle East COIN force.

According to historian Nicholas Bethell, Bernard Fergusson "knew several young officers" who matched his candidate specification for the squad leaders' jobs. Among them were members of the SIS/SOE, but his requests for Ran Antrim and Colonel David Smiley (who had fought in the SOE along with partisan groups in Albania, Yugoslavia and Thailand), were unsuccessful, as neither was able to take up the offer at that moment. (Smiley's participation was vetoed by his new wife!) Nonetheless, the SIS cooperated in allowing another newly-wed, James Alastair 'Angus' McGregor, to leave the "Foreign Office Political Intelligence Department" for a stint in Palestine, where he was to join his fellow ex-2nd. SAS squadron commander, Captain (later Major) Roy Farran, (while Col. Harold Perkins of the SIS mined insurgent supply ships in 1947). Fergusson was aware through his prior contacts with the Regiment of both men's outstanding, heroic wartime SAS exploits (under the command of Lt.-Col. Franks). They both had been trained by Fergusson's associate 'Tac Tac' as well.

Additionally, Farran was himself familiar with the Palestine problem, having served there after the War with the 3rd. Hussars, from October 1945 to August 1946, before going on to Camberley, where Calvert was currently posted. In September 1945, Farran had informed his C.O. that if he "should want me for any job .. you can always get hold of me" and, prior to Fergusson's arrival for talks at the War Office, Brian Franks wrote from the Hyde Park Hotel, to Calvert, on 3rd. February 1947, asking him to "give Roy my love when you see him".

Clearly, both former and current commanders of the SAS were centrally involved in recruitment for Fergusson Force, viewing its formation as a golden opportunity to further underline the SAS's COIN credentials. In addition, on 4th. February, a Private Roche wrote to Calvert, telling him that former SAS, Parachute Regiment and Commando soldiers were "interested in your special force", gossip about which was evidently circulating within special forces circles. Calvert secured at least Farran's involvement and, having studied COIN first hand, Farran and Captain (later Major) McGregor possessed the type of 'terrorist' experience that Fergusson sought, having fought alongside the *Maquis* and other partisan forces (such as in Italy), as well as in cooperation with the SIS and SOE. Fergusson later recounted that "Alastair and Roy had operated behind enemy lines with great success and I thought that their minds would work like terrorists' minds".[18]

As will be recounted, in the following months, Lt.-Col. Franks and his colleagues took a keen interest in the SAS-styled work that was done in Palestine. And Capt. Farran must have jumped at the chance to try out the kind of counter-guerilla operations that he and Franks had envisaged for so long. Farran agreed to take on the command of one of three PPF squads, with his own based in South Palestine. The North Palestine squad would be led by Capt. McGregor, who was filled in about the scheme by Farran at the Gent's toilet of the Berkeley Hotel in London!

A third SAS old comrade, David Sullivan, was assigned the task of stemming Zionist terrorism in Europe, by developing intelligence leads and trying to pre-empt further attacks like that carried out by the IZL on the British Embassy in Rome, on 31st. October 1946 (followed by an attempted but abortive assault on the Colonial Office in April 1947). It seems that one other officer was selected by Fergusson as well, but his departure from the UK was delayed, and so Fergusson personally took command of the third squad area, Jerusalem.[19]

It's interesting to note too, that the three special police squad areas did not correspond to the six PPF Districts (of Jerusalem, Haifa, Lydda, Galilee, Samaria and Gaza), but to the three military zones under the auspices of the GOC (namely 21 Area - South Palestine; 15 Area - North Palestine; and 156 Sub-Area - Jerusalem). Most historians have stated that the undercover groups were "answerable only to Colonel Fergusson, who, in turn, reported directly to .. [Col.] Gray". But Brig. Rymer-Jones asserted that Col. Fergusson additionally reported to the GOC, Major-General Sir Evelyn 'Bubbles' Barker,[20] indicating the Army's deep interest and involvement in the project. The War Office Directorate of Military Operations doubtless would have been kept apprised of developments, although it was the Colonial Office that gave the final go-ahead for the enterprise on 11th. March 1947.

The 2nd SAS veterans, Farran and McGregor, arrived in Palestine by 17th. March 1947 and, soon afterwards, they were instructed to put to good use their "knowledge of underground warfare", and to do "whatever" was required to undermine the insurgents. Maj. Farran reflected later that they had their superiors' "complete backing .. to do something to smash those 'thugs' .. [and that the units had] *carte blanche* [to act] .. as we pleased within our own specific areas .. [in] hunting dissidents".[21]

There was immense political pressure from London on Cunningham and Gray to commit the squads to the fray as soon as possible, in the hope of gaining some swift morale-boosting success that would stiffen the resistance of the security forces, government officials and the remaining ex-patriate community. This necessity limited the time that was available for the development of detailed tactical plans and techniques, as well as for their training. However, the squads' commanders tried to overcome this impediment by drafting into their ranks as much 'suitable' manpower as they could. The squads were each to consist of 10 men, and they were "largely [made up of former] .. SAS and Commando troops".

There were a considerable number of SAS/SBS old boys already in Palestine, both within the PPF and the armed forces. Indeed, the SAS had a long association with the Mandate going back to 1 SAS's reorganisation in March/April 1943. It arrived in the Holy Land on 6th. June 1943, where it was divided into the Special Raiding Squadron and the Special Boat Squadron. The SRS was tasked with preparing for operations in south-eastern Europe at Azzib, northern Palestine, while the SBS practised 'Mountain Warfare' techniques at Athlit, near Haifa, in southern Palestine. They - along with the Long Range Desert Group and the Greek Sacred Squadron - came under the auspices of the Middle East Raiding Forces HQ, which was based in Palestine. Its commander, Colonel (later General Sir) John 'Shan' Hackett, who had "special responsibility for supporting the SAS", in 1946 became the commander of the Trans-Jordan Frontier Force (which conducted Palestine border patrols).[22]

Further, on 15th. September 1945, the 6th. Airborne Division had been sent to southern Palestine as a Theatre regional Imperial Strategic Reserve, and it had strong associations with its fellow Airborne formation, the SAS. In March and April 1945, the 1st. and 2nd. SAS had operated in deep recce and penetration roles for the 6th. Airborne's thrust to the east of the river Rhine in northern Germany. Then, after the SAS Regiments' HQs were closed down and many personnel were transferred to other units, "some of the [SAS Regiments'] .. members .. join[ed] the 6th. Airborne Division in Palestine", such as Captain Holland. Others serving there included Messrs. Baker, Harding, Llewelyn, Ovenden, Briggs, Goodall and Herd, plus an SAS 'Original' who saw action in wartime Greece with the SBS, Lieutenant Ambrose 'Black Jack' MacGonigal.[23] While the identity of all Fergusson Force members is not known, Farran's group included five of his wartime SAS confrere (as well as two Commandos), and at least one of McGregor's men was an SAS colleague called Hillier.[24]

There has been some debate about the exact role(s) of Fergusson Force, and Col. Fergusson may well have given his colleagues some latitude in the way that they interpreted his instructions and went about their business. But it's clear that the squad commanders understood the need for undercover intelligence-gathering patrols, which were done during both the day and at night by moving "among the Jewish civilians in Jewish-type clothing", as the SNS had done among the Arabs. This mode of operation would improve their chances of gaining useful information without being compromised, as well as affording them the opportunity to make contact with insurgents by springing ambushes and making arrests.

As well as clandestine foot patrols, Farran adapted his wartime experience of travelling in jeeps with the French Resistance during 1944, using motor vehicles as " 'Q' ship[s] going into the heart of the enemy['s]" territory. Maj. Farran subsequently argued that mobility was "the first basic requirement for a success-ful underground operation" and, to this end, he utilised jeeps, vans, a citrus-fruit delivery truck and a dry-cleaner's lorry (a technique repeated in Northern Ireland in the 1970s). Several successful 'sting' operations were pulled off using these vehicles, with no less than four suspected insurgents arrested by Farran's squad thanks to a dummy road-block mounted with two vans. However, reportedly, there were occasions when a motor patrol was spotted by vigilant Zionists and, in one instance, Farran and his men had to shoot their way out of a tight spot in which Jewish irregulars used Palestinian Arab youths as 'human shields'. Hence, mobility was undoubtedly useful, but as Farran himself acknowledged, good information was the key to operational successes.

As has been mentioned, however, in the two weeks or so before the police squads went on active service, they had only a short time to prepare themselves, and so they focused on CQB drills. The squads were "taught to shoot in the Tac Tac way" (Tac Tac possibly being a French-schooled instructor, as his 'Tac Tac' epithet derives from the French phonological description of a 'double tap' report from a gun), although the rural training grounds that they practised in were not an ideal template for the streets of Jerusalem, Haifa, Tel Aviv, Nablus or elsewhere. Moreover, a fortnight was too short a time in which to devise effective battle drills, intelligence techniques and post-action review procedures, not to mention devel-op contacts with other security forces and the local populace. Still, as David Charters has intimated, Farran and his colleagues seem to have been working along the right lines, and he wanted the squads' undercover tactics adopted by the rest of the security forces in Palestine.[25]

A fortnight after the undercover police squads became operational, the Officer Commanding [O.C., or C.O.] the 1st. Infantry Division, Major(later Lieutenant)-General Richard N. 'Windy' Gale - based in Capt. McGregor's North Palestine - ordered more army small unit operations, including short off-road ambushes. This followed consultations with Col. Gray, and Maj.-Gen. Gale was probably more favourably disposed than many other soldiers in the Mandate to such experimentation, having commanded the 1st. and 2nd. SAS (including

Farran) at the start of 1945, when they operated in Germany with the 1st. Airborne Corps. Although it has been asserted that the Army "never progressed" to small unit counter-guerilla tactics in Palestine,[26] Gale led the way in this regard. At a time when the CIGS and CINCMELF were emphasising traditional Imperial-policing policies, it seems that he was following the lead of SAS men he had served with in the German campaign. Despite his initiative, however, it would take time for tactical innovations to make an impact upon the Zionist insurgents, which was a commodity that Fergusson's Force did not have. In the light of this, Capt. Farran may have decided to try to accelerate the intelligence-gathering process, and to induce speedier operational results by adopting extraordinary means.

The Farran Case

There has been considerable disagreement among historians about what Farran actually did in Palestine and, while it should be stressed that he was never convicted of any crime there, the PPF CID believed that he abducted an insurgent propagandist, 17-year old Alexander Rubowitz, who went missing on 6th. May 1947 and was not seen alive again. On 3rd. June, Farran was arrested and charged with kidnap and murder, and the police squads' operations were suspended. The South Palestine squad commander admitted later that his thinking was influenced by the example set by Wingate's SNS, which was disbanded in 1939 by the War Office, amid allegations (like those in Iraq in 2004) about the torture of suspects during interrogations. It's possible that Farran likewise sought to extract 'hot' information about IZL or LHI terrorists by oppressive physical or psychological methods. Some historians have even claimed that he was engaged in a " 'shoot to kill' policy" (preceding the RUC/SAS controversies of the mid-1980s), and that numerous insurgents were "eliminated" without trace.[27]

One LHI source has asserted that the teenage leafleter "was captured by civilian-clad persons in the middle of .. Jerusalem .. dragged into an unmarked police car" that sped away, killed, and then buried by a Bedouin native. The source added that "his body was found in the desert a few miles outside Jerusalem" some time afterwards, although there was nothing to link the corpse to Farran. However, as Captain Philip Brutton (serving in Palestine at the time) noted, "in a careless moment, Farran left his hat at the scene" of the abduction, which damned him in the minds of much of the Jewish community.[28]

Farran was tipped off about his impending arrest - doubtless by a security force colleague - and he fled over the border to Syria. On 14th. June, an extradition order was served on him, and a series of surreal events followed, about which there are differing accounts. It appears that the authorities captured and arrested their quarry three days later, but that he escaped on 19th. June, causing a minor sensation in the British and Middle Eastern press. Col. Fergusson was then despatched swiftly to try to persuade Farran to give himself up, which he did, on 30th. June.[29] In the interim, on 25th. June, the Chief Secretary (who headed the administrative machine in Palestine), Henry Gurney, contacted the Colonial Office about the squads' powers and their rules of engagement, and he explained rather confusingly that, while they had been "employing unorthodox methods against terrorists .. no authority has ever been given for the use by any member of the police force of other than ordinary police methods". This probably means that the undercover squads were not given any special extraordinary powers, and attention should be drawn to the fact that the police were "bound by regulations which were very clear on powers of arrest" and the use of fire-arms.[30]

On the other hand, Col. Fergusson reportedly stated that he was "to work to the [orders of the] GOC" as well as the Inspector-General, which may call into question whether, in practice, the squads came under police or military authority. Moreover, a week after the Cabinet's decision of 15th. January 1947 to back Gen. Cunningham in carrying out whatever COIN action he deemed fit in the circumstances, the GOC, Maj.-Gen. Barker, issued a new Order, dated 23rd. January 1947, which was ratified by the Theatre commander and the High Commissioner. It stated that, "the object [of] .. operational policy [was] .. to kill or arrest terrorists and to obtain .. their arms".[31] If the squads were answerable to the GOC, as well as to the police chief, Farran may have felt that he was within his rights to bend but not break the rules, and this loose interpretation led to his fugitive status in Syria. Once he was back in custody, Farran was committed to trial by a military court (indicating whose ultimate authority he operated under). The remaining police squads were demobilised and plans to send another officer to assist Fergusson were dropped.[32]

Eventually, Roy Farran was tried by a court martial on 1st. October 1947 and, due to the lack of evidence against him, he was acquitted on 3rd. October. He was hastily escorted "under close guard" out of the country, leaving a furore in his wake, and he arrived in Liverpool on 13th. October. Col. Fergusson and his own bodyguard left shortly afterwards, and the inauspicious conclusion to the special force experiment in Palestine was all but over. Except for Alastair McGregor, who - in spite of having given evidence in open court in support of his SAS colleague - to the ire of the Zionists - was inexplicably left to fend for himself while the uproar died down. This put him in considerable danger, as his opponents sought revenge. (The insurgents achieved this by default, when a letter bomb addressed to Roy Farran was opened by his brother, killing him in the explosion). Capt. McGregor was obliged to go undercover once more, he and his wife (armed with a revolver) spending about six weeks dodging Jewish extremists while trying to make their way surreptitiously out of the Mandate. McGregor headed for Egypt and, after a journey across the desert and an "awful" spell hidden in a German nunnery (!), they ended up at Alexandria. The Captain then approached the Fayed MEF HQ, which posted him late in November 1947 to another mission in the Theatre. He was to become an SAS advisor to the Greek Commandos,[33] (as detailed in the next chapter). During his own stint on the run, Capt. Farran also contemplated getting in touch with some of his "many friends in Greece", and he noted that, in the months preceding his trial (July through to September 1947), "only the interest of friends like Brian Franks and Bill Stirling had persuaded me to put up a defence".[34]

Clearly, there were strong links between those dealing with COIN in Palestine and Greece during 1947, including the transfer of personnel and expertise. This network of contacts extended between SAS old comrades in the Middle East Theatre and the new Regimental HQ being established in the UK. Calvert, Franks and their associates kept their finger on the pulse with regard to all SAS activities, acting as a coordinating fulcrum, as well as a standard bearer for the Regiment as a whole. Indeed, it appears that the SAS nucleus continued to be involved in developments in Greece, where, after the disappointments experienced in Palestine, and renewed criticism from the vocal anti-special forces lobby in the War Office, the SAS needed more than ever to try to maintain its presence there.

The International Squadron
Bending the rules in Greece

While Brian Franks' friends were trying out innovative and controversial counter-guerilla techniques in Palestine, the SAS in Greece was facing some potentially significant problems. Early in March 1947, political complications arose, as the Foreign Secretary, Ernest Bevin, sought to cut Britain's aid programme in Greece and draw in the Americans (into what would become a keystone of the 'Truman Doctrine'). In view of this, covert British advisory teams were ordered to withdraw from combat areas.[1] But, contrary to the professed wishes of the British government, some British soldiers decided to adopt a broad interpretation of their revised instructions and to persist in helping the Greek military in certain vital respects. At least one small British army group carried on instructing the GNA Commandos, and two British Majors continued to offer "Combined Operations and Irregular Warfare Training" at the Combined Operations Training Centre in Volos, and at the Commando Training Centre at Vouliagmeni, near Athens. They also continued to "be mobile" in the field and, Maj. Keep, for one, "made frequent visits to the Parnis Mountains inspecting Commando squadrons under training" in the battlezone, offering them advice about their deployments.[2] By April 1947, no fewer than half the Commando Companies (from a total of 40, comprising over 3000 men) had undergone six-week training courses. Thereafter, they would be deployed on operations in 'A', 'B' and 'C' Corps districts, although those Companies in 'B' Corps were still waiting to be instructed in air support procedures (for which there was a specific three-day course), having had an initially slow start to their tuition when only a "few hundred men .. reported" for duty.[3]

Hence, it appears that SAS advisors were determined to supervise their wards when they went into battle against the KKE's military arm, the DSE (*Demokratikos Stratos Ellados*, or Democratic Army of Greece). It's not clear how many members of the SAS International Squadron remained engaged on advisory duties, but as the military campaign escalated, there must have been a good number observing and/or partaking in the fighting. It is known that, in addition, other British Army formations diverted manpower to I.S. tasks and furnished the Greek Commandos with training support, notably the Royal Artillery (to which

Bob Bennett was officially attached), and the 10th. Infantry Brigade, which, during May 1947, ran a four-week battle assault course for trainee Commandos. SAS soldiers could have operated under the Brigade's auspices, and one renowned SAS 'Original' (and friend of Bob Bennett), Johnny Cooper, is known to have been serving with the Green Howards in Greece at this time.[4]

The influence of the SAS can be seen also in the nomenclature used by the GNA Commandos in 1947, which operated in "Squadrons", following the SAS template.[5] Further, the Operations Officer of the RAF Delegation to Greece [RAFDG], Wing-Commander Philip Broad - who was advising the Royal Hellenic Air Force [RHAF] on air support - noted, on 21st. June 1947, that he had had "discussions with British officers who have played a bandit role (S.I.S. *etc.*) in the last war" (emphasis added). From these, "it appears that the average bandit fears paratroops more than anything else". He added that, "the mountains of Greece are by no means an impossible terrain for a small force of picked paratroops" to work in, and they could be used "to carry out surprise raids on bandit-held villages" in combination with "air action" (meaning air-strike fire-support missions). He envisaged a unit of "2-400 men of [the] Commando type, of which not more than 100 (4 Dakota [DC-3] loads) would be dropped in any one operation". The Wing-Commander noted that they could be supplied from the air, although usually they "should .. be relieved in 12 hours by surface troops". Moreover, he noted that, "I now find that some of the GNA Mountain Commandos [*Lohos Oreinon Katadromon*] are, in fact, receiving preliminary ground training as airborne troops [and that the] .. BMM(G) are arranging" this. He continued, in somewhat disgruntled fashion that, "I do think that they might have told us about it earlier".[6] If the SAS were involved in this, then it would explain why the RAFDG were kept in the dark until late in the day. Taking into account Broad's discussions with the "S.I.S. *etc.*", the SAS's parachuting expertise, and their place at the cutting edge of tactical innovations in Greece, the International Squadron's participation in this endeavour would certainly make sense.

The Greek Commandos' first clashes with the Democratic Army did not result in any major breakthrough and, in June 1947, Maj.-Gen. Wickham referred in a BPPM report to the "rottenness of the methods applied" by the Greek forces to date. The Commandos' lack of effectiveness must have caused their SAS advisors great concern and, in spite of the restrictions that had been imposed on British personnel with respect to COIN advising, the BMM(G) felt that more British support was needed. On 4th. July, it set up a new Infantry Branch to provide this, particularly by bolstering Britain's ongoing Commando training programme in the GNA's 'B' and 'C' Corps areas. In stark contrast to the British Cabinet's previous decision to cut back Britain's COIN commitment, the Mission arranged "visiting rights" for its soldiers to carry out "Fd. [Field, or Forward] Tr[ainin]g of Commando units".[7] The British military authorities on the ground invested considerable faith in the Commandos as the vanguard of the GNA counter-guerilla effort and, in August 1947, D.A.P. Reilly, the *chargé d'affaires* at the Athens Chancery, wrote that, "experience indicates that these .. [intelligence-gathering and raiding forces] are likely to play a decisive part" in the overall military campaign.[8] Indeed, despite the reduction of the BMM(G)'s War Establishment on 23rd. July by 308 (to 1144), in order to save money, the Mission retained its two official Combined Operations/Irregular Warfare Major instructors, along with their two Assistant ORs and two Drivers.[9]

Furthermore, on the day before the slimlining of the BMM(G) - 22nd. July - the Secretary of State for War, the Rt.-Hon. F.J. Bellenger, was asked during parliamentary questions by Mr. S.S. Tiffany, MP, if "he will give an assurance that members of the British Military Mission in Greece have not taken any part in operations against the guerillas"? Quite why Mr. Tiffany made such a query at this point is unclear, but Mr. Bellenger responded simply, "yes sir". Yet, two days later, the War Office DMO informed the Chiefs of Staff that Major R.M. Archdale was actively engaged in counter-guerilla operations with the GNA's 8th. Division, and the War Office commented that, "it would appear that [the] Mission has omitted to recall him". In reality, some of the BMM(G)'s staff were only selectively applying the government's edicts, so that the British could continue to assist the GNA in a crucial aspect of its COIN drive.[10] Additionally, in the quarter-year up to the 30th. September 1947, Maj. Keep of the 2nd. SAS was "temporarily attached" as a Staff Officer to the Volos Training Centre. There, he implemented his Commando training programme and, as Major Archdale had done, he took part on a "very hush-hush" basis in GNA counter-guerilla operations in the remote mountain regions through 1947 into 1948.[11]

As a result of the ongoing talks between the British and American administrations, by October 1947, the BMM(G) was preparing for the increasingly likely prospect that, at short notice, it would renew an official COIN advisory role in Greece. This would be undertaken along with an American military mission to Greece and, partly with this in mind, on 22nd. October, the BMM(G) reviewed the current position for the War Office and estimated what the prospects might be for

the new year. At long last, Maj.-Gen. Rawlins agreed with his more forward-looking colleagues that it was imperative for the GNA to reorient its counter-guerilla
approach away from large-scale sweep operations to small unit intelligence-
based patrolling. This had been pioneered under SAS tutelage by the Greek
Army's Commandos (which, by 1948, were expanding and redesignated as the
Greek Raiding Forces [GRF], echoing British wartime practice). Rawlins added
that, "it is felt that th[e] .. all important question of training .. the key to the problem .. is not wholly appreciated by those [Greeks] in authority", which amounted
to a plea for the despatch of more 'expert' British counter-guerilla advisors to the
Balkans.[12]

At this juncture, the War Office was weathering the storm created by the
Farran Case, which allowed those enemies of special forces both within and outside
it to press the case for their abolition, and an end to unruly "private armies". But, as
Brig. Calvert noted, each time that the anti-special forces elements tried to put the
final nail in the coffin of the SAS, the pro-special forces lobby pointed to the War
Office DTI's 1946 report and used it to retain a special force capability in the shape
of the SAS.[13] Manifestly, by the end of 1947, the War Office accepted that, if the
GNA was to make appreciable progress, then more specialist British advisors would
be required in Greece, as the BMM(G) had urged. By that winter, efforts were being
made to recruit personnel for a new covert British taskforce - many with a special
forces background - who would join those already involved in COIN in Greece.

One of those who joined Ray Keep et al by December 1947 was Capt.
Alastair McGregor, who was attached to the BMM(G) as G2 and worked as a BLO
with the Raiding Force Commandos. In Athens, he met members of the wartime
Greek Sacred Squadron, including Colonel (later Maj.-Gen.) Kalinski Andrews - the
Greek Commandos' 50-year-old C.O. - and Bombardier Bennett (still sporting his 1
SAS insignia). He was assigned to McGregor as his liaison, guide, driver and bodyguard, while the newcomer familiarised himself with the situation. McGregor's two
missions were to actively help the GRF in the field in their fight against the
Communists, and "to drink as much retsina as possible"![14] They would soon be
joined by other advisors, as the War Office busily organised reinforcements totalling
no fewer than 96 officers and ORs for advisory duties in Greece. This included a
special forces contingent, one of whom, Major Brian Dillon, had helped train
Kalinski's GSS in the War and fought in the SAS/SOE. Among others that Keep
apparently sought for his taskforce were Sgt. Clarke (1 SAS), Sgt. Barnes (2 SAS)
and Sgt. Bowles (SAS).[15]

It's likely that Lt.-Col. Franks was involved with recruitment once again, for he was both the O.C. 21 SAS (the Territorial Regiment), and Chair of the Regimental Association. Hence, he was well placed to locate any old boys who might want another adventure in the sunnier climes of south-eastern Europe (following one of Britain's worst recorded winters), and he was "collaborating closely" with Maj. David Smiley of the SIS "over proposals for the role of the SOE to be taken over in any future conflict by [the] SAS". Indeed, there were major developments afoot in London as well.

The SAS and the Artists

James Ladd notes that the SAS's Territorial Regiment, 21 SAS (Artists' Rifles), was formed in September 1947. But preparations for its manning were well in hand by April, when the War Office was planning for it to become part of the new 16th. Airborne Division (TA). It asked the GHQMELF to pass on to the 6th. Airborne Division in Palestine (which had SAS veterans in its ranks) details about the SAS's TA unit, and how to go about enlisting in it. The communication revealed that it had been "decided to form at [an] early date [an] SAS B[attalio]n as [a] TA unit of 16 AIRBORNE DIV[ISION]". It was commanded by Major-General Roy E. Urquhart (who had fought with the Independent Companies in Norway in 1940, then the Paras at Arnhem; later becoming GOC Malaya, 1950-52). The War Office message, which was circulated by, *inter alia*, 2 Para., added that the "unit will be designated 21 B[ATTALIO]N SAS REG[IMENT] T.A.", and it was "proposed to form [it partly by the] transfer [of the] ARTISTS' RIFLES to [the] A[rmy] A[ir] C[orps]". This had been proposed by Brian Franks, who knew that the Artists were looking for a new home in order to save themselves from the budgetary axe, while they offered him the advantage of having a drill hall available on the Duke's Road in Euston, central London.

The SAS "Permanent staff", the War Office outlined, "will comprise [the] following regulars or short service commission .. engagement[s]", over and above a C.O.: a Second-in-Command, Adjutant, Captain Quarter-Master, Regimental Sergeant-Major, two Warrant Officers Class (II), and two Sergeants. The Service Department asked that any nominations for these posts be forwarded to it directly, and it was stipulated that, "personnel nominated must be trained parachutists", illustrating the War Office's acceptance of the SAS TA unit as a component of the Airborne Forces. Further, it was "desired [that,] if possible, personnel selected be ex-Rifle Brigade [of which the Artists' Rifles was a part, and which, at first, the SAS would be too], and have served with [the] SAS REG[IMEN]T". Among those kept informed about developments in May were Calvert, Franks and Major Hart, who was told by Maj.-Gen. Dempsey that he "intended to keep up his connection with" the SAS. Franks added that he would as well, and he informed Calvert that, having been offered command of the revamped force, he would take charge of it for a year, in order to "have a nucleus of ex-SAS chaps [joining it, as they] .. would not [do so] .. unless there were a few people [that] they knew" within it.[16]

By 24th. April 1947, the War Office SCAPP was considering a paper entitled "Re-formation of [the] Special Air Service Regiment", prepared by the War Office DAW and the Chair of the Army Council Secretariat [ACS]. This record-ed the fact that the SAS "was disbanded with effect from 30th. June, 1946", and that it was now "proposed that the new Special Air Service Regiment should con-sist of one Territorial, and no Regular, Special Air Service battalion". It would be attached to the 16th. Airborne Division (TA) as part of the Army Air Corps, by virtue of its soldiers' parachute training and expertise. But, the War Office under-stood that the SAS had a distinctive wartime mode of operation, and so its affiliation with the Glider Pilot and Parachute Regiments in the AAC was deemed inappropriate in the long term. The SCAPP agreed with the report's findings and,[17] after some debate over whether to include "Army Air Corps" in the full title of the new SAS unit,[18] by 19th. June 1947, it was decided that "the design[ation] of the battalion shall be '21st. Battalion, The Special Air Service Regiment (Artists' Rifles) (Territorial Army)' ".[19]

Other historians have argued that the TA unit became "2 1" or "21st." SAS because, when a simple amalgamation of 1st. and 2nd. SAS was suggested - producing 12, or 12th., SAS - it was rejected for the "mundane" reason that there was a 12th. Airborne Battalion (TA) in existence, which could be confused with 12 SAS. Hence, the numbers were simply reversed, giving rise to 21 SAS.[20] Equally plausibly, Brian Franks may have wanted to make a political statement to the War Office that, at a time when COIN advisors were being withdrawn in Greece, he and his beloved 2nd. SAS had not be killed off, and that they were now in the ascendant, leading the SAS forward into the future: hence 2,1.

Either way, the day after 21 SAS's title was settled - 20th. June 1947 - a Royal Warrant for the Special Air Service Regiment was drawn up and, in an attached "Explanatory memorandum", it was explained that "it is proposed to reconstitute the SAS Regiment .. and to transfer it to the Artists' Rifles (Territorial Army)". This may imply that the SAS was already constituted in some form, so that it would need to be *transferred to* (rather than simply created in) the TA, under whose auspices all SAS affairs would come. The memo added that 21's maintenance within the AAC was not deemed "appropriate to the role of the new unit". The Royal Warrant went for assent to King George VI on 7th. July 1947, and it was returned on the following day. Hence, 8th. July is effectively the official birthday of 21 SAS (and arguably of the units that it would spawn as part of the broader SAS family).[21]

By mid-1947, the War Office Directorate of Personnel Administration [DPA] was coordinating recruitment for 21 SAS with the 16th. Airborne Division (TA) HQ. With reference to the "provision of Permanent Staff Instructors for 21 Bn. SAS Regiment, AAC", it referred to an SAS 'Original', Colour Sergeant-Major "Bob Tait, who had been nominated for employment with [the] above unit [by] .. MELF".[22] By August 1947, Lt.-Col. Franks and his second-in-command, Maj. Hart, were busy inducting other old hands into the ranks of the new London-based unit. James Ladd asserts that some 180 former SAS officers and ORs rejoined the SAS in September 1947, but in Franks' *Annual Report* on 21 SAS, for the (extended) period up to the 31st. October 1948, he recorded that, of the 196 personnel then making up its "actual strength" (36 officers and 160 ORs), only 59 (21 officers and 38 ORs) had any previous SAS, SBS "or other special unit" experience. Other newcomers had arrived from the Artists' Rifles, other Army units, the RAF, and the Royal Navy, with a total of 224 having been accepted for service by October 1948.[23]

In addition, Lt.-Col. Franks noted that, "in raising the regiment I have aimed at the creation .. of a unit ready to undertake a variety of SAS tasks at short notice [while] .. maintaining in conjunction with the SAS Regimental Association [which had over 1000 members by 1948], an up to date register of those ex-SAS officers and men .. who are volunteers for this type of unit in the event of mobilisation" - what would become known as the 'Z' Reserve.[24] Further, in order to tap the considerable pool of SAS manpower residing outside of the Regiment's south-eastern England wartime stamping ground, 21's commander formed (not for the first time) a "phantom SAS troop. [It was] attached to the 10th. Yorkshire Parachute Battalion" and led by a hero of 1 SAS who'd returned recently from service in Greece - another legendary figure in the history of the Regiment (and even a subject of TV's *This Is Your Life*), Major Johnny Cooper.[25]

The battle for Greece

Whatever the involvement or otherwise of the SAS's London HQ behind the scenes at the turn of 1947/48, scores of new British covert COIN advisors joined the BMM(G) from the start of 1948. Among them were a number of "experienced Commando officers [who] were sent out [by the War Office] under Brigadier [Ronnie J.F.] Tod". He was a good friend of Roy Farran's and a colleague of Lt.-Col. Franks, from the days when they had both served in the 2nd. Special Service Brigade.[26] Another leading figure in the British special forces community who went back to Greece to help out the GRF and his old GSS friends was the erstwhile commander of the SBS (and a Commando/Layforce officer), Lt.-Col. David 'Dinky' Sutherland. He recalled that, "in January 1948, I was called to the War Office Personnel Branch [actually the DPA]. A senior officer [there] said, 'I have been studying your personal file. The Civil War in Greece is a real problem for the West. I note that you have spent a lot of time in Greece liberating the country from the Germans. Officers with your experience are badly needed now to help train the Greek Army and special forces against the Greek Communists. We have a large Military Mission based in Athens .. [and] we think that you should [join it']". Lt.-Col. Sutherland arrived in the Greek capital "later that month", having been tasked first with contacting "Colonel Kalinski, commander of [the] Greek Raiding Forces". Next, the ex-SBS C.O. was to lead the SAS advisory effort in Greece and "examine ways of improving the performance of [the expanding] Raiding Force Groups in their battles against Greek Communist gunmen in the mountains".

David Sutherland "knew Col. Kalinski well [from the time that they had] .. served together in 1943-44" during joint operations by the SBS and GSS. Sutherland adds: "I told Kalinski [that] I wanted to visit the most accessible GRF group in the mountains", and arrangements were made for him to travel to a unit based in a region unsettled by an estimated 5000 DSE fighters. Sutherland went there with three companions who made up a British Instruction Team [BIT which became, in SAS parlance, a BATT, or British Army Training Team]. The Team (which did not have any other SAS/SBS members) "drove in a jeep to the village of Oiti in [the district of] Roumeli, [where] .. the previous day, two GRF men had been shot dead approaching a spring in [broad] day light". This was a costly error and an obvious breach of the rules that was frowned upon by Lt.-Col. Sutherland. He took note of this and other GRF mistakes, and then, he recounts, "we moved out of Oiti on the track .. [where] two Red gunmen opposed us and disappeared, killing one and wounding another GRF" soldier. He concluded from his experiences in Roumeli that at least some of the Raiding Forces were in a state of "disorder .. [as it seemed that] no one knew what to do .. no standard operating procedures [SOPs] existed", and the Greeks were in dire need of his BIT's direction. "After 10 days in the mountains", the Colonel reminisced, "helped greatly by Paul Pourlios .. I decided that *all* GRF [units, emphasis added] .. should undergo a six-week SAS type training course", which was not currently the case.

Lt.-Col. Sutherland's standard SAS fare had various elements to it, including "basic training with guns and [the] use of ground" *a la* Tac Tac, which took place at the "Vouliagmeni [GRF Training Centre, as did training in animal transport, welfare and] load carrying in the mountains of Parnis". Although the new American military mission, the Joint United States Military Advisory and Planning Group [JUSMAPG], was organising and providing the overall logistical and equipment requirements of the GNA from the beginning of 1948, the Raiding Forces were an exception.

The British supplied them with the additional specialist kit that they required, which included familiar SAS weaponry like the .303 Bren gun, Thompson M1 sub-machine gun, .303 Browning, .303 Enfield, .30 Springfield, 9mm Sten, Webley service revolver, Sykes-Fairburn Commando dagger, .303 Vickers machine-gun, 2", 3" and 4.2" mortars, and various munitions. At that time, "British NCO instructors [were doing] .. tactical training and demolition[s]" courses with the Commandos, and the total package of indoctrination and drilling in essential techniques and procedures lasted for eight weeks. Lt.-Col. Sutherland felt that the courses were vigorous and worthwhile, and he "proposed that Col. Kalinski should present .. new badges to all [GRF trainees] .. who passed the course. This, [noted Sutherland,] he accepted and did".[27] Indeed, during 1948, a future commander of the regular 22 SAS, Colonel John Waddy, visited Greece and noticed that Raiding Forces personnel, many of whom had served in the Greek Sacred Squadron and/or the SBS, "wore SAS berets and badge[s]".[28]

Another noteworthy advance was the establishment of a new Greek Raiding Forces HQ by spring 1948. This mirrored the Middle East Theatre's Raiding Forces HQ, created by 1943, which was responsible for overseeing the activities of, among others, the Special Raiding Squadron, Special Boat Squadron and the Greek Sacred Squadron, until mid-1945. Further, the Greek Raiding Forces were reorganised along SAS lines, with four Groups labelled 'A',

'B', 'C' and 'D' (as were the wartime SAS's own Squadrons), each with three Troops and, within them, three Sections (much like the SAS).[29]

From January to September 1948, the BMM(G) had extensive clandestine COIN operational advisory commitments in Greece. British 'special' advisors worked with the GNA and its GRF Groups throughout this period (and some beyond it, as will be seen), providing vital support upon which future Raiding Force successes were based. The Commandos were regarded as a vital component of the Greek security forces' campaign and, in February 1948, the British Military Attaché to Athens, Colonel A.C. 'Peter' Shortt, told the War Office DMI that the lack of GRF units was the key reason why there had lately been little counter-guerilla progress. He added that, even when they were ready to go into battle, they were committed as a vanguard force in huge encirclement operations orchestrated by GNA commanders who had no appreciation of their true worth in pursuing small guerilla bands, which was essential if the authorities were to prevail.[30] Still, by the time that Lt.-Col. Sutherland left Greece in November 1948, he had overseen the training of some 2850 GRF soldiers,[31] and they achieved ever more impressive results from their increasingly protracted patrols against the DSE.

Another battle behind closed doors?

At this point, there is yet another odd twist to the SAS story that warrants some conjecture based upon the available evidence. In 1956, Major C.L.D. 'Dare' Newell wrote a little-known article about the SAS's contemporary operations in the jungles of Malaya, and the background to them. In this piece, he noted that, "at the end of the War in Europe preparations were made to move the SAS Regiments to the Far East, but these plans were cut short by the surrender of the Japanese forces" in mid-August 1945. He continued that, "the Regiments were disbanded in June 1948", which at first sight appears to be a typographical error - it should, perhaps, read "1946" instead of "1948" (or "1945", if the persistently repeated date of the SAS's supposed disbandment is accepted - although the HQs were closed down in November 1945, not June). However, the idea that Newell meant "June 1946" rather than "June 1948" does not tally with the passage that followed. He noted: "However, in September 1947 a Territorial SAS Regiment *had been* formed and amalgamated with the Artists' Rifles" (emphasis added).[32]

His use of the past tense indicates that "June 1948" was indeed the date that the 'Father of the Regiment' had in mind. If this is the case, it begs intriguing questions as to which "SAS Regiments" he was referring to, and why they were disbanded in the middle of 1948?

One possibility is that Maj. Newell was referring to the SAS's War Crimes Teams, and Tony Kemp has shown in *The Secret Hunters* and elsewhere that Maj. Bill Barkworth was signing correspondence as Officer Commanding, 2 SAS War Crimes Investigations Team, until at least 23rd. June 1948. Yet his unit continued to function until "as late as 1949".[33] On the other hand, Newell may have been alluding to the SAS's International Squadron operating in Greece, which certainly comprised men from both 1st. and 2nd. SAS Regiments. According to official documentation of the time, 2 SAS, at least, had its own distinctive, officially-recognised individual identity. These units could well be the "SAS Regiments" referred to in Dare Newell's article in *The Sphere* magazine, and it is plausible that he learned about the Greek venture from colleagues who had served there.

Maj. Newell had worked as an SOE operative during the War, including a tour with Force 136 in Malaya during 1945, and he could have been told about the Greek situation by former SOE colleagues who served in Athens. Alternately, in 1950, Newell was called up by 21 SAS HQ to fight in Korea as a member of an SAS "independent squadron" (details of which are related in another chapter). The concept broadly followed the example set in Greece by the International Squadron and, among those recruited for the Far Eastern trip, were veterans of the Greek campaign, such as Sergeant-Major Bob Bennett and Major Alastair McGregor. Newell could have learned about developments in the Balkans from old stagers like them, or from others at 21 SAS HQ familiar with the situation there.[34]

Assuming that Maj. Newell was at least partly aware of what had gone on in Greece, and that "SAS Regiments" actually were "disbanded" in June 1948, it could be that, at that point, the War Office withdrew its tacit support for 'shadow' SAS units in Greece. This could have come about due to developments that occurred in that war-torn country; in other areas, which impacted on them; in the War Office or Cabinet; or because of a combination of such factors. Various possibilities will be examined to try to determine what may have triggered this down-turn in the SAS's fortunes with respect to its Greece mission, which may have meant that, from then on, SAS personnel were obliged officially to work solely under the purview of normal British Army formations in Greece, rather than as a distinct entity linked to the London SAS HQ.

The first factor to consider is the attitude of War Office opinion-shapers and decision-makers about the whole question of British "private armies" and the possibility that Greece could set an unwanted precedent and lead to their proliferation in the future. These fears could have been heightened by the influx into Greece in 1948 of a considerable number of special forces advisors from various wartime forces that might seek to use the conflict as a starting-point to press the case for the resurrection of their own units, such as Phantom and the Army Commandos. Anti-special forces elements in the War Office also would have been concerned by the recent re-formation of the Royal Marines Commandos and, in particular, that "significant parts of [the] SOE [still existed within the SIS, and] fought on in the post-war period" in Greece. Indeed, it has been asserted that they were "assist[ing] regular British forces against [the Communist] guerillas .. as late as 1948". The SIS Head of Station in Athens, Commander Patrick Whinney (who had commanded the wartime African Coastal Flotilla, transporting SOE and other special forces personnel) was even gun-running for the Greek government "in the first half of 1948", and maintained a radio monitoring post in Corfu.

Furthermore, concurrently, "renegade" ex-SOE officers were supporting Karen insurgents against the authorities in Burma, in flagrant contravention of the British government's declared foreign policy.[35] The activities of former SOE personnel (and those of other special forces) inside and outside Greece could have contributed to a War Office clamp-down on the activities of special units by June 1948.

Another point worth considering is the fact that, at precisely this time - June 1948 - the British authorities were facing an Emergency situation due to another Communist insurgency, this time in Malaya (see later chapters). To a large extent, this revolutionary campaign emulated those undertaken in Greece and China and, unusually, the British military in the Far East Theatre immediately backed the formation of an unorthodox counter-guerilla Jungle Guerilla Force [JGF], code-named "Ferret Force". This was formed by local ex-servicemen who possessed wartime special forces experience, including action with the SOE's Force 136 and the Chindits (with whom Calvert and Fergusson served). It appears to have been organised by the GOC Malaya, Major-General (later Sir) Charles H. Boucher, and the CINC Far East Land Forces [FELF], General Sir Neil M. Ritchie (who had championed the SAS concept from its inception in 1941). They took action in the light of their studies of the concurrent Greek and Chinese conflicts, and the Malaya Ferret Force was assigned tactical roles that mirrored those of the GNA's Raiding Force Commandos: namely, deep patrolling, and spearheading large offensives. Further, from the outset, General Ritchie intended to use 'Ferret Groups' as a counter-guerilla training cadre that could speed up the army's training in these techniques, as was the case with the GRF during 1948. The Ferrets were meant to "spread the doctrine" to other units once the COIN campaign in Malaya had been invigorated by the JGF's operations. Ferret Force personnel did this from January 1949, following its disbandment,[36] (details of which are elaborated later).

The parallels between Malaya and Greece in mid-1948 are obvious, and it is feasible that, when the idea of creating another counter-guerilla special force for use in South-East Asia was contemplated by the War Office in June 1948, those sections of Departmental opinion that were opposed to the idea of special forces on principle acted to make sure that the Jungle Guerilla Force's formation could not be utilised by the pro-SAS lobby to exert greater pressure to have the SAS officially re-Established as a line Regiment in the British Army's Order of Battle. Indeed, it seems that, at about this time, there were more moves afoot behind closed doors with regard to the status of the SAS and the other components of the Army Air Corps - the Glider Pilot and Parachute Regiments - which raised the possibility of enhancing the SAS's current status and its long term prospects.

Major-General A.J.H. Cassels - who had commanded the 6th. Airborne Division in Palestine during 1946, and who, in 1948, was in charge of the new War Office Directorate of Land/Air Warfare [DL/AW] - noted, on 29th. July 1948, that, "the CIGS has suggested to me that the AAC as a separate Corps was not necessary and that the individual Regiments .. should exist as separate regiments". This indicates Field-Marshal Montgomery's continued support for the idea of a post-war SAS, and Maj.-Gen. Cassels minuted that the CIGS's proposal had "much to commend it". The recipient of the DL/AW's communications on this subject, the War Office Directorate of Personnel Administration [DPA], wrote, on 23rd. August, that "the SAS Reg[imen]t is not a regular peacetime f[or]m[atio]n, but consists of one TA B[attalio]n which would form a nucleus for expansion in war" (as Brig. Calvert and Lt.-Col. Franks had envisaged). The Directorate's officials understood that the SAS's "work and training are highly specialised, more so than in the Parachute Regiment, while its members have to be carefully picked and must volunteer for S.A.S. duties". In the light of these facts, and the proposed disbandment of the AAC by the Army's most senior officer, the War Office

DPA suggested that the Parachute Regiment ought to be granted separate Corps status, with "the SAS Reg[imen]t (TA) [authorised] to become an ungrouped regiment of an Inf[antry] Arm" of the Army.[37] Not long afterwards, in 21 SAS's yearly review of 31st. October 1948, Franks referred to the unit being currently "the only SAS or similar unit in existence".[38] This remark tallies with the idea that there had been 'shadow' SAS Regiments operating prior to this that had had their wings clipped after mid-1948.

There is one other vital area that merits attention when considering the possible thinking behind the decision to withdraw support for the activities of the SAS International Squadron. The first and perhaps the most telling thing that could have had a bearing on this was growing American military opposition, by the spring of 1948, to the whole concept of a special force of Commando Raiding Forces. At that juncture, the US Army had no special forces of its own (and did not officially have any until 1951), and the Americans' opposition to the GRF probably stemmed both from military principle and also because of the political circumstances in which the British and American Armies found themselves during the first 'hot war' of the Cold War era. Both governments deliberately deceived their publics and their respective elected bodies about the level of British involvement on the ground in Greece. They gave the appearance that the COIN effort was led by the Americans, who would bear by far the greatest burden, with the British cast in the role of junior partners, carrying out only minor but psychologically important support tasks. The maintenance of this image of America as the saviour of the free world (rather than as the backer of an imperial power with an acquisitive influence in the Near and Middle East), was vital, in order to secure the sceptical and traditionally isolationist American voters' tax-dollars and their support for this entangling commitment. Anything that threatened to undermine this 'Allied' front had to be addressed, and so the Americans were understandably nervous about Britain's ongoing advising about the training, organisation, equipment and deployment of the GRF, and the involvement of British soldiers in combat operations.

Indeed, a related factor in British thinking at this time could have been the conduct of some British covert military advisors (who greatly outnumbered their American colleagues). On 23rd. February 1948, the Foreign Office Minister of State, Hector McNeil, declared that no British troops were authorised to "become involved in the fighting unless attacked, or when their security is directly threatened". Yet, some Britons were engaging with the enemy by this stage, leading to a public statement on the subject. This involvement threatened to blow the carefully constructed British-American cover story about their Missions' roles, which would cause both governments serious domestic and international embarrassment and difficulty, possibly leading to Congress blocking further US aid to Greece, or even encouraging Stalin to interfere there. The growing trans-Atlantic Cold War partnership could come under strain as a result, possibly even jeopardising Bevin's efforts to form NATO.[39]

Consequently, the British government needed to ensure that the Americans were content with their Balkans commitment and, therefore, SAS personnel prosecuting the war as they saw fit would have to be reined in. This could be done by pulling the plug on the SAS 'shadow' organisation, so that, henceforth, their personnel should be monitored and employed solely under the auspices of 'normal' British Army channels in Greece. This action would have sent a clear message to the SAS nucleus in London that they had to play by the War Office's rules, while their vital special forces expertise was retained on the ground, thereby keeping both the Americans and the Greeks happy.

Unsung heroes

There is ample evidence that some British soldiers were in the thick of the battle during 1948 - by which time the conflict had become a classic civil war, with two rival 'governments' and armies - and that they included SAS personnel. Their active participation in operations was deliberately covered-up by the British military and political authorities, and it was UK government policy that, even when British soldiers carried out acts of bravery or distinction, these must not become public knowledge. Hence, they were to remain "ineligible for permission to accept Greek awards for their services". Despite this, the Greeks themselves recognised the distinguished and meritorious service of several Britons in the pay of His Majesty's Government [HMG], and the GNA made awards for their outstanding conduct and gallantry in battle.[40]

In August 1948, the CINCMELF, General Sir John T. Crocker, noted that GNA "Corps Commanders are empowered to make immediate awards of the Greek Military Cross for meritorious service in the field .. [and that,] recently, two British officers have been awarded this decoration and we have had to tell the Corps Commander concerned that, in accordance with our present policy, we are unable to accept these awards". Gen. Crocker continued that it was likely that there would be "further instances" of this potentially thorny situation arising in the near future, and he expressed his dissatisfaction that he was in such a "difficult and delicate" position. He clearly saw that it was crucial not to affront the GNA hierarchy at a critical point in its battle with the DSE, while ensuring that the wider world was kept in the dark about the true extent of the British military commitment to Greece. Crocker - who had served alongside a champion of the SAS, Maj.-Gen. Dempsey, in France in 1944 - thought that a compromise ought to be reached, whereby "the special position of British officers serving in the field with Greek formations should be recognised [but not publicised]. I therefore recommend that the policy .. be relaxed in the[ir] case .. and that they be allowed to accept and wear Greek awards, but only for service in the field". The CINC sought approval for this proposal from the War Office, which was fully apprised of the situation. But, before any action could be taken, the Service Department needed to coordinate with the Foreign Office, which had outlined HMG's policy on foreign citations for it. Major-General Sir R. Mansergh, writing from the War Office, noted that, "under the existing rules, foreign awards cannot be accepted by British subjects for services rendered to a foreign state in connection with actions against persons who are fighting the established, recognised Government". He went on, somewhat cryptically, that, "in any case .. none of the British officers concerned are on loan to and paid by the Greek Authorities", (possibly implying that others might have been before, such as 'soldiers of fortune' like Roy Farran's associate, Xan Fielding). Be that as it may, the General recommended "that these [field-decorated] British officers should be given restricted permission to wear Greek awards .. [but] only in Greece and when employed with the Greek Military Forces". However, doubtless because of the possibility that this could set a precedent and lead to a flurry of awards in future - which might be picked up by British press and radio correspondents in Greece, thereby endangering the government's clandestine COIN assistance programme and cover arrangements - the Foreign Office refused to agree to this.[41]

Even so, on 16th. September 1948, the Greek Army's Orders of the Day included "the names of five British officers .. all of whom had been decorated [by the GNA]" and, at least one, Lt.-Col. Hugo F. Meynell, was presented "the Greek Military Cross .. by the [local] Greek GOC for services in connection with operations in [the] GRAMMOS" Mountains. Another British Army officer in a similar situation was Rory O'Connor and, in his case, the Foreign Office was "adamant" that they must stick to the same policy as that applied by HMG "over French decorations for our [I.S.] actions in Indo-China [during 1945] and Dutch decorations for operations in Java and Sumatra [in 1945/46]" against guerillas operating there. When, in March 1949, the War Office and Foreign Office pondered whether Meynell and others should be allowed to keep their decorations and to wear them in public, they agreed that the established policy of disapproval must be adhered to, and permission for them to do so was denied.[42]

How many of those who received Greek Army awards were SAS men is not known, but one who did was Sergeant Bob Bennett. It could even be that his (and others') gallant conduct, and the unwanted publicity that it might (and subsequently did) generate, contributed to the demise of the SAS International Squadron as a separate agency in the Greek Civil War by summer 1948. Indeed, Lt.-Col. Sutherland recalled working with Bennett during that year, and that 'Benno' was posted as a Sergeant in the Grenadier Guards - his parent regiment prior to enlistment in 1 SAS - to which he may have reverted for administrative purposes after mid-1948.[43]

Delicate questions

The greatest fear for the British authorities during this vital period of the war would have been the public exposure of the supposedly non-existent SAS contingent in Greece. And this was realised in March 1949, when the MP for Mile End (East London), Mr. Piratin, learned of an unusual award having been made to his fellow Londoner, Bob Bennett, who had returned to the UK on leave two months before.

In the House of Commons, on 2nd. March 1949, Mr. Piratin asked the Foreign Secretary, Ernest Bevin, "if he was aware that ex-Staff Sergeant R. Bennett of the Grenadier Guards has been awarded the Greek Military Cross; whether he has served in the Greek Army with the authority of the British Government; whether such authority has been granted to other British ex-soldiers; and if he will make a statement?" about this matter. In response to this enquiry, Bevin stated that, "I understand that a Greek Corps Commander made an unauthorised award of the Greek Military Cross to Staff Sergeant R. Bennett" (interestingly, not referred to as "former Staff Sergeant"). The Foreign Secretary continued that, "the Greek authorities are .. fully aware that members of the British Armed Forces are not permitted to accept foreign decorations in peace time". He added that, "as Sergeant Bennett has never served in the Greek Army, the second part of the question does not arise" and, as to the question of other British citizens having done so, "the answer .. is 'No Sir' ".

In spite of this denial of active British military involvement, Mr. Piratin pursued the issue, asking, "is the Foreign Secretary aware that, according to the statement made in the Greek press, quoted in this country, Sergeant Bennett was awarded this distinction because of his gallantry in action and, irrespective of the gallantry - I am discussing the action - is the Right Honourable Gentleman aware that this is evidence of the fact that British troops are taking part [in operations] alongside the Greek Army?" Bevin once more made a blanket denial of the allegations, despite evidence to the contrary, of which he was patently aware. Indeed, in tackling the Honourable Member for Mile End's queries, Mr. Bevin said that, "British troops *are not* taking part alongside the Greek Army" (emphasis added), which, at the time that he was speaking - March 1949 - was in all likelihood the case, thanks to the diminution of the BMM(G)'s COIN role by then.

But Bevin's response was disingenuous, and his words certainly do not ring true with regard to events prior to 1949. Mr. Piratin, finally and exasperatedly, asked, "then what was Sergeant Bennett doing?" The Foreign Secretary simply reiterated that "British troops are not taking action alongside the Greek Army" and, clearly having been briefed about Bennett's activities by his Foreign Office officials, he said, "I have no evidence that Sergeant Bennett took any action with the Greek Army. He was serving with the British Military Mission [to Greece] and helping to train the .. [Greek National Army], but he did nothing in connection with operations". He rounded on Mr. Piratin in order to try to demolish his accusations - "In my answer I have given the facts, not what is in the newspapers".[44]

Despite Foreign Secretary Bevin's belittling of Mr. Piratin's questions, however, on 8th. March 1949, "Mr. Platt-Mills [MP] asked the Secretary of State for War, if he was aware that ex-Staff Sergeant Robert Bennett, MM, Grenadier Guards [currently resident in Oxford] .. on release leave from the Army, has been awarded the Greek Military Cross?" He followed this up by pointing out that the Greek Army "citation affirms that this British NCO has been serving with the Greek Commandos for over three years past". Actually, the Greek Commandos were not formed until late in 1946, and so Mr. Platt-Mills' question was phrased inaccurately. But, if the essence of what he said is true - that the Greek citation showed that Bob Bennett had served with the GNA for more than three years - and there seems to be no reason to question this, then this confirms that he was in Greece prior to March 1946. Greek documentation additionally revealed "that he has helped with the training of Greek Raiding Forces and participated in tasks which they undertook". Hence, it is clear that, at least as far as the Greek authorities were concerned, Sgt. Bennett had served gallantly in the field with the GRF in their fight against the DSE's forces, and they recognised the fact, even if the British government refused to do so. The Right Honourable Mr. Platt-Mills concluded his questions by asking whether the Secretary of State could "give an assurance that no other British Service personnel have been or will be so employed in Greece?".

Predictably, in a Written Reply to these requests, the Secretary of State at the Foreign Office, Emmanuel Shinwell MP, noted that "a Greek Corps Commander [had] made an unauthorised award of the Greek Military Cross to this NCO .. [but that] this amounts to an unofficial memento only, as all Greek awards are subject to confirmation by Royal decree, and this award has not been so confirmed". This statement rather missed the point - in that it did not explain why Sgt. Bob Bennett had been awarded the Military Cross in the first place. But the Secretary of State tried to forestall any further awkward questions by asserting that "the NCO served as an instructor with a British Liaison Unit attached to a Greek Corps from April 1947, until he left Greece, in January 1949".

(It is worth recalling that, just before the former date - April 1947 - British covert COIN advising had been brought to an abrupt halt by political developments orchestrated by London, and so it seems more than a coincidence that this April date was cited). Once more, it was officially proclaimed that Bob Bennett "did not personally engage in operations", and that the BMM(G) was providing only training assistance to the Greeks.

Indeed, Foreign Office Minister Shinwell reinforced the joint War/Foreign Office policy-line by affirming that, "no member of the Mission has been or will be authorised to take an active part in operations". This was demonstrably untrue and, despite all the official protestations of innocence designed to conceal Britain's clandestine COIN role in the Greek Civil War, once the conflict came to an end, by 1950, and the attention of the press, public and statesmen had shifted elsewhere (for instance, to China, Tibet and the Korean War), it appears that Bob Bennett's Greek citation was confirmed,[45] slipping through unnoticed and without raising any more uncomfortable questions about the actions of SAS (and other special forces) soldiers in their first post-war COIN campaign.

The US and special ops

During 1948, the GNA, supported by the British and Americans, made major progress against the DSE. By October, however, the Western military missions had fallen out over operational policies and priorities (with the BMM(G)'s chief, Major-General Ernest Eric 'Dracula' Down - who was aware of the SAS in 1941, when he took up command of a new Parachute brigade - calling for a greater emphasis on small unit/Commando operations, much to the displeasure of the JUSMAPG's commander, Lieutenant-General James A. Van Fleet). Hence, by October 1948, the BMM(G) was restricted by HMG to advising the GNA on training matters. There were, as usual, though, some exceptions to the rule - namely the British special forces fraternity.

Some British soldiers continued to accompany Greek Raiding Forces Companies into the field until at least December 1948, and BLOs trained them at the Vouliagmeni Training Centre until March 1949. (At this juncture, on 13th February 1949, the British Cabinet approved a scheme for covert subversion operations against Albania. Planned by SIS officers including William Hayter and ex-SBS commander, the Earl Jellicoe, the venture began in May 1949, when ex-SOE/SIS officers, Julian Amery, Lieutenant-Colonel Neil 'Billy' Maclean, Alan Hare and Palestine veteran, Col. Harold Perkins, put together teams of Albanian dissidents in Greece. They were trained by ex-SOE men, Captain Robert 'Doc' Zaehner and Bill 'Gunner' Collins, along with two former SBS sergeants, Terence 'Lofty' Cooling and 'Derby' Allen). Early that March, the BMM(G)'s commander, Down, finally accepted in the face of American pressure that the British should stay out of all operational affairs,[46] although some SAS personnel like Alastair McGregor remained in Greece until the end of 1949 (by which time the Communists had accepted defeat), prior to a low-key return to the UK.[47]

While their efforts were not widely recognised at the time, the British special forces community had made a significant contribution to the COIN campaign in Greece, and their presence there gave the case for the SAS Regiment's survival a major boost. The fresh limitations that the British government imposed on the BMM(G) by October 1948 meant that, potentially, there was a pool of surplus manpower with SAS and other special forces experience in Greece that could be utilised in the future for other Cold War missions. The extant documentary evidence suggests that this fact figured heavily in the thinking of planners at the MEF HQ and the War Office during their concurrent discussions about Theatre preparations for a Third World War, in which the SAS - in the right place at the right time, thanks to the Greek conflict - would be assigned a new and important role.

"Too funny to be true!"

The Middle East Rangers (SAS)[1]

O
ne more episode of which few are aware stems from the period after September 1948, when the British Army was winding down its commitments in Greece, and contemporary preparations were being made by the Middle East Forces HQ and the War Office DMO for a new Theatre conventional war plan, 'Operation SANDOWN'.[2] It was an operational blueprint for "the defence of the Middle East and .. control of [the] Middle East['s] sea communications" in the event of an outbreak of all-out war with the Soviet Union in the year up to July 1949. The SANDOWN plan had been in development from the start of 1948 and, by April of that year, combined planning with the Americans was underway. It included, *inter alia*, "special operations and the military aspect of psychological warfare", for which the British were given the lion's share of responsibility. This was probably because they had retained more expertise and capabilities in these fields than their trans-Atlantic partners (although the CIA was cooperating with the SIS by 1947). It was self-evident to the British military planners that they would need to organise a dedicated special force to undertake the various special duties that might be required in another world conflict, and the SAS naturally came into the picture once again.

Middle East strategic plans and the SAS

In the strategically vital Middle East and southern border areas of the Soviet Empire there would be plenty of scope for a special unit to conduct sabotage operations directed against road and rail Lines of Communication, oil refineries and other key targets. And in drawing up plans for this, the Joint Planning Staff of the British Chiefs of Staff noted, on 30th. April 1948, that, "it would of course be necessary to consult C's organisation ['C' being the Head of the SIS] and the Foreign Office". Both of these agencies were involved in the Greek campaign at this time, and both retained propaganda and paramilitary specialists whose knowledge could be drawn on by the military planners.[3] When the time came for the British COIN effort to be downgraded in Greece, in the autumn of 1948, the MEFHQ found itself with a ready-made pool of talent that could be utilised for SANDOWN, including SAS teams that would be an ideal foundation upon which to establish a new Middle East special force. Additionally, this would fulfil the War Office DMO's desire to create an SRG there, as the 1946 DTI report had recommended, as well as allowing immediate training in General War special forces techniques.

Within weeks of the changes affecting the BMM(G), on 4th. November 1948, the CINCMEF's chief of staff, Major-General (later Sir) Harold Pyman, recorded the fact that he had recently visited the War Office for consultations with the DMO and the DMI (both of which had been dealing with the Greek situation). Further, he spoke to officials from the War Office's Directorate of Staff Duties [DSD], who were responsible for assigning military personnel tasks ascribed to them from higher authorities within the Service Department. Maj.-Gen. Pyman noted that the DMO staff had told him that, "it was likely that we [i.e. MEF] should get a[n] SAS Regiment of between 200 and 350" men,[4] (which, incidentally, was a figure similar to that suggested for SRGs by the War Office DTI).

Unfortunately, there's no mention of how many soldiers working in Greece could be transferred from there to the new Unit's location. Nonetheless, it's reasonable to assume that Greece was seen as a potential source of manpower for the special force, and a Middle East GHQ note of 7th. November 1948 refers to a mysterious "GREEK PROJECT". In addition, a "Review of [the] Mobilisation Situation" viz the SANDOWN plan, dated 15th. November, points out that, "there is a scheme for the recall of 'Z' Reservists", and that this was over and above that for "Regular Reservists". This implies that SAS resources from the UK could have been called upon, while 21 SAS itself was currently training for special operations in a Middle Eastern war (on the basis of a War Office Directive of 17th. August 1948). Furthermore, in 21 SAS's *Annual Report* of that October, its commander, Lt.-Col. Franks, referred to volunteer reserves that could be called up for service at short notice and who could then join "this *type* of unit"[5] (emphasis added). This implies that he had in mind the future expansion of the Regiment beyond the TA, and he was most likely aware of concurrent planning for a Middle East special force.

It appears probable that, as the BMM(G)'s COIN enterprise was drawing to a close in October 1948, the pro-SAS lobby in the UK pressed the War Office to employ the SAS on other tasks in the Middle East Theatre, namely the proposed wartime special unit (thereby taking the first step to creating the world-wide network of SRGs that the DTI had championed). The War Office evidently accepted the arguments of the SAS's backers, that it was best placed to undertake this role. In November 1948, the MEF HQ expected that it would acquire shortly an SAS force (at least in name) of no less than 200 men, some of whom could have come from the ranks of the SAS or other special forces advisors who had confronted Communist opponents in Greece. The SRGs were meant to undertake intelligence-gathering, long-range "deep penetration behind-the-lines" patrolling, demolitions, raiding, and other "harassing activity", which would admirably suit the SAS. But the anti-special forces lobby must have fought a rear-guard action against this new development, playing on the fact that the Armed Forces were still subject to ongoing cut-backs and reorganisation.

On 25th. November 1948, Maj.-Gen. Pyman reported that he had been informed by the Vice-CIGS, General Simpson, that new arrangements for national conscription and the TA were draining the Army's financial resources, and so, while the War Office accepted the military logic of a ME special force, it now looked as if "our [i.e. MEF] chances of getting an SAS regiment are small". Further, at the end of 1948, the War Office traditionalists welcomed more good news when the Jungle Guerilla Force in Malaya was disbanded.[6] This must have heartened the anti-SAS clique, and Lt.-Col. Franks et al doubtless feared the worst for 21's future. Still, the pro-SAS camp would have had their spirits raised by the appointment in November 1948 of a new CIGS, Field-Marshal Sir William Slim. He had supported certain kinds of unorthodox forces and operations during the War (notably in Burma), particularly behind-the-lines small unit action. Indeed, at the turn of 1948/49, the tide seemed to turn more in favour of the War Office 'progressives', boosting the prospects for the SAS as a whole.

Early in 1949, the War Office's planners were considering revisions for the SANDOWN plan and, by 16th. February - only days after the Attlee Cabinet approved of SIS-directed and ex-SBS designed subversion operations against Albania, which originated in Greece, and just before the impending termination of the BMM(G)'s advisory role in March - the MELF was again looking at the "forma-tion of [an] SAS force". Worries about finance must have been overcome behind the scenes, and it was noted with regard to the establishment of a new SAS unit that, "there is an urgent paper on the subject as agreed between [the] B[rigadier] G[eneral] S[taff] (Plans and Operations) and S[taff] D[uties]".[7] A couple of days before this, Maj.-Gen. Pyman also wrote that, at the request of the Deputy Adjutant-General [DAG], he had asked the BGS (Staff Duties) to authorise the inclusion of "an AG representative .. in the SD team which was to visit GREECE on 18[th.] February 1949, for eight days to examine certain establishments".[8]

Although there are no further details about this intriguing sojourn, there clearly was a flurry of activity at the MELF HQ in connection with the formation of a new SAS unit, at the time that the BMM(G) was withdrawing officially from all COIN operational training. The Adjutant-General and Staff Duties branches were at the forefront of this initiative, even to the extent of making a fact-finding tour to Greece and reporting their views forthwith to the Middle East Command. Given their role in the creation and organisation of new army units, it seems that they went to Greece to enlist British special forces personnel for the new SAS Middle East Unit. Indeed, in a memo on "special operations" of 2nd. March 1949, Maj.-Gen. Pyman stated that, "the 12 vacancies have been filled",[9] and that many more would be in the near future. Even more tellingly, on 18th. February, in a Top Secret document written for the Theatre CINC, his chief of staff observed that, "within MELF we have the potential to form a small SAS Group", indicating the current availability of at least a core of personnel who were deemed to be qualified for special forces duties. This Group would comprise "all armes [sic.] based on one squadron of armoured cars and two troops of Royal Engineers". Training in the former arm, Maj.-Gen. Pyman believed, could be provided by the "13/18[th.] Hussars [who came] under [the] GOC, 1 Division, in CYRENAICA", eastern Libya.

The SAS and Libya

Cyrenaica was familiar to the SAS from its wartime desert days and, in 1949, the former Italian colony was a U.N. Trust Territory (or Mandate, like Palestine), under the control of a British Military Administration [BMA]. While its long term future was uncertain and under review at that juncture, the area was considered an ideal location for a small SAS force to organise itself in secret, ready for a future deployment anywhere in the Theatre. The implementation of the scheme cannot have been considered so urgent as to warrant any immediate reconnaissance for potential base sites by personnel on the ground, but there was already a large British garrison there which could be utilised by the SAS. Indeed, "a major part" of the British army presence in Cyrenaica was made up of "engineers and RASC units", which could be incorporated swiftly into an SAS Group should the circumstances dictate this.[10]

The planning for the new Special Air Service force included the pre-positioning of stores and other essential wartime kit at the proposed forward base of operations. Over and above fire-arms, munitions, signals equipment and the like, the SAS would need desert-adapted motor vehicles, especially armoured jeeps fitted with twin Vickers-K machine guns - just as in the last War - and this materiel could have come from the Middle Eastern armoured squadron contingent, as Pyman proposed. The requisitioning and transfer of all this hardware would be supplementary to that required for training purposes at the Cyrenaica rear HQ, and all of these arrangements could be made surreptitiously, given that the location chosen as the peacetime pre-positioning point was "HABBINIYEH" - Habbaniyah - a British military base around 80km. west of Baghdad, in Iraq.

The SAS and Iraq

In 1949, the Habbaniyah RAF base was one of two remaining British treaty-garrisons in Iraq (the other being Shaiba). It was in close proximity to a strategically vital area for the West in the event of Soviet invasion. The SAS would be given the job of hindering a Soviet armoured thrust towards the Middle East's oil reserves (particularly in Iraq and Kuwait), and the all-important trade artery of the Suez Canal. They would do this by interdicting the invasion route in the same way that the SBS had planned to halt a threatened German incursion into the region during 1942. (Indeed, numerous members of the wartime 1st. SAS had been recruited from British army units in Iraq, and some of them could well have returned there after the War).

The SAS's key missions now were to carry out surgical strikes on the main bridges, highways and road junctions, and strategic communications links, thereby slowing the Red Army's onslaught. However, reflecting on high level discussions about SANDOWN and the SAS, Maj.-Gen. Pyman argued that there were advantages to "keeping the training of the SAS Group less particular than" had been suggested by those who appreciated the SAS's strategic capabilities (possibly the likes of Brian Franks). Pyman believed that this would "make it [the SAS] a more flexible tool in the event of war" and, after all, it (alongside the Secret Intelligence Service) was being trusted to execute the numerous tasks that had been allocated to a variety of special forces and organisations just a few years before.

A broad-based training programme would also mean that the SAS was less likely to attract unwanted attention and unwarranted criticism from other quarters, and Lt.-Col. Franks undoubtedly would have accepted the necessity (albeit rather begrudgingly) for the SAS to be flexible in its approach, in order to enhance the case for the Regiment's survival. The fact that the SAS had to demonstrate that it could be "a more flexible tool" implies that proponents of the SAS Middle East Group still had to convince the War Office sceptics that it was both militarily and financially justifiable to establish the unit. Maj.-Gen. Pyman reassuringly (from the SAS's perspective) added that, in any case, during any pre-war crisis, the Group's training and logistics could be switched "from the general to the more particular", depending on the needs of the current situation.[11]

The growing interest in special forces

During March and April of 1949, the MELF HQ continued to work on its plans for "special operations"[12], and it's evident that the supporters of special forces were making headway in the continuing policy debate about them at this time. By 22nd. March 1949, Field-Marshal Slim was enthusiastically recommending the creation of more Raiding Force "Pursuit Groups" in Greece, following a visit to British and Greek forces there.[13]

Shortly afterwards, on 1st. April, during a review of the current I.S. position in Malaya undertaken by the Prime Minister, Clement Attlee, and his ministers - including the Secretaries of State for the Colonies and War - it was agreed that they should look at "any suggestions .. for further measures [that could be taken to improve the COIN campaign], for example, whether it would be useful to recruit a special corps of commando or guerilla type [soldiers] (including ex-members of Force 136) for service in Malaya". The senior Cabinet members present thought that the High Commissioner of Malaya, Sir Henry Gurney (who had faced insurgency in Palestine), and the Commissioner-General for South East Asia, Malcolm MacDonald (who had prior experience of Palestine and was now Britain's regional security coordinator), should be consulted on the matter.

On 4th. April, the War Office DMO loaned its support to the initiative - demonstrating its consistent backing for such developments - and it was in touch with the CINCFELF, General Ritchie, about this. Despite his high regard for the SAS (and key role in its wartime foundation), however, the Directorate noted that Ritchie had already contacted the War Office, asserting that, with the ex-Ferret trainers that he had at his disposal, he possessed adequate resources to tackle the Malaya insurgents.

Consequently, the DMO did not follow up the matter at this stage,[14] (more details about which are outlined later). Despite this, parts of the British Army hier-archy still backed the special forces concept with some conviction, and it appears that, by the spring of 1949, opinion was moving more and more favourably in this direction.

The Middle East special force

Preparations for Operation SANDOWN continued apace in the Middle East Theatre and, on 15th. April 1949, Maj.-Gen. Pyman "saw [the] Chief Engineer, and [he] agreed that we [i.e. MEF] should attempt to get [the] 200 personnel which had been allotted to us by the War Office". Therefore, a decision to go ahead with the organisation of an SAS Group (now with a more definite ceiling) seems to have been taken, at least in principle, with the new unit consisting of "SAS troops made into engineers". This implies that up to 200 SAS personnel had been earmarked for the project and, presumably, they would be trained by Royal Engineers [RE] units in Cyrenaica, with the focus on demolitions and sabotage work. Just where these SAS men would come from is not revealed in the public record, but it's safe to assume that only a portion of the total were currently available within the Theatre.

Indeed, it appears that a lack of sufficient manpower or other resources led to a delay in the formation of the Group. In mid-May 1949, when the Middle East Forces Command was preparing to relocate and restructure its military assets, it sought permission from London to "retain the Army Engineer Reg[imen]t [so as] to form the basis of a[n] SAS element", indicating that reinforcements would be attached to the Group as and when suitable personnel became available. This would probably include men with SAS and other special forces experience from the UK and from Greece, where British NCOs had themselves taught demolitions courses to the GRF.[15]

Another GHQMELF memorandum on Operation SANDOWN, written by the Brigadier in charge of Staff Duties on 19th. May, focused on "Demolitions Training". This reported that the 35th. Army Engineer Regiment in Cyrenaica had been selected as the core of a unit that would carry out wartime demolitions work (thereby becoming the nucleus of the Theatre SAS Group, when it was estab-lished). Their target area would be the "RUWANDEZ GORGE" - Rawandiz Gorge - some 120km. north of Kirkuk, in the mountains of Kurdish northern Iraq. The new force was to deploy in wartime to the Rawandiz valley, utilising the "necessary vehicles and stores" that would be housed at special facilities set up at "HABBANIYA" before any wartime emergency, in line with previous SAS planning. Immediately prior to any outbreak of hostilities, extra materiel would be flown into the air base, including fresh rations, fuel, medical supplies and ammunition. Operations would be planned in cooperation with RAF Liaison Officers on the ground - who would arrange for the air-supplying of SAS behind-the-lines parties - and with SIS officers, who would organise civilian resistance efforts and coordinate them with SAS activities. The MEF's 35 Royal Engineers Regiment was to be reorganised and retrained in order to carry out these tasks and, in addition to its existing manpower, the War Office agreed that it would provide "200 additional" men at a later date, bringing its strength up to just under 400. If the SAS was to supply a good proportion of the other 200 soldiers, it can be presumed that the Regiment's London HQ would have been called on to help by providing volunteers over and above any transfers from Greece.

The stated objective of the Middle East Command was "to produce a unit which, a) is suitably org[anised] and equipped for its primary [special] role of demolitions [and,] b) will [at the same time] provide a nucleus [for] .. an Army Engineer Regiment with a normal wartime role". However, the 19th. May memo noted that, "no attempt is to be made [yet] .. to form an SAS Unit in [the] MELF" Theatre, again indicating that there were problems in acquiring the additional manpower required for the Unit at this time (when, incidentally there was a flurry of activity by the SAS's senior officers in Britain - described in more depth in the next chapter). Still, an initial target date for "re-positioning to HABBANIYA" was set for October 1949, and the Unit was to prepare for its "special role when future manpower for MELF" was secured. Furthermore, the Middle East Forces' "Demolitions" paper stated that the "completion of such preparatory action as is possible in peace[time], and training for the RUWANDEZ GORGE demolition task", should be accomplished by February 1950. However, as well as the problems re personnel that had to be resolved, it was made clear that no training of this special unit was to commence "until the necessary cover arrangements" had been made by the authorities,[16] underlining the need for the customary strict secrecy surrounding SAS operations.

At this point, Maj.-Gen. Pyman was transferred from the MEFHQ, and so the account that he provides peters out. Nevertheless, while there are no further direct references to the MELF's special force initiative in his papers, on 4th. July 1949, the Middle East Command chief of staff noted that the HQ "had now got priority for [its] R.E. officer reinforcements",[17] which in all likelihood went some way to meeting the requirement for the 200 additional personnel needed by the October 1949 deadline. If all went to plan, the new Iraq-based SAS Group would be ready to take up position there early in 1950, and SAS-type operations in another global conflict would become a crucial element of overall Western war-planning. As will be seen, however, other developments delayed the formation of what became known as the "Middle East Rangers (SAS)", probably until mid-1950,[18] (although possibly, if less likely, until 1951).

Fighting for Corps status

The SAS's commitment of what became its International Squadron in Greece from 1945 was essential for the Regiment's continued survival, and it helped to spur on plans for its expansion. On 11th. May 1949, Lt.-Col. Franks wrote from the Hyde Park Hotel to General Sir Miles Dempsey - erstwhile commander of the Middle East Forces, and currently retired to Basingstoke, Hampshire - about the SAS's current position within the Army. It would appear that Dempsey had taken on the role of SAS Colonel Commandant-designate by this stage (as well as Honorary Colonel of 21 SAS). Undoubtedly, he lent the weight of his support to the campaign to retain and expand the SAS. Lt.-Col. Franks informed him that, "as I think you already know, the status of the SAS has altered very much for the better recently" (due to the developments in the Middle East Theatre). Franks noted that this was in contrast to the previous state of affairs when, "in fact, [the SAS] were scheduled [by the War Office] for disbandment in the event of mobilisation" for War. Although 21's commander did not elaborate when this had been made clear to him, presumably it was around the end of summer 1948, after the unsettling changes affecting the International Squadron in Greece, and prior to the groundswell of opinion nurtured by the pro-SAS lobby for the formation of a Middle East special force. This illustrates just how precarious the Regiment's position was during 1948, and how hard the SAS stalwarts and their allies must have fought in Whitehall's back channels to preserve it.

It's most likely that they were able to point to the SAS's achievements in the 'hot war' against the Greek Communists (despite some politically sensitive incidents there), and to use the episode as a springboard upon which to press their case to slot the SAS into the new conventional war plans being considered by the War Office and Cabinet's decision-makers. This is implied in Franks' letter to General Dempsey, which relates that, "without going into details [about the SAS's covert activities in Greece, with which Dempsey would have been familiar] there is now [among the powers-that-be] a recognised requirement for it [the SAS] both in peace [for I.S.] and [in] war".[1]

Besides his letter of 11th. May to Gen. Dempsey, Lt.-Col. Franks attached "a summary of the position which [his second-in-command, Maj. L.E.O.T.] Hart has put on paper after a discussion with me". Maj. Hart's paper of 10th. May 1949 reveals that the Regiment's sponsor, the War Office Directorate of Land/Air

Warfare, had been in touch with the Directorate of Staff Duties (which assigned Army personnel their duties). Hart commented that letters from them had "clarified our position", and they confirmed that "recruitment for [the] SAS both in peace and war" could proceed. In addition, they accepted "the tasks and role of the SAS in War on [the] lines already represented by us" to the War Office. Patently, the SAS HQ was involved in the development of the new Middle East unit, and it helped to frame policy with regard to its organisation, composition and roles. Indeed, Maj. Hart confided that relations between 21 SAS, which was currently "the only SAS unit in the Army", and both 16 Airborne Division (TA) HQ and the War Office DL/AW, were "better than ever before".[2]

Tony Kemp has argued that, with Brian Franks being only a part-time Commanding Officer of 21 SAS, and his second-in-command only a Major, at this juncture the SAS would have had little political clout with senior military authorities. Therefore, it couldn't favourably influence high-level policy-making. At first sight, such a view appears justified. But, with the likes of Generals Dempsey, Browning, Laycock and other senior officers, possibly including the CIGS, as well as politicians such as Sir Winston Churchill, full-square behind the retention of some SAS/special force capability in the British Army, when danger loomed, the SAS could call on considerable assets to fight its corner. Although, as Tony Kemp notes, "none of the officers on the staff [of the War Office DL/AW] had any [first-hand] experience of SAS methods", it is not the case that the SAS was regarded "as simply a variety of parachutists, albeit exotic".[3]

The Director of Land/Air Warfare, Maj.-Gen. A.J.H. Cassels, had commanded the 6th. Airborne in Palestine and was well aware of the SAS's record. Further, the Regiment had influential opinion behind it, and it had played an impressive role in gradually achieving military successes in Greece. All this must have counted in the SAS's favour and contributed to the War Office DL/AW's appreciation of its capabilities, as outlined by 21's Command. It was this, along with perceived future wartime requirements for the Middle East Theatre, that allowed the SAS to win the debate about its future, despite persistent opposition from the Service's enemies in Whitehall. Indeed, in his paper, Maj. Pat Hart stressed that the point had to be reiterated forcefully to the War Office, that parachuting was only a small part of the SAS's repertoire. Fortunately, this message got through, and key Service Department personnel understood the military arguments presented by Lt.-Col. Franks and his colleagues. Hence, by the spring of 1949, the distinctive nature and value of SAS-type operations was recognised within the War Office.

Maj. Hart continued, however, that "our present satisfactory position depends entirely on the goodwill of a number of individuals having certain appointments", so that, in spite of the late up-turn in the Regiment's fortunes, its future was far from secure. While there was a pro-SAS faction within the Army and the Service Department in mid-1949, "their successors .. may not necessarily take the same view". Hart added, "as we know there are some senior Airborne officers who are not in favour of the SAS" at all. Therefore, the second-in-command of 21 SAS felt that the Regiment had to vigorously press the case for establishing a regular SAS formation, while simultaneously capitalising on recent developments that had been instigated by the former CIGS, currently Colonel Commandant of the Parachute Regiment, Field-Marshal Montgomery.

Montgomery had pressured the War Office to clear up the issue of the Paras' future status in the Army, and a Service Department memo of 26th. April 1949 stated that, "it has been decided [in the light of Montgomery's approach] that the Parachute Regiment should be withdrawn from the Army Air Corps and be constituted as a separate Infantry Corps", thereby securing its position in the longer term. Mindful of this, Maj. Hart thought that, "it would be most dangerous from the point of view of the SAS *as a whole* [emphasis added] to miss this opportunity to raise the basic question of the status of the SAS Regiment in the Army",[4] especially if the AAC were to disappear. Clearly, Maj. Hart and Lt.-Col. Franks visualised the future expansion and incorporation of the Regiment into the regular Order of Battle, and it was well on the way to achieving this objective quite separately from Field-Marshal Montgomery's intervention on behalf of the Parachute Regiment, although the SAS sought to take advantage of this.

In fact, Maj. Hart was rather worried by the moves regarding the Parachute Regiment's proposed secession from the AAC. This would leave the Corps with only the SAS Regiment and the Glider Pilot Regiment, and without any obvious reason why they should remain grouped together, the Corps' future would be far from clear. Indeed, the War Office DL/AW recognised that, "in peace[time], the SAS has nothing to do with" the AAC Depot and HQ, and Maj. Hart argued that, "we believe that the SAS Regiment is wrongly grouped in the Army Air Corps". He indicated that this matter had been "thrashed out .. before" in private discussions between the SAS and higher military authorities, although plainly it had not been resolved to the Regiment's satisfaction. He went on that there was a concensus "that individual SAS *units* [emphasis added] may often be organised with advantage for training in Airborne formations". But if the Special Air Service was to raise new units like that being planned for the Middle East Theatre, then a new framework was necessary.

Consequently, Maj. Hart recommended that the SAS should have its own Corps status or, failing that, it should be attached to another Corps outside of the soon-to-be defunct AAC. Indeed, he recounted that, already, the Greenjackets Brigade had been approached about affiliating 21 SAS to it as an "interim solution", while remaining "in [practice within the] 16th. Airborne TA under [the War Office] DL/AW". This set-up was proposed "in view of the 'Artists" background", and Maj. Hart made it clear that "the Greenjackets [should] be asked if they will accept the affiliation to them of this [21] TA unit [but] .. not the SAS Regiment" as a whole. If and when the SAS expanded with a Middle East Group and others in future - a prospect that seemed likely to occur sooner rather than later - then the SAS would require its own Corps, to ease the path for the formation of such units under the War Office's auspices.

Evidently, the SAS had sought approval for temporary affiliation to the Greenjackets before, as Hart reflected that, in the past, "[we] were told that a decision must be left in abeyance until our position was clearer". Now, though, in May 1949, he felt that "our position is .. clear", implying that authority for the Middle East special force had been given by the Service Department. Therefore, finally, steps could be taken to secure the Regiment a new, more assured status. As a first step to this, Maj. Hart thought that "we must ask the Greenjackets for a decision", and then press the case for separate SAS Corps status while the time was ripe.[5]

Irrespective of the issue of granting the SAS a Corps Warrant, there were other questions that the 21 SAS Command also needed the War Office to answer. "The question of the SAS Regiment's peace-time organisation has not been covered", Maj. Hart lamented, with decisions taken to date "merely [having] confirmed the need for and the role of the SAS in the Army, and .. clarified the position of the TA Unit". Yet, there remained outstanding points of contention, like the Regiment being "left in the Army List as a Regiment .. grouped in the AAC [but] without [having the normal, permanent positions of] a Colonel Commandant or officers". In view of the fact that "the continuance of the SAS in the Army is now apparently settled", wrote Hart, it was time to make an official request for the appointment of a Colonel Commandant. Indeed, he pointed out that, in 1945, General Dempsey had asked to be considered for this post, should it arise in the

1. Brigadier Calvert (SAS C.O.), with men of the SAS's overseas regiments, at their final parades in October 1945

2. Corporal McDiarmid of the SAS (with Desert Rats, January 1943). He
was in an SAS Mobile Team in Greece in 1946

3. SAS jeep patrol in Cyrenaica, December 1942. The SAS planned to return covertly to Libya in 1949

4. The Greek Sacred Regiment (SAS) on patrol in March 1943. The SAS deployed covertly from the UK to Greece in November 1945

5. General Dempsey, a staunch SAS supporter, in Greece, 1945, just before covert counter-insurgency activities began

6. The Habbaniyah air base, Iraq, 1941. The SAS (Middle East Rangers) planned to set up a clandestine depot there in 1950

7. SAS parade with Roy Farran (right), October 1943. He led controversial secret operations in Palestine in 1947

8. SAS (Malaya Scouts) ready to embark on a Valetta of 48 Squadron in Malaya, 1952

future. Brian Franks was in close contact with Gen. Dempsey and he would have been pencilled-in for this position. Maj. Hart also identified the need for an office or "Depot Party" for the more efficient peacetime running of the SAS Regiment, as well as "to ensure continuity" when old hands like himself and Brian Franks came to the end of their contracts. Tours of duty with the TA were only meant to last for three years, so there was a need to establish "a small permanent cadre", which would put the SAS nucleus (and the 'shadow' structure that preceded it) on a more stable and secure footing. Maj. Hart elaborated that they had been "unable to raise [a permanent cadre] .. before, since the permanent requirement for [the] SAS in the Army had not been laid down by the War Office" (with the International Squadron having been viewed as a transient COIN body). But the SAS's fortunes had changed, largely due to its own efforts.

Now there was the prospect of a transformation in both the organisation of the Regiment and its status. In order to achieve this, 21 SAS was prepared to make further sacrifices. Maj. Hart suggested that some of the Artists' present complement could be culled to make way for the new core SAS staff. He included his own position, along with a clerk and a driver and, if needs be, even some of the Warrant Officer and Sergeant Instructors.

Maj. Hart recommended too that the SAS's records (which did not all disappear in 1945 as has been supposed by other historians) should be transferred from their current repositories at the Airborne Forces Depot and Museum in Aldershot, and in the War Office, to the Infantry Records Office at Exeter. Once the new, permanent SAS cadre was in place, it could take over from the current "TA permanent staff" and deal with all the matters that had been delegated to it. This included "office work [which] .. at present deals as much with the Regiment as a whole as with the TA unit". Hart gave examples of this as "inquiries [sic.] about past events, correspondence with the [existing] French and Belgian SAS, SAS Association matters, etc.".[6] In this case, the apparently innocuous "etc." would have included secret activities connected with the Middle East Theatre, about which only a select few were fully cognisant.

Lt.-Col. Franks sent Maj. Hart's "Summary of the position" to Gen. Dempsey the day after it was written, and 21's commander observed that, "anything that is done now will obviously have a great effect upon the Regiment's future". He admitted to Dempsey, however, that "as the whole matter is now a question of higher policy, and also, quite honestly, I am in two minds as to what might be [the] best for the future, I would very much like the chance of discussing it with you". Lt.-Col. Franks therefore appears to have been undecided about whether the SAS's future could be best secured by achieving separate Corps status, or by becoming affiliated to an Established Infantry Group that might be less subject to the vagaries of financially-dictated higher-policy on organisation.

Either way, in view of the fact that Franks' own "appointment [would] end .. fairly soon[, in 1950, he wanted] to feel that [the SAS's] .. affairs were in as satisfactory [a] position as possible when I go". Hence, he put his weight behind Hart's recommendations for a permanent SAS cadre, a Colonel Commandant and, ultimately, Corps status.[7]

Evidently, the battle over the SAS's official standing was hotting up by mid-1949. On 20th. June, the War Office Director of Land/Air Warfare, Maj.-Gen. Cassels, noted that the Parachute Regiment was about to gain its own Corps Warrant, thereby leaving open the question of what would happen to the remaining AAC elements - the SAS and the GPR.[8] In another letter to Gen. Dempsey, dated 7th. July 1949, the SAS Territorial Army Command informed him that Lt.-Col. Franks' replacement would be the highly decorated and respected former leader of 2 Commando and author of the widely-read HMSO handbook of 1943, *Combined Operations, 1940-42*, Lt.-Col. A.C. Newman, who would take over in 1950. The correspondent added, "incidentally .. that the Parachute Regiment have now split from the AAC and become a separate entity in the Inf[antry] .. [which] should rather strengthen our case for the SAS Regiment" to do likewise.[9]

As has been mentioned, early in July 1949, the Middle East Forces Command had acquired permission from London to press on with its Engineer reinforcement plan (as the basis for the MELF special force). A few weeks after this, on 28th. July, the War Office Director of Personnel Administration - responsible for arranging personnel transfers - Major-General J.E.C. McCandlish (who had dealt with the wartime SAS), wrote to the Directorate of Land/Air Warfare about contact made on 26th. July between Gen. Dempsey (the SAS's Colonel Commandant-in-waiting) and the War Office Adjutant-General (responsible for raising new Army units). According to Maj.-Gen. McCandlish, the Adjutant-General had been asked by Gen. Dempsey - currently the "Hon[orary] Col[onel of the] SAS Regiment" - to "consider [a] proposal (put forward unofficially by the SAS Regiment) to remove the SAS Regiment from the AAC and to form it into a separate group of Inf[antry]".

The logic behind the SAS's argument was "that their role was a special one [that was] .. separate and distinctive" from any other Army formations. The Regiment consistently put forward its proposals for a fresh status based on their own merits, rather than doing so solely on the back of the changes affecting the Parachute Regiment - although these added grist to the SAS mill. Its initiative was undertaken, like much of the Regiment's business, via unofficial back channels in the Whitehall corridors of power, through the good offices of some of the Service's most influential backers. As was the norm too, the endeavour emanated from "the commanding officer of the unit", Lt.-Col. Franks, who, along with Maj. Hart, was responsible for leading the quiet but critical campaign to ensure the SAS's continued existence and future expansion.

The recommendations drawn up by Lt.-Col. Franks for the perusal of the Adjutant-General were:

> Firstly, "[the] establishment of a Colonel Commandant and [a] small staff for [the] SAS Regiment .. [which] could be found by giving up .. [a] proportion of instructors from [the current] permanent staff of [the] TA unit".

> Secondly - and a point upon which he must have settled after being reassured by Gen. Dempsey - was the need to establish a separate SAS Corps.

> Thirdly, he wanted "SAS Records .. to be located at [the] Inf[antry] Records Office [in] .. EXETER".

> Fourth, was his requirement for the War Office "A[djutant-]G[eneral] 2(0) to adminster [SAS] officers".

> Fifth, he wanted 21 SAS to remain under the wing of 16 Airborne Division (TA).

> Sixth, for an approach to be made to the "Greenjackets .. to accept affiliation of this TA unit [21 SAS] in view of the background of the Artists' Rifles".

Maj.-Gen. McCandlish concluded that, should 21 SAS's suggestions be implemented, this would raise questions about the viability of the Army Air Corps.

Hence, he sought clarification from the DL/AW about whether it supported Franks' and Hart's proposals, as he recalled that, at some point in the not too distant past, "you [DL/AW] said that you could foresee no possibility of there ever being an Active Army element" of the SAS.[10] Once again, this shows just how tenuous the SAS's existence was around 1948, with even the Regiment's sponsoring War Office Directorate harbouring no hope that a regular SAS would ever be formed. It can be deduced, therefore, that SAS developments in the Middle East, combined with pressure from its lobbyists, and the appointment of Maj.-Gen. Cassels as Director of Land/Air Warfare, reversed its fortunes, greatly enhancing the Regiment's prospects of achieving Corps status and a berth in the regular orbat. Apparently, Brian Franks was given the opportunity to present the SAS's case in person to the War Office Adjutant-General early in August 1949.

In notes on "The future of [the] 21st. SAS Reg[imen]t (Artists') TA", written on 15th. July 1949, the 21 SAS Command's recommendations are outlined, and they imply that Franks had been "asked to attend a meeting [at the War Office] and [to] state the case" for the changes that were desired by the SAS. It may well be that, at this meeting, Franks presented a paper - dated August 1949 - which offered greater detail on his vision for the future of the SAS Regiment and its wartime roles. 21's Commanding Officer underlined the importance of SAS strategic behind-the-lines missions rather than its deployment on tactical operations (although he no doubt accepted that the SAS would have to be ready to undertake them).

He additionally pointed out, probably mindful both of recent developments in the Middle East Theatre and documentation that was being circulated in connection with this, that the SAS was not a quote-unquote "Unit .. in the sense [of the word that is] generally accepted". Rather, he stressed that "the SAS *Regiments* [emphasis added] are NOT organised and CANNOT be employed as Units" (made up of hundreds of men). While the British Commandos had been employed in that manner in large-scale operations during the last War on numerous occasions, Lt.-Col. Franks sought to get over the idea that "all operations undertaken by SAS troops are carried out by parties especially picked and equipped for the occasion". The SAS was "merely a force of SAS troops from which a large number of SAS parties can be found, controlled and maintained".[11] It's patent that Lt.-Col. Franks hoped that, in time, other SAS forces would follow in the footsteps of the Middle East Group, and that eventually there may be a presence in each Theatre around the world (in line with the War Office DTI's recommendations). Indeed, he favoured the foundation of an SAS peacetime organisation consisting, initially at any rate, of a base unit with 192 personnel (21's actual strength in October 1948 was 196 All Ranks), and three operational squadrons of around 350 officers and men in total (or 118 each).[12]

This figure tallies precisely with the upper limit of the "200-350" SAS personnel that the MELF's chief of staff, Maj.-Gen. Pyman, recorded on 4th. November 1948 as the special demolitions manpower that the GHQ should be acquiring in the near future, by arrangement with the War Office. (The lower limit corresponds to the SRG unit ceiling cited by the 1946 DTI report for special units). Hence, it could well be that the figure of 350 soldiers for the Middle East special force emerged from consultations with Franks on the subject (following the reduction of the BMM(G)'s role in Greece from October 1948). Whether or not this is the case, by 9th. August 1949, the War Office DL/AW informed the DPA that, in response to Lt.-Col. Franks' current proposals (presented by him to War Office officials at the start of that month), it was "agree[d] that [21 SAS] .. should, if possible, become part of the Greenjackets Brigade". However, as regards the SAS as whole, it was felt that "the only solution is to make the SAS a separate Corps".[13]

It is known that, by the beginning of September 1949, the "advantages and disadvantages" of an SAS Corps had been thoroughly debated by those concerned. (It's also worth bearing in mind that, according to the initial timetable proposed for the formation of a SANDOWN special force, arrangements for its deployment were to have been completed by October 1949). On 7th. September, the Assistant Adjutant-General, P.H. Man, referred to a draft paper in his possession on the development of "a new Corps from the SAS", which would be of approximately battalion strength (i.e., 500-600 men, which closely matches Franks' request for an SAS force of 546 All Ranks). The AG representative had one reservation about the endeavour, however, which was that, "when the [wartime] Emergency Powers cease, it will be difficult to transfer volunteers from, say, an 'SAS Corps', if they prove to be unsuitable, or if suitable employment cannot be found for them",[14] which would presumably be in limited wars and I.S. campaigns. In spite of this concern about the retention of such a sizable number of special force troops, a meeting was convened on 20th. September to consider what to do with the remaining components of the AAC.[15] For the SAS, at least one possibility was COIN action, especially with the concurrent upsurge in insurgent activity in Malaya.

In readiness for the Conference on the Army Air Corps, which was to be held at Lansdowne House in central London, under the Chairmanship of Maj.-Gen. McCandlish of the DPA, he wrote a review of the position on 13th. September 1949. McCandlish noted that the SAS currently had "no regular content", and that its "present composition" was one TA battalion, which came under 16 Airborne Division (TA). He recounted how decisions had been taken after the War "to reconstitute the SAS Regiment as a component of the AAC .. that the Artists' Rifles (TA) should cease to be a component of the Greenjackets [Brigade and, subsequently, that the SAS] .. should be entitled the 21st. Battalion SAS Regiment". He went on that, "the present grouping of the SAS [in] .. the Army Air Corps does not appear to satisfy the unit" and, as a consequence, "strong representations have been made, based on the unique role of this regiment", for a new status to be afforded it.

The next step for the SAS was to push for its own Corps Warrant, and this "was taken, since it was considered that neither the Parachute Regiment nor the Glider Pilot Regiment were appropriate regiments in which to include the unit", noted General McCandlish. These developments contradict assertions by some historians that, in the eyes of the Service Department, the SAS was "little more than an appendage of the Parachute Regiment". Rather, the SAS's own special role was recognised as the key determining factor in its case to become "a separate Corps on their own .. or .. [if necessary,] a component of the Greenjackets Brigade".[16]

In conclusion, Maj.-Gen. McCandlish referred to the "advantages .. and .. disadvantages" of the tabled changes, foremost among the former being that "the identity of the [different] regiments will be assured". Furthermore, he realised that the "SAS Regiment would afford a suitable 'home' and basis for expansion in wartime for 'special agents' and the numerous 'irregular' personnel and 'bits and pieces' [that are] necessary to modern warfare". Thus, the War Office was coming round slowly but surely to accept the worth of unorthodox Army forces and to see that it made sense to gather them all under the SAS banner. The General's only worry was one about "the problems [traditionally] connected with 'special agents" etc., [in that they] .. might become a burden on the Greenjackets Brigade" if the SAS was affiliated to it.[17]

Notwithstanding the fact that a few potential difficulties were foreseen, the Service Department was edging towards authorising a separate SAS Corps by the time that Maj.-Gen. McCandlish met, among others, Colonel G.H. Cree of the War Office Adjutant-General's Office (AG(2)) and Lieutenant-Colonel T.C.M. Pearson of the DL/AW (Air 2).

On 20th. September 1949, the interested parties mulled over the future of the Army Air Corps, and the SAS's sponsor Directorate stated that, due to problems envisaged over things like terms of service, recruitment, and dress, it was thought that the Colonel Commandants of the Greenjackets Brigade, the King's Royal Rifle Corps and the Rifle Brigade "would not show any real interest in [acquiring] this [SAS] unit". The DPA representative added that, at the same time, it could see "no connection" between the SAS and the GPR in the AAC as it stood at present.

Hence, some change was necessary and, taking into account the probable reticence of other formations to take over responsibility for the SAS within their establishment, it was deemed wise to form a new SAS Corps. The Conference delegates agreed that Lt.-Col. Franks' recommendation for "a depot was necessary", although this "would have no training commitment", so that, presumably, existing arrangements for training with the Airborne Forces would continue. The Conference further concurred that "Permanent staff [for the SAS Corps] should be found from those Arms and Services which supplied recruits for the Regiment" in the past, such as the Guards Brigade and Airborne units.

Additionally, with reference to the "future status of the SAS Regiment .. it was agreed that the SAS Regiment should continue to be a Rifle Regiment. It should retain the precedence of the Artists' Rifles in the TA" - given 21's constitution during 1947 - and the SAS would be entitled to a regimental band. As for recruitment from this point onwards, the DL/AW thought that National Servicemen could be enlisted as volunteers "when doing their part-time service in the TA" and, generally speaking, "only volunteers could be accepted for service for the SAS Regiment". Finally, the War Office "DPA said [that] Sir Miles Dempsey had unofficially consented to become Colonel Commandant of the SAS Regiment".[18] Shortly after the War Office's AAC Conference, the Service Department got down to the business of making provision for an SAS Corps. On 17th. October, the Adjutant-General to the Forces, General Sir James S. Steele, informed the Colonel Commandant of the Glider Pilot Regiment, Field-Marshal Lord Alanbrooke, that the decision had been taken to "form the SAS Regiment into a Corps of its own" in the near future.[19]

James Ladd has written, somewhat cryptically, that when the Special Air Service was being given Corps status, arrangements were made so that its higher HQ at Brigade level would be directly "responsible to the Army Staff in some situations of political delicacy". This was said to be because of "reasons of security", particularly in terms of weapons procurement for the SAS's future deep penetration role, which was understood best by SAS officers themselves. This certainly could be applied to the secret formation of the Middle East special force and, indeed, Ladd linked the above reasons to the decision to make 21 "the senior regiment of the SAS Corps .. with power to raise other regiments as and when the War Office .. required them".[20] (In the case of the Middle East Rangers, this would be fairly soon).

A MEF unit was not the only factor in the minds of those considering the expansion of the SAS into a Corps, though. There was the broader contribution that the SAS could make to the British Army, notably in a major war. On 2nd. January 1950, "the War Office .. issued a new directive for the use and training of 21 SAS" that focused on preparing to "harass the enemy .. destroy military stores .. etc., gain information, operate as the recce element of an Airborne Division .. in deep penetration .. [and] provide a disciplined background to partisan movements". A week later, the DL/AW's Colonel R.C. Elstone wrote a paper on the "Organisation of an Airborne Division", and he reiterated that, if the SAS was to form its own Corps, it should assist with "deep penetration .. in an airborne assault" and in a "quick link-up role" between Airborne Forces. He noted, in regard to the "deep penetration role in airborne assault[s that,] .. should there be a requirement for a reconnaissance element, this will be provided by [the] SAS on an 'ad hoc' basis" and, similarly, if a "quick link-up" was needed, "the SAS will again provide it".[21]

Hence, by the start of 1950, the SAS's sponsor Directorate was preparing for the establishment of an SAS Corps and earmarking it for future wartime special operations in coordination with the existing Airborne Forces (with whom joint training would continue, along with the newly reconstituted SBS). The SAS was to provide the expertise for unusual military missions as and when it was demanded by the Army, thereby demonstrating the flexibility and adaptability Franks saw as a necessity for the Regiment to flourish. Even so, the anti-special forces faction within the upper circles of the military - which included opponents of the SAS in the Airborne Forces who disliked the planned expansion of the SAS and its likely 'interference' in Airborne operations - persisted with their rearguard action to try to prevent the SAS obtaining its Corps Warrant. This delayed things for a while, the War Office Assistant Adjutant-General noting on 24th. January

1950 that the SAS was still part of the AAC, even though it was meant "to be taken out .. and constituted as a separate all-arms Corps" (in line with plans for the Middle East Rangers and the wider SAS Corps). In attempting to block this, the Army traditionalists appear to have reverted to the old arguments against special forces, with two "alternatives" being floated by the AG branch in the light of these.

The first option was for the Parachute Regiment to remain "as at present constituted .. and the Army Air Corps composed of only the Glider Pilot Regiment and the SAS Regiment .. to be retained". Alternately, "the Parachute Regiment and Glider Pilot Regiment [were] to be amalgamated into a NEW Corps, NOT an Inf[antry] Corps, and the SAS Regiment [was] to be constituted as a separate Corps". In assessing the former proposal, the AG's staff identified an "advantage [that,] .. although it may be desirable to form the SAS into a separate Corps from the operational and security angle" - which were central and broadly accepted reasons for having an SAS Corps - it was felt, "nevertheless, that the AAC does in fact provide a very adequate 'home' for any of the 'hybrid' units which modern warfare demands", thereby obviating the need for an SAS Corps.

In addition, a supposed "disadvantage" to the option of forming an SAS Corps was that, to do so would be "a lengthy and complicated business" requiring, among other things, the issue of a new Royal Warrant. To summarise, it was readily admitted that "the SAS Regiment being formed into an independent Corps would satisfy operational/security requirements", but, on balance, the AG felt that the first option should be adopted.[22]

Yet again, therefore, the SAS had to muster all the support that it could to fight its corner, with Pat Hart reportedly orchestrating the lobbying of the War Office.[23] This paid off, and the doubters were overwhelmed by the pro-SAS lobby once more. In another meeting at Lansdowne House, held on 14th. February 1950 and chaired by the Adjutant-General's Colonel F.R. Armitage (AG 1(A)), a final decision was reached in the SAS's favour. The Service Department agreed that the SAS should be reconstituted as a separate Corps, thereby fulfilling the operational and security requirements arising from the formation of the SAS's Middle East Unit (whose deployment in battle-ready condition was, initially, scheduled for February 1950).

The Conference directed that "officers who serve with the SAS Regiment will be commissioned into that Regiment [while] .. Other Ranks who join .. will be re-enlisted into the Regiment, or if they are already serving in another Corps, will be permanently attached to a unit of the SAS Regiment [such as the planned MELF one] whilst remaining in their original Corps".[24] However, Captain C.W. Weston, AG1 (Records), wondered whether this might not "lead to certain criticisms by individuals", as only ORs who enlisted in the SAS "can be given the substantive ranks in the Regiment". Consequently, he proposed that, "if men are to serve all their service in the SAS Regiment, they should be entitled and transferred to the [SAS] Regiment and Corps", while even those who did "only .. a tour of duty .. should be permanently attached and enlist[ed] .. except [for] military bandsmen".[25]

The Captain's arguments were accepted and, henceforth, SAS officers were to be appointed to commissions and administered by the Infantry Records Office in Exeter, Devon, while ORs would be enlisted into the SAS and "administered by Combined Records, Bournemouth", Dorset.[26] This would put the SAS and its soldiers on a far firmer footing than hitherto and provide the solid foundations upon which the Regiment could fight for its survival.

Soon the necessary documentation to establish an SAS Corps was being prepared by the War Office and, by at least 28th. March 1950, the Adjutant-General had produced a draft Corps Warrant to which amendments were added regarding the "Constitution of the Special Air Service Regiment as a new Corps". In a memorandum of 24th. April it was explained that, "to allow for the expansion of the Special Air Service Regiment without having to amend the Corps Warrant [in future,] a specific reference to the 21st. B[attalio]n (Artists' Rifles) TA has been omitted". This was most important, because it would more readily allow the future formation of various SAS units that the Regiment's leading officers visualised, such as those for the Middle East, the Airborne Forces and, as will be seen, for the Far East Theatre. (The Special Boat Squadron also became operational again at this time, possibly, as some historians speculate, in view of the Malaya situation - where SBS men were sent in 1950 - but, more likely, on the back of these behind-the-scenes SAS developments).

Preparations re the SAS's Warrant were nearing completion by late April 1950 and, on 13th. May, the Secretary of State for War, John Strachey, signed Corps Warrant Amendments Number 20 (Miscellaneous 2986) for the Glider Pilot Regiment, the Parachute Regiment and the Special Air Service Regiment. This paperwork declared "that the Special Air Service Regiment shall be constituted as a separate Corps for the purposes of the Army Act, the Reserve Forces Act, 1882, and the Territorial and Reserve Forces Act, 1907". As a consequence, and with the King's consent (which followed on the next day), the SAS Regiment was authorised to become a Corps of the British Army with effect from 22nd. May 1950, when the fact was announced at a Staff College Conference held at Camberley. Some historians have asserted that Corps status was not granted to the SAS until early in 1951, but, in reality, the 'official' birthday of the contemporary SAS (aside, arguably, from that of the Territorial Army formation, 21 SAS) can be dated to 22nd. May 1950, when the new Corps was proclaimed under the title of "Special Air Service Regiment (consisting of all units and personnel of the Special Air Service Regiment)".[27] Some five years after the SAS's top brass had begun the campaign for survival, a major victory had been won.

At this time, the SAS's records were transferred to their new repositories, including "documents of Army Air Corps reservists with SAS experience", which went to the Combined Records Office at Bournemouth. These files could be utilised by the 'Z' Reserve in future, and they were considered "essential for mobilisation planning", not least because a "Joint Staffs Memorandum laid down .. that, if any special force was required for the future, it would be provided by the SAS".[28] In the light of all that had gone before, it would be surprising if, having gained its Corps Warrant, the SAS did not set about organising the Middle East Rangers (SAS) with all due haste, utilising the 'Z' Reserve for this purpose. Unfortunately, no records about this matter have emerged to date, but there is evidence to suggest that this is what happened, as will be seen.

By the middle of 1950, the SAS had at last become an Established part of the British Army orbat, if not yet a universally accepted one. This was a great achievement for Brian Franks, Pat Hart, Sir Miles Dempsey (its new Colonel-in-Chief) and the other champions of the SAS, among whom was Mike Calvert - by then back on the scene (in Malaya) and doubtless fully aware of what was going on (more details of which are outlined later). In addition, the saviours of the SAS had not only won the argument about the Regiment's continued existence and expansion, they had managed to drill it into some key elements of War Office officialdom just what the SAS was and was not about.

This does not mean that the SAS message sank in completely across the board there and, because of personnel changes and continued resistance to the idea of special forces, the SAS would face further opposition from within Whitehall. But, by mid-1950, the Regiment was much better understood than in the past, or, at least, less misunderstood. This is illustrated by an explanatory memorandum drawn up in May 1950 to accompany the Corps Warrant Amendments during their passage through the bureaucratic process. This explained that "all members of the Special Air Service Regiment are normally parachutist[s]. This, however, in no way means that the role of the unit is analogous to [that of] the Parachute Regiment". The SAS was not looked down upon by everyone working in the Service Department as "little more than an appendage" of the Red Berets, and the assumption that "nobody [in the War Office hierarchy had] .. any true understanding of what the SAS was capable of" is demonstrably not true.

In reality, the War Office memo argued that "the tasks and principles of employment of a Special Air Service unit differ fundamentally to those of a normal Parachute battalion, as Special Air Service units will not normally operate in contact with the tactical battle and their operations are coordinated directly by the HQ of the Theatre of Operations concerned", (just as David Stirling had stipulated during the War). The SAS Warrant addendum elaborated that an SAS Corps was required so that there was "a suitable 'home' and basis for expansion in wartime for 'special agents' and .. 'irregular personnel' ". Further, "the qualifications of officers and ORs who serve with the SAS Regiment are of a highly specialised and strictly confidential nature, and [so the] interchange of personnel between units is impracticable".[29]

Another related memorandum described how, "whilst members of the G.P.R. always reach the battlefield by air, units of the SAS Regiment do not always do so .. [and their] tasks and principles of employment differ fundamentally". The paper observed that the Glider Pilot and Parachute Regiments' troops acted in a normal infantry capacity, but that the SAS's *modus operandi* was quite different and, being strategic in nature, it was outside the realm of the "tactical battle".[30]

Soon after the Corps Warrant was effected, the War Office Directorate of Military Training [DMT] raised no objection to the idea of the SAS providing " 'ad hoc' " forces for strategic deep penetration patrolling and link-ups with the Airborne forces in future wartime operations.[31] Hence, the SAS's strategic role was understood more widely within the War Office than at any time since the War and to a greater extent than has been assumed by historians. Coincidentally, the

Regiment was given the chance to demonstrate its strategic capabilities almost immediately, when, just as Calvert was developing the SAS's COIN arm in Malaya, the Korean War broke out in June 1950. This offered the Regiment further possibilities to consolidate its burgeoning position, and this was soon seized upon by its senior ranks.

Korea: the war that never was?

On 25th. June 1950, the Communist North Korean Army crossed the 38th. Parallel and invaded its southern, non-Communist neighbour, the Republic of South Korea. The United States and its allies and friends were faced with a major test of their resolve to stand up to "the Red menace" and, on 29th. June, President Harry S. Truman ordered his proconsul in Japan, General Douglas MacArthur, to organise assistance for South Korea in the form of air and naval forces. On the following day, MacArthur arrived in South Korea to assess the situation, and he began to sketch out plans for a land campaign. The British government also favoured a firm approach to the crisis, as it had done in Greece. But, at the same time, it did not want to unduly antagonise the USSR or China. Hence, the Cabinet was somewhat concerned by "the sweeping nature of American policy-making [and] .. the tendency to over-react". Notwithstanding this worry, with the Soviet Union boycotting the U.N. Security Council, the United States was able, by 7th. July, to get U.N. authorisation for the creation of a Military Command headed by General MacArthur, and a recommendation that all member states contribute military forces to the U.N.'s "police action". The Attlee Cabinet went along with this,[1] and so the possibility of an SAS involvement in a conventional war, for the first time in five years, loomed large.

Predictably, the SAS would have viewed this conflict as an opportunity to prove to those in charge in the War Office and the Cabinet that the Regiment could and should have a vital wartime role, thereby boosting the case for the formation of the Middle East Rangers and other units in various Theatres around the globe. Although little has come to light about this episode in the SAS's history, it appears that Gen. MacArthur, impressed by the Regiment's reputation - having reportedly "made an outstanding contribution .. to the Anglo-American relationship" thanks to the work of its touring Team in the US during 1945 - initially made a specific request to the British government to send an SAS force that could undertake operations behind-the-lines in North Korea. MacArthur's interest in the SAS may have been sparked not only by their renowned wartime exploits, but also by recent joint Allied planning in which a role for special forces had been identified and allotted to the Service (while the US Army lacked combat-ready special forces until 1952).

Either way, the Americans apparently appreciated the potential of the Regiment by this stage,[2] and the SAS used this fact to press the War Office to allow the Regimental HQ to set up a new SAS unit for deployment to Asia. In view of the British government's worries about the scope of the US' war plans, at first, the War Office was reticent. Thus, 21 SAS's Adjutant, Major Anthony Greville-Bell, was given the task of convincing the Service Department to allow another special force to be raised. David Stirling's youngest 'Original', Johnny Cooper, later recounted how Tony Greville-Bell was "brimming over with this thing" and how, with the backing of Lt.-Col. Franks and Maj. Hart, he "was battling with the War Office to send .. [a] squadron to Korea". During the summer of 1950, Army staff officers at Great Scotland Yard were "badgered to find a place" for the SAS in the orbat for Korea and, evidently, the War Office gave the green light to create an SAS force, ready for action should the British government decide subsequently to send it off to Korea.

Greville-Bell "sent letters far and wide to old comrades", telling them that "we are forming an independent [SAS] squadron to go to Korea". This implies that the SAS decided to follow the Greek example and send a unit in some shape or form, come what may. Among those that the Adjutant contacted were Captain (later Major) Johnny Cooper (who had been made responsible by Brian Franks for SAS affairs in northern England, where he ran a 'phantom' SAS troop in Yorkshire). Cooper was told by Greville-Bell, "I am asking all old comrades if they would like to rejoin" the Regiment, and Cooper enthusiastically agreed to take up the Corps' offer "to get back into a fight".[3]

Tony Greville-Bell had fought with 2 SAS in Italy and north-west Europe during the War. Afterwards, he become O.C. 'A' Squadron, 21 SAS, then its Adjutant. One of those old campaigners whom he contacted in mid-1950 was his companion for several months behind-the-lines in Italy, Maj. Alastair McGregor, who had returned to the UK from Greece, late in 1949. He was asked to organise recruitment of other SAS old boys in southern England, and among those who decided to join him were Sergeant-Major Bob Bennett (who had been living in Wales since 1949), Jock Easton, and John Woodhouse (both august figures in the annals of the SAS). Another who tagged along was Dare Newell, who had fought alongside the partisans in Albania and Greece, and then as part of SOE's Force 136 in Malaya during 1945. It appears that they and a few dozen others gathered at Aldershot, ready for refresher training with the Airborne Forces at their Depot in the Maida Barracks. Greville-Bell met Bennett at Aldershot railway station and briefed him on what had been done so far. They met up with Maj. McGregor, who had mustered his recruits, including SAS stalwarts from the 'Z' Reserve. The new unit was dubbed "M Independent Squadron", probably designated 'M' after its field commander, McGregor - in line with wartime SAS/SBS practice for the naming of *ad hoc* forces - although it seems that Maj. Greville-Bell was to run the SAS's HQ in Korea himself.[4]

The volunteers from the SAS's 'Z' Reserve were "ex-regular officers and soldiers who had opted to remain on the reserve list [and could] .. be called into action in the event of a sudden need for reinforcements". Reportedly, they were "all enlisted for two years['] " service (which followed the War Office DTI's recommendations on SRGs) and, presumably, 'M' Independent Squadron (SAS) was to be raised under its Corps Warrant. It is not known whether this occurred before the Middle East Rangers were formed, but it has been established that some of the Korea-bound troopers "went to Sherborne-in-Elmet in Yorkshire, for a refresher parachuting course with the 12th. [sic.] Yorkshire Parachute Battalion" - Johnny Cooper's 'phantom' SAS unit.[5]

During summer 1950, Maj. Greville-Bell elaborated on the roles that the SAS might be called on to fulfil in Korea, following discussions with Lt.-Col. Franks and Maj. Hart. Greville-Bell suggested the deployment of SAS parties behind-the-lines, following coastal landings by folbots (a type of tough, customised canoe) in the manner of the SBS, which had recently been training the SAS in their use. They would then work their way inland and raid strategically important targets like air bases, supply depots, railways, road bridges and junctions, fuel stores, communications links, and command and control centres - in much the same way that the Middle East Rangers planned to operate. 'M' Squadron would undertake deep penetration reconnaissance as well, gathering information by patrolling on foot and, if possible, with armoured vehicles such as Land Rovers, once these had been shipped in. The SAS parties could be supported by air-supplying, depending on the availability of suitable Drop Zones in the Korean mountains - a technique that had been tried and tested in similar terrain in Greece. Hence, the SAS had the know-how, planning, organisation, materiel and manpower ready to go, if and when the word came to set off for Korea. The only real difficulty foreseen by Maj. Greville-Bell was not in the preparation of a speedy SAS commitment, but in the deployment phase, when white soldiers might be more easily spotted among an Oriental populace, thereby making protracted covert operations potentially much more difficult to conduct.[6] Still, the Regiment was raring to go and, by the end of the summer, it would have a well trained and motivated force ready, which, if the template for other SAS units was copied, would have numbered around 120 officers and men.

It's apparent that, right up until October 1950, the SAS and the War Office were quite convinced that 'M' Squadron would be despatched to Korea and, in fact, Maj. McGregor's force was ordered to prepare for departure at this time. The Major and his cohorts gathered at Farnborough airfield, made their final checks and preparations, and they were kitted out, ready to leave. Then, less than a week before their flight was scheduled for departure to Seoul, the rug was pulled out from under them. The North Korean Army had been halted by the U.N.'s combined forces at Pusan during August and, then, in September, they were pushed into retreat by MacArthur's audacious amphibious landings and counter-strike from Inchon.

As the American-led international forces advanced northwards back across the 38th. Parallel, taking Pyongyang by 17th. October, the Chinese Communist government decided to pre-empt any possible attack on China that would fulfil MacArthur's dream to 'rollback' Communism. The People's Liberation Army - battle-hardened from more than two decades of fighting - prepared for another "anti-imperialist" struggle and, on 8th. November 1950, the Chinese entered the Korean War. This development signalled the end of 'M' Independent Squadron's hopes of (at least officially) implementing the SAS's third active anti-Communist undertaking of the Cold War.

The exact reasons why the SAS's mission was dropped are disputed by historians. Some assert that it was MacArthur who made the "decision not to use them", and to deploy American Marines instead. But this does not fully explain the British authorities' decision to stop the SAS expedition at the last minute. It has been argued that the Attlee administration felt that, "with the entry of China into the Korean War, it was politically unacceptable for a British unit to operate behind-the-lines". James Ladd has added that such activities, "with their inherent risks of political involvement for those local people who might work with the [SAS] .. apparently deterred the British government from allowing" the Squadron to be deployed.[7] Whatever the truth of the matter, by the time that Chinese troops clashed with U.N. forces, early in November 1950, the SAS was obliged to depart the scene. Soon afterwards, some of McGregor's 'M' Squadron were reassigned to another anti-Communist campaign, this time in nearby Malaya, where they would carry out the SAS's other recognised post-war role, namely counter-insurgency.

Still, as Tony Kemp has noted, on 5th. November 1951, Maj. Pat Hart wrote that there had been some "operations in Korea by so-called SAS parties about which neither the War Office nor 21st. SAS had any knowledge". This escapade was deemed most undesirable. But, given the precedent and example set in Greece by senior SAS officers themselves, it was not entirely out of kilter and cannot have been that much of a surprise. Hart stated that this special force "had no SAS approval [and that, while] 'M' Indep[endent] Sq[uadro]n .. was withdrawn as a matter of policy .. an officer of only slight SAS experience, who had been turned down for [service with] the Sq[uadro]n, subsequently was permitted to operate as SAS". It is not known how this officer was qualified to lead SAS parties or how many men from the Regiment he led. Even more intriguing is the question of who "permitted" him to operate under the SAS banner. The implication is that it was somebody linked to the Regiment and, if this was the case, then the finger would point to the outgoing commander of 21 SAS, Brian Franks. Alternately, it's possibile that the episode involved Major Ellery 'Bill' Anderson, a "former SAS officer", who is known to have set up a small force for behind-the-lines sabotage missions by April 1951. This consisted of half-a-dozen Koreans who were given specialist training, including parachute insertion, with the knowledge of the 8th. Army HQ in Korea. After swiftly sustaining heavy casualties, however, its operations soon ceased.[8]

Irrespective of this mysterious episode, the SAS additionally was busy preparing another SAS unit for action in the Far East during 1950, and this was constituted under the SAS's Corps Warrant. It also included veterans of the Greek campaign, and it followed in the footsteps of the International Squadron by being organised for COIN against Communist rebels - this time in the jungles and rubber plantations of Malaya.

9

Malaya - hearts, minds & winged dagger

T he SAS Regiment's official historian, Philip Warner, rightly noted that "the Malayan campaign was of great importance to the Regiment, as it provided the experience on which the post-war SAS was built". But, it has been asserted time after time by numerous historians that the Malaya Emergency led to the re-creation of the SAS and that, without it, the Regiment would not have emerged from its post-war disbandment. As has been demonstrated in previous chapters, this is manifestly not the case, and to claim that the Malaya campaign was "the first of the savage wars of peace [in] which the SAS took part in" is incorrect. Nor is it right to aver that, when a decision was made during 1950 to set up a new COIN special force for use in Malaya, "it was through a series of accidents" that an SAS unit was assigned this role.[1]

The establishment of another SAS force occurred because circumstances conspired to allow it, but various factors played a part in it. In particular, there was an upsurge in Communist insurgent activity in Malaya that required a response from the authorities. There were also developments that occurred in London with regard to the evolution of the SAS Regiment as a whole that had a critical bearing. And changes of personnel holding key posts in the military hierarchy allowed a new policy to be implemented. The genesis of another SAS force for Malaya was far from accidental.

Another Communist insurgency

The Malayan insurgency began in the spring of 1948, at a time when the BMM(G) and SAS International Squadron were embroiled in their secret COIN programmes in Greece. Just like the Communist insurgency there, the origins of the revolutionary war in Malaya are the subject of debate among historians, albeit less heated than that which rages about Greece. But, it's generally accepted by scholars that the Malayan Communist Party [MCP] was fomenting trouble in Malaya from the autumn of 1947 and, as was the case in Greece, individual Communist organs began to undertake terrorist and guerilla actions of their own volition. These gathered momentum in the spring of 1948 and constituted an insurgency campaign. Like his Greek counterpart, Zachariades, the MCP's chief, Chin Peng, appears to have harboured a flexible attitude to the means by which the Communists might attain political power. But, once the insurgency was underway, Peng adopted it as his own and, by May 1948, the MCP was directing the operations of around 3000 Communist irregular fighters (guerillas, terrorists and armed propagandists).

The politburo leader hoped to gain a relatively swift victory over the colonial government by disrupting the State's economy and dislocating its security forces, prior to creating "liberated zones" on the Greek and Chinese models, then toppling the British regime with the help of the masses. Later, he came to see the need for a more protracted struggle. But, by mid-1948, the former commander of the Malayan People's Anti-Japanese Army (who had fought alongside SOE's Force 136 during the War), was organising the Malayan People's Anti-British Army [MPABA], consisting mainly of ethnic Chinese Malayans (who made up just under half of the population, some 1.9 million), and a few ethnic Indians and Malays (the latter of whom were around half of the population, at 2.4 million).

The British security forces faced attack by irregular groups ranging in size from five-man terrorist cells to 200-man large MPABA units. Although the Malayan Security Service (the equivalent of MI5) had foreseen as early as 1947 the possibility of a Communist revolt like those in other countries, it had not discerned an insurgent threat at the critical time that it emerged, nor did it give the authorities any clear, unequivocal warning of impending danger. Therefore, at first, they were caught off guard, although the Federal government soon introduced Emergency legislation and set about trying to stem the insurgent tide. Initially, it did so by having the police and army conduct large-scale sweeps and short-duration small unit patrolling in the jungle (which covered four-fifths of the Federation).

The focus of the Communist offensive was on the rubber estates and villages at the jungle fringe, especially in the less mountainous areas (whose peaks rise up to 7000 feet), notably in the Sultanates of Johore and Perak. (The other States of the Federation created in February 1948 were Pahang, Negri Sembilan, Selangor, Kedah, Perlis, Kelantan and Trenggannu, plus the two Straits Settlements of Malacca and Penang, and Singapore). The MCP sought to gain the cooperation - willing or otherwise - of 600,000 Chinese illegal squatters residing in the jungle and its fringes, as well as around 50,000 jungle-based aboriginal *orang asli* ('original people'). As the MPABA offensive intensified during June 1948, the British Commissioner-General for South-East Asia (responsible for security coordination), Malcolm MacDonald, authorised the expansion of the Federation of Malaya Police Force [MPF] and, two days after, on 26th. June, he requested reinforcements from Palestine (with which he was familiar). Over the next two months or so, about 400 PPF men arrived in Malaya under their commander, Col. Nicol Gray, who took over as the MPF's chief, despite considerable local opposition to the involvement of outsiders. The new Police Commissioner cooperated, and coordinated his actions with, the military authorities, particularly the GOC, Major-General (later Sir) Charles H. Boucher, and the CINC Far East Land Forces - a wartime champion of the SAS - General Sir Neil M. Ritchie.[2]

The Jungle Guerilla Force

Over and above the security forces' ongoing counter-guerilla operations, it seems that Boucher and Ritchie decided, around the end of June 1948, that "there was a definite requirement for highly trained teams able to operate deep into the jungle for prolonged periods". General Ritchie later implied that this was his idea, though other sources say that the scheme was "first suggested" by a local civil government official and former British special forces operative, Richard N. Broome. Indeed, he and three other local men with special forces experience in SOE's Force 136 and the Burma Chindits - the entrepreneur, John P. Hannah, and two civil officials, (later Sir) Robert G.K. Thompson (who had served with Calvert in Burma), and Col. John L.H. Davis (former commander of Force 136) - met the GOC, and produced a memorandum on the type of operations that they might be able to conduct. Gen. Boucher subsequently appointed them as commanders of four Jungle Guerilla Force [JGF] units. But it's notable that Sir Bob Thompson recounted in his autobiography that it was actually Maj.-Gen. Boucher who had "called on [them] .. to form a small force" for deep jungle operations, and the GOC and CINCFELF appear to have been the driving forces behind the project.[3] Both were conversant with the COIN campaign being waged simultaneously by British forces in Greece, and it is likely that the example of the Raiding Force Commandos played a part in their thinking about the use of special forces in Malaya.

Indeed, the Jungle Guerilla Force's designated roles mirrored those of the Greek Raiding Forces, which was not "to seek intelligence by penetrating the terrorist[s]", as David Rooney asserts. Rather, JGF units were "to locate and destroy insurgent elements .. in [the] jungle [and] .. to drive such elements into the open country where they can be dealt with by orthodox Army and police units". At the same time, they were to act as an exemplar for other army units to follow, by adapting their training and operational procedures to the prevailing conditions in the Federation of Malaya and the Straits Settlements.[4]

Maj.-Gen. Boucher reportedly named the new special force as "Ferret Force", declaring that they would "ferret the [Communists] .. out of their holes" in the jungle. This appellation was adopted by FARELF HQ by mid-July 1948, and, from 6th. July, the Ferret Groups were organising themselves and training, so as to be ready for action by mid-August.[5] They were to carry out patrols of up to two or three weeks' duration, which was considerably longer than those being done by other Army formations in Malaya. In order to afford patrols of over 10 days' length, they would be supplied by the RAF. This followed recent precedents set in the jungles of wartime Burma, as well as in Greece, where air support was given to the GRF Groups by the RHAF, under RAF supervision. Indeed, in September 1948, the Army hierarchy on the ground in the Far East ruminated over the lessons of the Greek conflict to date, including the air-supplying of small patrols.[6]

Initially, the Ferret Force would consist of four Groups, although, according to some accounts, this was subsequently raised in practice to six. Different sources state that there were 65-80 men in each Group (the latter is a similar number to the Greek Commando Companies), and each Group had eight ethnic Chinese Liaison Officers acting as interpreters and guides. In addition, there were 12 Iban tribesmen (or Dyaks) from Borneo, who were expert trackers and had been, until recently, head-hunters. The rest of a Ferret unit's complement was made up equally of security force personnel and local volunteers who possessed knowledge of the jungle in their locales. In the field, teams totalling 15 All Ranks operated against the MPABA (including up to four Iban trackers). They conducted intelligence-gathering foot patrols, operating during the day or night in groups ranging in size from 3 to 15 men (with nocturnal movement from area to area in lorries). They also laid ambushes of between 3 and 12 hours' duration on tracks, near villages, and at water sources and other spots likely to be frequented by insurgents.[7]

From the very start of the Ferrets' activities, the top brass dealing with the campaign in Asia recognised that lessons must be learned as the fighting went on, and that the formation of a Ferret element in each and every army unit in Malaya would be desirable in the medium term. But, the GOC and the CINCFELF were anxious too that the Ferrets ought not become "the private armies of the local [MPF] CID". Hence, by 21st. September, it was decided that, once Ferret-style training and operations had become more widespread across the Federation, the Ferret Groups would be disbanded. This decision was implemented by the end of the year and,[8] on 22nd. December 1948, the War Office noted that the Ferrets were "gradually disbanding". This process went on into January 1949 and, from then on, a select few remaining Ferret personnel were employed as roving training instructors by the Army. They passed on their expertise to infantry and other battalions across Malaya and, while attached to them, they were used to "train up to one co[mpan]y of each of their units in FERRET tactics".[9]

Another police special force

Despite the dissolution of the Jungle Guerilla Force, the authorities in Malaya retained their interest in unorthodox COIN forces, and the police and army cooperated at the start of 1949 in running another unusual unit (as the two main security force agencies had done in Palestine in the case of 'Fergusson Force'). A "Chinese Assault Team" [CAT] was used by the Federation Police at the suggestion of the Army. Col. John Davis, the commander of Number 1 Ferret Group, asked his friend John C. Litton, a civil government administrator in the State of Perak, to "take charge [of] .. the Chinese squad" that comprised ethnic Chinese policemen.

They operated undercover and "dressed as Communists" in a pseudo-guerilla role. Davis' proposal implies that the army had had such a scheme on the drawing-board for some time. Indeed, a CAT may have been in use already, and the head of the Malayan Security Service in 1948, John D. Dalley, for one, had "raised and led DALFORCE [in 1941. It comprised] a detachment of locally-recruited Chinese .. as an observer corps, patrolling the mangrove swamps" in Singapore and undertaking "irregular warfare" training.

Whatever the case, Litton was asked to form his own Team at the start of the new year, and he had it manned and ready to undertake special duties by 7th. January 1949. The CAT was to carry out covert intelligence-gathering and pseudo-guerilla patrols, lay ambushes and make arrests. Litton oversaw the Team's organisation and, from 17th. to 26th. January, it trained in readiness for operations. Although this did not give the force much time to develop its tactics (as was the case in Palestine), the pseudo-guerilla guise was a step forward in Malaya. It's not known whether any of the PPF personnel who had transferred there from the Middle East to Malaya had any input to this endeavour, but the authorities would have been both aware of Capt. Farran's exploits and determined not to repeat his mistakes. The presence of ethnic Chinese officers in the Federation of Malaya Police Force lent itself to the development of COIN patrolling techniques, and men with SOE experience like John Davis - who had served with some of the insurgents only a few years before - would have recognised the possibilities that pseudo-guerilla action offered.

Some of the CAT policemen wore Communist khaki uniforms and badges, and carried captured weapons, papers and other kit. They travelled to their target areas - like Fergusson Force - in lorries, deployed on foot, and then layed ambushes, or mixed with the local population in search of 'hot' information. Pretending to be MPABA personnel on active service, they tricked local residents into divulging the whereabouts of MPABA units, 'Min Yuen' underground contacts, and hidden caches of arms and supplies. They received food, shelter and other material support from the populace, and, most importantly, intelligence that could be acted on forthwith. Their subtle ruses and interrogations led to several arrests of insurgent suspects in the "Chuk Pa" operation of February 1949, and more followed during March. The CAT surreptitiously returned to base on 2nd. April, having chalked up some valuable successes against the MPABA,[10] which, at that time, was relatively inactive, regrouping and reorganising as it was for a renewed and more protracted onslaught from September 1949. Unfortunately, the public record does not reveal any further clues about the CAT's subsequent activities, if any. But Litton's unit may well have inspired the formation of pseudo-guerilla police forces in other Malay States, where "Q" squads worked along the same lines from 1949 (not 1952, as one recent study asserts), often in cooperation with the army, such as operations early in 1951 with the 1st Battalion of the Suffolk Regiment (which had come from Greece in May 1949).[11]

Another SAS force?

Furthermore, by the spring of 1949, the War and Colonial Offices and their political masters were involved in another special force initiative, apparently at the behest of the civil authorities in Malaya, headed by the High Commissioner, Sir Henry Gurney. He had served in the Palestine administration prior to his transfer in autumn 1948 to Kuala Lumpur and, early in 1949, he followed the lead of his military partners and studied the Balkan conflict, including the Greek Raiding Forces.[12] Gen. Ritchie later noted that the civil arm of the Malaya COIN machine sought the formation of "ad hoc units of the Commando type for operations", and it seems that London responded to this call by March 1949. At a meeting on 1st.

April about the Malaya I.S. situation, ministers were briefed about the latest developments. They agreed that it would be wise to consider any fresh measures that may help the counter-insurgents to win, including the possibility of raising "a special corps of Commando or guerilla type" soldiers. The Colonial Office prepared to contact the High Commissioner and the Commissioner-General in this regard, and the War Office DMO went along with the proposal (while concurrently dealing with plans for a Middle East SAS unit).

Gen. Ritchie did "not consider that the formation of more jungle squads on 'Commando' or 'Force 136' lines" necessary, however, spurning the idea of "Commando type troops" on the grounds that, when they operated in large groups, they gave away their position to the enemy. He also repeated the misconception commonly held in the upper echelons of the British military that "small three men patrols were unable to maintain themselves" for prolonged periods in a taxing jungle environment. Moreover, he believed that the ongoing Ferret training programme for the army in Malaya was sufficient to meet all its small unit requirements, and that progress was being made in this respect. Indeed, the fact that the MPABA was relatively inactive during this period must have reinforced his view that the security forces were getting on top of the I.S. situation. The Police Force's organisation of scores of Police Jungle Squads would have further reinforced this conviction. Lastly, Gen. Ritchie declared that he was opposed to the dangers of "elitism" and "private armies", which he thought might be engendered by the creation of more special forces.[13] All these factors contributed to his rejection of Whitehall's forward-looking offer of additional special forces manpower during the spring of 1949.

Field-Marshal Slim and the SAS

Following the MPABA's shake up of its organisation, training and planning, and the revision of its strategy by the summer of 1949, it returned reinvigorated to the fray. Boosted by the success of Mao in China that October, and aiming to avoid going the way of their comrades in Greece - who called off their campaign at this juncture - the Malayan Communists intensified their military efforts across Malaya. In view of both this upsurge in Communist insurgent activity, and of the prospect that the SAS might soon be placed on a firmer footing within the British Army by Whitehall, it seems that the top brass in the UK (and later in the Far East), came to see that another SAS COIN force could be of use in Malaya.

In addition, early in September 1949, Gen. Ritchie was replaced as CINCFELF by General Sir John Harding, thereby removing one hurdle to the formation of a new special force for Malaya. By the end of the year, it was also clear to the authorities in London that the GOC Malaya, Maj.-Gen. Boucher, would have to return to the UK to recuperate from illness, and he left Malaya on 8th. February 1950. Replacing Boucher - initially only temporarily - was Major-General Roy E. Urquhart, former commander of the 16th. Airborne Division (TA), of which 21 SAS had been a part. His attitude to the SAS is not obvious, but he may have been one of the Airborne officers mentioned in SAS correspondence who did not want it to acquire Corps status. Indeed, he had witnessed a special forces debacle with the Independent Companies in Norway in 1940. Moreover, he favoured traditional Imperial-policing practices such as large-scale offensives with massed ranks of soldiers, artillery fire-support and air-strikes. He also accepted the use of normal 1-to-4 day small unit jungle patrols in Malaya, though Calvert asserted that Urquhart was even ambivalent about these.

The new GOC certainly had to be cajoled into adopting more protracted small unit counter-guerilla ambush and patrol operations by the new Director of Operations, General Sir Harold Briggs (who was appointed at the same time as him). As a result, there was no perceptible shift in tactical policy across Malaya until the autumn of 1950.[14] Even so, the deteriorating security situation, combined with the changes in key positions of authority, meant that a fresh opportunity arose to propose new I.S. policies. The CIGS, Field-Marshal Sir William Slim, decided to take the initiative by floating the idea of SAS involvement in the conflict (following the example that the Regiment had set in Greece - with which Slim was familiar).

It's been suggested by some that Slim was opposed to the idea of special forces *per se*.[15] But during World War Two, he did back their use in the jungles of the Far East and, in 1946 (at the time of the War Office DTI's review), he advocated small behind-the-lines forces. Then, in March 1949, he urged the formation of more Greek GRF "Pursuit Groups".[16] Despite others' assertions that an SAS Malaya Unit was proposed either by Gen. Sir John Harding or Major (later Lieutenant-Colonel) Mike Calvert, and that they were inspired by the Ferret Force,[17] other factors played a part in its origination. Brig. Calvert recalled in the 1990s that, in fact, he "was ordered to go to see [the] CINCFARELF [sic.], Gen. Harding, at Singapore", about the possible formation of a new special force, "on the recommendations of the CIGS, Field-Marshal [later] Lord Slim".

Gen. Harding is said to have accepted Slim's directive that Maj. Calvert be granted all the assistance that he required to investigate the potential scope for an unorthodox COIN force for Malaya, albeit "with [some] reservations". But with Field-Marshal Slim's support for the project, as well as that of the War Office DMO, Harding had little option.[18]

The leader returns

Field-Marshal Slim was well aware both of the ongoing saga of the SAS's application for a Corps Warrant, and of Mike Calvert himself. Slim had fought in Burma at the same time as 'Mad Mike' during the War, and he recognised that the one-time Chindit leader and SAS C.O. was "perhaps the greatest expert on guerilla warfare then serving in the British Army". Rather than have him continue "mouldering in a staff job in Hong Kong" - where, due to his air-support experience, he was GSO(I) Air - Slim felt that there was "perhaps .. a study role in Malaya" for Calvert. As well as having 13 wartime medals for gallantry and distinguished service - so that Calvert was "something of a legend" in military circles - Slim knew from his days in Burma that the former jungle warrior had an "analytical turn of mind [that] seemed likely to produce results".[19] Finally, as the SAS's erstwhile Brigadier and current Vice-President of the SAS Regimental Association, Calvert was in touch with Lt.-Col. Franks (who remained in command of 21 SAS until the autumn of 1950). Being an SAS 'insider', it was likely that Calvert would be able to quickly organise and recruit a force with relative ease.

No record of the meeting between Maj. Calvert and Gen. Harding has come to light, but it appears to have taken place around mid-January 1950 (given that the Major studied Malayan security conditions for "just under seven months", prior to being given permission for SAS operations to commence early in August 1950). During their confabulation in Singapore, Gen. Harding remarked to Calvert, "Slim says [that] you know all about guerilla warfare [and so] .. I give you *carte blanche*" to look into future COIN requirements and to report your findings.[20] From the available evidence, it seems that the formation of a new SAS counter-insurgency force was on the cards from the outset, Brig. Calvert pointing out that Field-Marshal Slim "probably foresaw the necessity of such a force and got me to recommend it". Indeed, as early as mid-February 1950, the War Office's Colonel Field "mentioned [to Colonial Office officials] that the Army has started training a 'long-range penetration squad' on Chindit lines with one of General Wingate's officers [i.e. Calvert] in charge".[21] This implies that he quickly put together a core of manpower for the new special force (possibly including some of the ex-Chindits from Hong Kong who are known to have joined him in Malaya), and that some basic training was swiftly underway. But with the SAS's Corps Warrant yet to be finally approved, Calvert concentrated on his study task and, thereafter, he travelled the length and breadth of the Malay peninsula, scrutinising the operations of various British military units including the King's Own Yorkshire Light Infantry, the Scots Guards, the Gurkhas, the RAF, Royal Navy, and the locally recruited Malay Regiment.

By April 1950, the SAS's Corps Warrant was at last ready for Royal Ascent. In that month, Calvert "sent [a] manuscript report direct to Harding" on what he'd learned thus far. Calvert argued that a special force was vital in order to take the war to the insurgent army - now restyled as the Malayan Races Liberation Army [MRLA] - with the focus on jungle operations. He recommend-ed the raising of an SAS unit for this task, as it "had been the best organised, staffed and recruited special force in the War and had [a] great tradition". Indeed, David Rooney asserts that Calvert "saw the chance to re-create the SAS", while Adrian Weale goes further, arguing that "by insisting on associat-ing his new unit with the SAS, Calvert succeeded in establishing a [COIN] .. role for the regiment which would not necessarily have come about otherwise".

While Calvert's overall contribution to the post-war SAS has been severely underestimated by historians and soldiers alike, such statements over-state his role and influence at this point, as they ignore the SAS's previous activities and the fact that the SAS would soon have the power to raise new units in any event. Not long after Gen. Harding received Calvert's paper, he "recommended it to Slim" (while the SAS's Corps Warrant was signed by the Secretary of State for War, John Strachey, on 13th. May 1950). The authorisa-tion to proceed with preparations for an SAS Far East unit seems to have been given around this time and, on 17th. May, the FELF HQ informed the War Office that both Gen. Harding and Gen. Briggs had been apprised of Lt.-Col. Calvert's findings and concurred with his view that a special COIN force should be set up.[22] Over and above Calvert's recommendation for a special force, he found that "many of the [army] battalions in Malaya were commanded by [competent but intellectually] .. dead-beat colonels .. [who] had not learnt the lessons of Burma .. [such as the] air supply[ing of ground forces] .. jungle tactics, etc.".

Furthermore, he noted that one of the top advisors to the COIN military authorities, General Francis I.S. Tuker (Retired), had done his best to prevent any mention of the wartime Burma campaign, as he reportedly "loathed Wingate and was [therefore] anti-special forces". Gen. Tuker had considerable experience of India's North-West Frontier and, in August 1944, had been a member of a War Office's Mountain Warfare Committee that assessed the Army's future Mountain Warfare requirements in the light of recent experiences. The Committee urged that, after the War, Army Mountain Warfare units should be created, consisting of "paratroop, Commando-type" soldiers who could "seek .. out and destroy .. illegal organisations and bandits".[23]

Yet, according to Calvert, Tuker was unenthused about such novel ideas and, in Malaya, he played down innovations like the air-supplying of foot patrols and the air-lifting and deployment of troops by helicopter. (This had been pioneered by the Chindits in Burma, using American Sikorsky S-55 choppers, two of which Lt.-Col. Calvert later acquired from the Royal Navy for use by the SAS, when the RAF was unable to furnish it with any). In addition, there was a prevalent attitude among many army commanders in Malaya and also "the medical lot, [that] no man could service [properly] in the jungle for more than a week, which", as Calvert stated, "turned out to be utterly untrue". There was opposition to the idea of a special force too from some Gurkha officers, who, having proven their worth in jungle fighting many times, "thought that the formation of a special force was an insult to the Gurkhas".[24]

Notwithstanding this opposition to an SAS deployment in Malaya, the CINCFELF and Director of Operations gave Lt.-Col. Calvert their support. In May 1950, they backed his plans to form a force of four Companies (with sub-units of 15 men, like the Ferrets), plus a HQ. This would give a total of 142 All Ranks, and it could well be that Lt.-Col. Calvert was following Lt.-Col. Franks' template for a Squadron of 118 men, supported by a small HQ staff. On 19th. May 1950, just three days before the new SAS Corps was publicly announced, the War Office Director of Military Operations, Major-General H. Redman (who'd deployed the SAS in 1942), agreed "that there is [the] scope for a special force on the broad lines" laid down by Calvert. The CIGS specified a "limitation to [the] size" of the force, however, as he understood "the reluctance of battalion commanders [in the Far East] to lose their best men" to it. On 13th. June 1950, the Chiefs of Staff authorised the activation of another Special Air Service COIN unit, and Field-Marshal Slim suggested that it be manned by ex-Chindits andpersonnel from "other similar special operations units", including SOE Force 136. The War Office commended this and, according to Calvert, Pat Hart was "backing [Calvert] .. up" in London, using "General Rowell's report and my [i.e. Calvert's] letter to the CIGS in 1945" to silence the SAS's critics within the Service Department.[25]

The SAS in the Middle East and the Far East

By the end of June 1950, the War Office Adjutant-General's office - which was responsible for organising the administration of the new special force - was preparing to deal with "the .. regular element of the SAS Regiment .. when the unit is formed". Hence, the Far East force was to be established as a regular unit under the new SAS Corps Warrant. The Directorate added that, "personnel for [this formation] .. would probably be found from volunteers from other Corps", although which ones wasn't specified.[26] It's also likely that, at about this time, the SAS's Middle East unit, the Middle East Rangers (SAS Regiment), was raised under the Corps Warrant. This can be deduced from the fact that, when the SAS was sanctioned to proceed with its Far Eastern venture, Lt.-Col. Calvert "suggested the [nomenclature of the] South Pacific Rangers (SAS Regiment)". His use of this particular terminology is more than a mere coincidence.

For while Calvert asserted that he wanted to name the Asian unit "according to the area in which it was operating", and he "anticipat[ed] .. further trouble in the Far East after Malaya", this doesn't explain why he used such an unusual term - "Rangers" - for the SAS special force. "South Pacific Rangers" wouldn't reflect the role that it would be called upon to fulfil, so, on the face of it, it doesn't make any sense. However, the "Middle East Rangers" was a far more apt title for the Middle East unit that, in the main, would undertake wartime demolition operations (like wartime Rangers). Thus, it appears that Calvert proposed "South Pacific Rangers" in the light of the existing Middle East Rangers epithet, thereby adhering to the SAS HQ's official unit-naming policy. The Middle East Rangers designation was certainly in official use by the SAS HQ by May 1951,[27] and it's highly likely that the unit was raised under the SAS's Corps Warrant a year before this, in the middle of 1950.

If the Middle East SAS unit was indeed formed in the summer of 1950, it would've been sent to that Theatre, ready to face a Soviet incursion into Iraq. This could have given a further boost to the case for the SAS's Far Eastern unit, although the War Office was apparently unwilling to let the Regiment use Malaya to establish another Theatre special force similar to that for the Middle East. Instead, the Department only permitted the Far East force to be sustained for the duration of the COIN campaign in Malaya (echoing the temporary deployment of the SAS International Squadron to Greece), and the FELF unit was made the direct responsibility of the GOC and the CINCFELF. With a strictly local rather than a regional purview, the "South Pacific Rangers" title was dropped (and not because it "had too much of an American ring for the British military", as David Rooney contends).

Indeed, Brig. Calvert revealed that Maj.-Gen. Urquhart's chief of staff, Brigadier Cottrell-Hill (an ex-Indian Army officer), "recommended [that] we be called the Malayan Scouts (like the Tochi Scouts and other regiments in [the] N[orth] W[est] Frontier [of India]). So, we became the Malayan Scouts, SAS Regiment, from the beginning". Rooney's view that the adoption of the 'Scouts' title was a "great personal achievement for Calvert" is misplaced.[28] By mid-June 1950, this label was being used by the War Office, although Calvert observed that "it was NOT [given a blessing] by [the Service Department's] traditionalists!"[29]

The Calvert Plan

Tony Geraghty has noted that, some two months after delivering his findings to Gen. Harding, Lt.-Col. Calvert was directed by him to start preparing the Malayan Scouts for combat,[30] which would be some time in June 1950. But at this stage, Calvert was still busy studying the broader campaign in the field and, on 11th. July, he attended a Conference of Malayan army Commanding Officers. Others present included the GOC Malaya, Maj.-Gen. Urquhart, the GOC Singapore, Maj.-Gen. Dermot Dunlop, and numerous local Army formation commanders. The idea was for them to pool the most up-to-date thinking on military/security operations and COIN action in general. Lt.-Col. Calvert was called on to present to the gathering a paper outlining his ideas. He identified the need for carefully planned, intelligence-based small unit offensive patrolling, as well as the "necessity of establishing a base deep in the jungle [where the MRLA was active,] and patrolling outwards" for lengthy periods. He underlined "the value of small patrols wh[ich, he believed] .. ha[d] the greater chance of locating bandits" and ambushing them. Hence, he "recommended [the] use of very small patrols as the normal [method of] patrol" for the army, which should be reoriented towards 'modern' counter-guerilla patrolling.

Calvert's presentation caused "considerable disagreement" among the battalion and brigade commanders, some of whom were the colonels that Calvert despised for what he saw as their lack of imagination and innate conservatism. After a vigorous debate, however, a concensus was reached. The Conference accepted "that the use of 2-3 man [patrols as suggested by the CINC's special advisor] could be of considerable value" for operations of limited geographical and chronological scope. But the commanders added that strong reinforcements had to be available to back up the patrols at short notice, and not all of them accepted that the army should alter its tactical outlook wholesale and adopt pro-tracted small unit patrolling as the norm.[31] Thus, Calvert still had some way to go to convince all his colleagues that the SAS example should be followed, though the key decision-makers once again backed the use of the Scouts.

Following the commanding officers' conference, Lt.-Col. Calvert complet-ed his field investigations and wrote "a 42-page typed report which was sent to Harding and Slim". The CINCFELF allowed Calvert to present it in person to the War Office, where, apparently, his treatise was commended by officials. Although historians disagree about the number of points that Calvert made, he recalled that there were seven. Among them was a proposal (already being considered and, subsequently, adopted by the British COIN authorities), that there should be "one commander, one man, with one plan, and the power to carry it out". Calvert suggested this post should be filled by either Lord Casey (whom he knew from Hong Kong) or Lieutenant-General Gerald Templer (who was based in southern England, and who had worked with Calvert on unconventional warfare projects when they were seconded to the War Office's Military Intelligence (Research) sec-tion in 1940). In the event, Templer took up the role of COIN supremo in February 1952. But far from the Prime Minister's first choice, Templer was about the tenth candidate that Churchill considered.[32]

Points two to six of Calvert's report covered details about the organisation, composition and technique of jungle patrols, as well as his observations about the importance of winning popular support from the Chinese squatters and *orang asli* in the jungle and its fringes, thereby denying the MRLA the material resources and safe havens that it relied on. Further, Calvert praised the idea of population resettlement into "New Villages", but claims by some historians that this "origi-nated in Calvert's fertile brain" and that his report inspired the Federal resettle-ment programme and the whole "Briggs Plan" are groundless.[33] These projects were already in the pipeline and Calvert can only have reaffirmed their value. The need for population relocation was appreciated by the British COIN civil and military authorities as early as September 1948 (once more, in the light of the Greek and other I.S. campaigns). A major effort to this end was espoused by a Federal Squatter Committee in January 1949, and the administrations of the nine Malay States were urged to act on this by the High Commissioner. However, the federated nature of the Malaya government and the lack of centralised powers at Gurney's disposal meant that he and his advisors were frustrated for over a year by ill-coordinated and half-hearted attempts at squatter resettlement. There was no widespread, concerted action until Gen. Briggs addressed the issue after February 1950. He ensured that the measure was pushed through and, by 1st. June, he had organised and started to implement a Federal resettlement programme. It is to this that Calvert gave his support.[34]

Calvert's seventh point in his COIN report was the most telling: the requirement for "a special force which would .. live in the jungle and, like quinine, move into the blood stream of the bandits so that they would" be subsumed by better trained and armed counter-guerilla opponents.[35] These would be men of the Malayan Scouts (SAS Regiment).

The Malayan Scouts

By July 1950, Lt.-Col. Calvert had his Kota Tinggi training camp up and running near Johore Bahru, and he was then authorised to set up an SAS Regimental HQ at Ipoh, in Perak, which would start operational planning posthaste. However, Calvert was hindered by having to almost singlehandedly "form, train, operate, administer [and] recruit" the Malayan Scouts, the latter being his first priority. He needed to acquire volunteers who were prepared to undergo all the ravages of jungle warfare, but he had to adhere to the top brass' various "stipulations on how to form" the force. He was told that he could seek officers from wherever he liked, but that he "must recruit Other Ranks only from units in Singapore and Hong Kong", in order both to avoid charges of elitism, and the alienation of formation commanders in Malaya. Additionally, the procedure would minimise the time and cost that it would take to form the Malaya Scouts and deploy them.

Calvert subsequently reflected that, "I should perhaps have held out for an 'elite'. But this would have upset the battalion commanders". Hence, he "tried to do things through the proper channels". Calvert admitted that "Harding said I could come to him whenever I wanted [for assistance,] but I did NOT do it often enough and [I] never made a friend of him and fully take him into my confidence" - a mistake that Calvert regretted. However, Field-Marshal Slim's proposal to man the Scouts with former special forces personnel was not followed up and, possibly in an attempt to make a point and demonstrate his own capabilities, Calvert decided to press on without asking for help from the SAS HQ or other interested quarters.

Consequently, he recruited whichever officers and men he could, and Calvert acknowledged that some were "not very fit", others were "rather too old" and, while many were enthusiastic and willing, "few .. had any jungle experience at all". Despite their flaws, Calvert thought that his recruits could be moulded into an effective special force, which was a philosophy that he had acquired from General Wingate. Calvert also had some "Hong Kong Chinese .. who had fought in Burma" with him while in the Chindits. One of their officers, Major John Harrington, became the Scouts' second-in-command.[36]

During the summer of 1950, Calvert devised a Scouts training programme featuring "leaping for cover exercises", in which - in typical Calvert fashion - an element of realism was introduced by using live grenades! He and his Chindit comrades also taught recruits the basics about the jungle environment and survival techniques, weapons handling and kit maintenance, and various methods that they should adopt when conducting small unit patrols from strategic jungle bases. This included "how to stalk each other in jungle", and Calvert had the trainees tackle each other with "air guns. Protected by goggles .. they had to shoot each other" while an umpire kept score. This was meant to teach the art of movement and concealment, as well as to develop camaraderie.

Lt.-Col. Calvert also attempted to build team-spirit and to test whether a volunteer could cope with the strains of jungle living by having his men drill after a hard night's drinking - the unorthodox idea behind it purportedly being that, if a man could function effectively while suffering from a bad hangover, he could cope with just about any situation that the jungle and the enemy could throw at him!

Unfortunately, Calvert's eccentric methods didn't lend themselves to the nurturing of a good reputation for the Scouts among other army units in Malaya, and it led to major problems of indiscipline thereafter. Irrespective of this, senior officers who inspected Calvert's training camp gave him glowing testimonials. They were particularly impressed with his novel scheme to enhance soldiers' ability to use cover and, around the beginning of August 1950, the SAS demonstrated their methods for an Australian military delegation boasting several expert special forces advisors and led by the Australian Army's Quarter-Master General, Major-General W. Bridgeford. He spoke to the assembled Scouts about guerilla warfare and, specifically, about the Independent Companies that had operated as guerillas in wartime New Guinea. The CINCFELF, Gen. Harding, thanked Maj.-Gen. Bridgeford for his comments and then pointed out that Lt.-Col. Calvert was "the man who [had] started and trained them", which, Calvert stated, "put Bridgeford back a little!"

Before the Bridgeford Mission left the Malayan Scouts' training camp, Gen. Harding enquired about the procedures used and whether being shot with air pellets hurt? Brig. Calvert remembered how, "I told one SAS man to shoot me in the body .. [and] this he did twice .. Harding then asked [the soldier] to shoot him, which he proceeded to do .. Bridgeford then had to ask for this to be repeated on him". Following this display, "the SAS corporal who had done the shooting bragged afterwards that it was the first time [that] he had shot a colonel and two generals in one day!"[37]

Learning lessons

Lt.-Col. Calvert additionally provided regular tuition to the Scouts on "lessons learned with the Chindits in Burma [and from] .. the Special Night Squads led by Orde Wingate in Palestine" during the 1930s.[38] As part of his ongoing recruitment drive, Calvert drew on the informal links between SAS personnel once again and wrote on 10th. August 1950 to Maj. Roy Farran, offering him a position with the SAS COIN force. Farran accepted Calvert's offer, but it was vetoed by the powers-that-be in London. On 17th. August, the Malayan Scouts' commanding officer informed Farran that higher authorities had intervened - an unusual step with regard to Army recruitment - because there was the "most unfortunate official view .. that your presence .. however desirable from the military point of view .. would be [a] considerable source of embarrassment". This was expressly said to be because of the "large number of government and police [personnel in Malaya] including GURNEY and GREY [sic., who were] .. from PALESTINE" - a far from triumphal episode for the British government. However, it is far more likely that it was Farran's notoriety due to his controversial I.S. record that prevented his secondment to the Malayan arm of the SAS's counter-insurgency effort.[39]

Nevertheless, by the middle of August 1950, Lt.-Col. Calvert had about

100 men, which was enough to form 'A' Squadron of the Malayan Scouts (SAS), under Major Rex Beatty. They were organised into four Troops of 12-15 soldiers each. Having been authorised to undertake operations once they were ready, they reportedly went into action during August 1950. They attempted to deny the MRLA food sources and to harass and hinder its fighters. This activity was very limited in scope and met with little initial success, which is hardly surprising given the Scouts' relative lack of experience and training. Thereafter, Calvert and his officers concentrated on the latter at their new camp at Dusan Tua, in Selangor,[40] as well as raising more manpower for another three planned SAS Squadrons (each of Company size).

Expansion and consolidation

Brig. Calvert recalled that Gen. Harding suggested to him that he may find recruits for the SAS in Rhodesia, and it's known that, in September 1950, its government offered to supply volunteers.[41] This would take time to organise, however, as Calvert had to fly out to southern Africa to whittle down 1100 volunteers to a Squadron of 120 before the end of 1950.[42] In the meantime, the Korean 'M' Independent Squadron had been prevented from deploying there and found itself in limbo. Consequently - and contrary to Tony Kemp's assertion that the Malayan Scouts had "nothing to do with the SAS Territorial set-up" - in October 1950, Maj. Pat Hart "recommended that the 21st. Squadron" send a contingent to Malaya for COIN duties and, along with a core from 'M' Squadron, a fresh intake from the 'Z' Reserve plus some "reservists from other wartime special forces", became 'B' Squadron, Malayan Scouts.[43] Calvert contacted Maj. McGregor ('M') and asked him to assist in the organisation of the new Squadron, and the Major agreed - though he only arrived in Malaya early in the new year, because the War Office was "so tardy over posting our volunteers". He was accompanied by five officers and 20 or so ORs from 'M' Squadron, including Sgt. Merryweather, formerly of the SBS, and a group of SAS signallers (making up a contingent of similar strength to that initially sent out to join the ASC(G) in Greece some years before). Some French Foreign Legion deserters also joined the SAS in Malaya at the start of 1951, though there was "obstruction from .. the Parachute Regiment", which sought to dissuade any of its "personnel from volunteering".

Among the new recruits to the Malaya Scouts were Captain (later Major/Lieutenant-Colonel) John M. Woodhouse. Another giant in the history of the SAS, he became 'B' Squadron's intelligence officer (having fought alongside the Resistance during the War, prior to going on to Hong Kong and thence 'M' Squadron). Another old campaigner who went to Malaya was Maj. Dare Newell and, unsurprisingly, there was the ever-present figure of Sgt.-Maj. Bob Bennett, who is said to have been "a significant factor in the re-forming of the SAS in Malaya".[44]

Most intriguingly, Brig. Calvert subsequently asserted that the commanding officer of the 21 SAS contingent, Maj. Greville-Bell, "thought that he was taking over from me, so I had to get rid of him", though Greville-Bell pleaded to Calvert that he "had got hold of the wrong end of the stick" and that 'M' Squadron was "willing to be commanded by anyone with jungle experience". In fact, they clashed over the indiscipline of 'A' Squadron and the lack of facilities made available to 'B' Squadron. Adrian Weale asserts that the latter's commander "resigned in disgust", but a distraught Greville-Bell apparently took his legitimate complaints about his men's conditions direct to Gen. Harding. This was not considered 'the done thing' (even if he was right) and, as a result, he got "the biggest bollocking" of his life and was obliged to leave.

Therefore, it's clear that the link between the London SAS HQ and its overseas branches continued to flourish during the COIN campaign in Malaya, albeit marred by disputes between Calvert and some senior figures in the Territorial unit over how the SAS's Far Eastern off-shoot should be run. Lt.-Col. Calvert also recalled facing further difficulties with the anti-special forces "die-hards" at the War Office, as they pounced on both the internal wrangling and continued reports of SAS indiscipline to snipe at the Regiment from the sidelines.[45] Despite the efforts of the SAS's detractors to undermine it, the Scouts continued to expand in the Far East, and James Ladd dates the unit's formal establishment to October 1950. (It appears that the decision to officially establish the Scouts was probably taken at this point, though the actual establishment followed some months later).

Ladd adds that 'A' Squadron patrolled the jungles of Perak during October, and then in November around Ipoh, in an attempt "to ambush known guerilla routes". In that month, 'B' Squadron was organised as well and, by December 1950, 'B' and the newly drafted Rhodesian contingent of 'C' Squadron underwent jungle training. 'A' Squadron concurrently carried out "patrols to deny food to terrorists", with the assistance of government Chinese Liaison Officers, the police CID and specialist trackers (including Surrendered Enemy Personnel - SEPs).[46] The Scouts' fourth Squadron ('D'), was created in the new year, following initial training at the Airborne Forces Depot in the UK. "The second half of

1951 saw a steady increase in the efficiency and effectiveness of the Malayan Scouts", and most historians concur that they were actually established as a regular regiment under the SAS Corps Warrant in January 1951.

Along with the Middle East Rangers, the establishment of the Malayan Scouts (retitled as the "Malayan Scouts (22 SAS)" in 1952),[47] marked the return of an SAS regular regiment after a gap of only six years - a major achievement in view of what had happened to most of Britain's other wartime special forces.

A detailed description of the SAS's subsequent activities in Malaya and elsewhere lies outside the scope of this book.[48] But by 1951, the SAS 'family' had grown on several fronts and set down roots that its opponents would find more difficult to dislodge. Hence, the Regiment's continued survival was far more assured and, despite persistent hostility to it within some parts of the Army and the War Office (not to mention the unhelpful R&R antics of some of the Scouts during 1950/51), the SAS had laid the foundations upon which it could grow from strength to strength.

The SAS family

During 1951, the SAS's critics focused on the behaviour of some of the Malayan Scouts - notably their drinking, casual dress and occasional brawling (although most of their misdemeanours have been exaggerated) - to try to have it disbanded. But over the course of the year, the Scouts were knocked into shape, Lt.-Col. Calvert having to leave Malaya for the UK in August 1951, due to serious illness. The command of the Scouts was handed over to Lt.-Col. John 'Tod' Sloane (Argyll & Sutherland Highlanders), who expelled troublemakers, improved the unit's disciplinary record and made a six-week SAS training course compulsory for all members of the outfit. By the end of the year, the prospects of the Special Air Service as a whole looked rosier than at any time since 1945, and Calvert - one of the two 'founding fathers' of the post-war SAS - saw the force grow and prosper. By December 1951, the Scouts numbered 426 All Ranks, and the FELF HQ sponsored its redesignation as 22 SAS Regiment (which was approved in 1952).[1]

Above and beyond the 400-plus SAS men in the Far East Theatre during 1951, there were 200 or so personnel attached to 21 SAS and the London HQ. In addition, on 23rd. May 1951, Maj. Hart wrote about the "Middle East Rangers (SAS Regiment)" and, assuming that the unit was raised on the basis of previous planning (and fresh missions for it were floated by the following spring), its complement would have been anything between 200 and 400 officers and men. Hence, by 1952, the SAS Regiment had up to 1000 soldiers on its books, with an additional pool of emergency manpower in the 'Z' Reserve of a similar order. This considerable figure indicates the SAS's ability both to fight its own corner in the bureaucratic minefield of Whitehall, and to demonstrate its worth to the powers-that-be in both peace and war.

Further, it appears that in mid-1951 the London HQ contemplated even greater expansion to extend the SAS family in pastures old and new. In May 1951, Maj. Hart informed Colonel Newman, the C.O. of 21 SAS, that "the policy within the SAS Regiment is that all special units formed under the SAS umbrella will have their own name, for example, Malayan Scouts (SAS Regiment), Middle East Rangers (SAS Regiment) etc.".[2] This "etc." bodes the question of what other unit(s) may have been on the drawing board or even already in existence at that stage, and the matter of new units was certainly under serious consideration for the issue to have been raised with the new commander. In this regard, it's interesting to note that, on 2nd. July 1951, Maj. Hart asked 21 SAS's Adjutant (who was tasked with planning the organisation of any new SAS unit), whether he wanted 'B' Squadron of the Malayan Scouts to be reassigned for COIN duties in French Indo-China. The French SAS (with whom 21 SAS had tried - unsuccessfully, as it transpired - to arrange joint training exercises in raiding operations during the previous spring), were entangled in a bitter civil war with the Communist insurgent *Vietminh*.[3] Such a mission would have appealed to 'B' Squadron globetrotters like Bob Bennett and Alastair McGregor, as well as supporters of the SAS cause in London. However, nothing more has come to light about this intriguing initiative, although it is known that 'B' Squadron remained in Malaya rather than going to Vietnam.

Even so, some "SAS parties" appear to have fought other Asian Communists during 1951 in Korea. In November of that year, Maj. Hart wrote a report about this 'unofficial' SAS commitment, and he called for better coordination of SAS activities across the globe, as well as a clearer top-level definition of the Regiment's future role and areas of likely deployment. He pointed to the urgent need for "a proper common [training] standard [to be adopted] among SAS units", as well as the standardisation of each establishment's organisation. Finally, and most significantly, he expressed 21's desire to be given permission to "propose and/or advise on the use of SAS units as and when situations arise in various parts of the world, both in peace and war". In September 1952, in response to an enquiry from Brigadier Fitzroy MacLean MP (an SAS confrere from north Africa in 1942), the Ministry of Defence elaborated on the policy covering the SAS and its possible future deployments. MacLean was informed that the SAS unit currently serving in Malaya "could be used elsewhere in emergency", but "in general, for operations of this nature .. suitable personnel will come from civil life". Indeed, the Ministry continued, in illuminating fashion, that "it is for this reason that the War Office maintain a Territorial Unit (The Artists' Rifles) of enthusiasts for SAS work", indicating that 21 and the 'Z' Reserve would be utilised as and when other "emergencies" arose (as one was soon to do in Kenya). The Brigadier was informed that if there was another major war and partisan-support activities were required, then the SAS would provide the backbone to local Resistance groups. For this purpose, the Ministry explained, "we maintain a lot of regular and reserve officers who are suitable for operations of this nature", available at short notice.[4]

There appeared to be plenty of scope for the SAS to carry out both I.S. and conventional warfare missions during the period in question. Over and above the Greek Civil War, the Malaya Emergency and the Korean War, there were many conflicts in far flung places where the British had strategic, economic, political or socio-cultural interests. In the Middle East Theatre, there was still tension and border skirmishing after the First Arab-Israeli War over Palestine in 1948-49 (which had involved British military forces). There was fighting in the former British territory of Kashmir, especially between 1947 and 1949 (as well as in India after the partition). And bloody civil conflicts emerged in the late 1940s in three other areas that had been ruled or administered by the British in the aftermath of the War, namely the Dutch East Indies, southern Indo-China and Burma (where renegade SOE elements were actively involved in fighting against the native government during 1949, while a British Military Mission offered the regime I.S. advice in 1950-51). Further, there was the concurrent Chinese invasion and subjugation of Tibet, following China's own civil war (which embroiled the British in the famous Yangtse incident). And another Communist insurgency flaring up in the neighbourhood was one prosecuted by the *Hukhbalahap* movement in the Phillipines from 1950 onwards. American military advisors were sent to assist the Magsaysay regime there, and they were in regular contact with British counter-insurgents in Malaya.

The British also had a military advisory group in Siam (Thailand) at this time and, during 1951, British sovereign territory was under direct attack from irregulars in the Suez Canal Zone. British citizens and interests were endangered too in numerous other states in 1951, notably by coups in Panama and Syria, while there was a civil war raging in Colombia from 1946 onwards. Other potential flashpoints included Madagascar, where the French had bloodily put down a rebellion between 1946 and 1948, and after the Second World War, several countries were rocked by coups, such as Venezuala (which bordered British Guiana and had a long-running border dispute with it), as well as Haiti, Bolivia, Nicaragua, El Salvador, Paraguay and Czechoslovakia. Rebels were also being backed by the SIS in Albania, the Baltic states and the Crimea.[5]

Patently, in 1951 the SAS envisaged various I.S./COIN and wartime activities in the foreseeable future and, while it took another few years for the SAS to become more broadly accepted by the British Army hierarchy, and to organise itself more effectively for its designated tasks, it was well on the way to achieving its long term goals by 1952. It should be emphasised that this was not solely down to the Regiment's participation in the Malaya Emergency, critical though this was for consolidating the Regiment's position and ensuring that it flourished thereafter. Rather, there were a whole series of crucial SAS exploits and ventures in the UK, Greece, Palestine, Libya, Iraq and Korea - over and above the accepted seminal commitment to Malaya - that contributed to the rebirth and growth of the SAS.

Contrary to the popular myth that the Regiment was "forgotten" by the British Army until the demands of the Malaya Emergency made it necessary to resurrect the SAS from post-war oblivion,[6] a group of SAS die-hards kept the flame alive through numerous quasi-official and little known but extremely important endeavours. They illustrated to those in power just how useful the SAS Regiment could be in a post-war world racked by 'hot wars' and limited conflicts within the Cold War context. The constant behind-the-scenes activities of a few fortuitously well-placed and influential SAS stalwarts in Britain, the Middle East and the Far East allowed the pro-special forces lobby in the War Office and the back channels of Whitehall to gain ascendancy over those who despised the concept of elite or special forces, and who feared that they would lead to the growth of "private armies".

The historian Richard Aldrich has written that, "after 1947, two distinct patterns of British special operations appear to have emerged, one under the general direction of the SIS, and the other under the auspices of colonial and military authorities in dependent territories".[7] To this must be added a third, highly significant pattern of development engineered by the SAS. By demonstrating its flexibility, willingness to adapt and its effectiveness, while simultaneously retaining almost complete secrecy about its missions (which has lasted for over half a century), the SAS saved itself from extinction. This was a major feat in the context of post-war demobilisation and financial retrenchment, and one repeated by very few of Britain's other wartime special forces. The greatest credit for this achievement must go to the small band of SAS visionaries and their supporters about whom very little has been known until recently. That band of SAS saviours was led by Brig. Mike Calvert and Lt.-Col. Brian Franks. As David Stirling acknowledged, without them it is unlikely that the SAS would exist today, making them and their supporters the true fathers of the modern SAS.

Appendix

Deception in Malaya

Since the publication of my *Postwar Counterinsurgency* book, further details on deception techniques that involved the SAS have come to light. As I noted previously, in June 1950, Slim visited Malaya and supported the Malaya Scouts' recruitment of wartime special forces personnel. Prior to that, on 2 June, the Chiefs of Staff considered the question of deception operations - 'VISTRE' techniques - including "sonic devices simulating .. small operations behind enemy lines" - as well as the employment of an adept at "black propaganda" who had served during the War with Col. Dudley Clarke (a key player in the founding of the SAS in 1941, as elaborated in my *SAS: Zero Hour*). Further, the Chiefs considered the deployment of an officer and four ORs from 421 Independent Field Troop (RE), which was based in Hong Kong (where Mike Calvert was serving prior to Malaya) and had a host of tricks up its sleeve. These included the spreading of misinformation; the use of dummy parachutists, troop movements and stores; and battle simulations and "patrol noises".

On 21 June, the FELF HQ asked the Ministry of Defence to provide Special Branch with an SOE advisor. Col. H.N.H. Wild, the "representative of MI5 and MI6 in the London Controlling Section [the post-war deception techniques organisation]" was sent to investigate the position. While the Far East GHQ felt "there is little scope for SOE on a big scale", its staff could be useful "in the tactical sense". On 26 June, the Chiefs of Staff considered drawing on MI5, MI6 and Army expertise and agreed on the provisional appointment of the former Chief Instructor of SOE Force 136, Lt.-Col. S.D. Calvert. Wild visited Kuala Lumpur on 8-10 July and, with Harding's backing, Lt.-Col. Calvert and Flight-Lieutenant Charles Cholmondeley (who had "wide experience of [wartime] deception work"), were sent to Malaya by December 1950 to coordinate their efforts with Security Intelligence Far East (MI6) and Special Branch re deception in both Malaya and Thailand. In August, the Director of Operations, Gen. Briggs, and High Commissioner, Sir Henry Gurney, had asserted that they saw no merit in wider SOE assistance, and the Chiefs of Staff agreed. But by 1951, Calvert surveyed the work over the last year of 'R' Force (one officer and 13 ORs) and noted that its deception programme had expanded thereafter, involving the SAS by 1952 in schemes such as the doctoring of ammunition and booby-trapping.[1] Once more the SAS and SOE/SIS were cooperating in COIN operations, to the benefit of both agencies and to the wider ongoing campaign.

Footnotes

Introduction- Dare all to win all

1. For example, Gen. Sir P. de la Billiere *Storm Command* (London: Harper Collins, 1992); A. McNab *Bravo Two Zero* (London: Corgi, 1993); C. Ryan *The One That Got Away* (London: Century, 1995).

2. For example, J. Adams/R. Morgan/A. Bambridge *Ambush- the secret war between the SAS and the IRA* (London: Pan, 1988); M.P. Kennedy *Soldier 'I' SAS* (London: Bloomsbury, 1989); P. McAleese *No mean soldier* (London: Orion, 1993); H. McCallion *Killing Zone* (London: Bloomsbury, 1995); M. Curtis *Close Quarter Battle* (London: Bantam, 1997); G. Stewart *Silent Heroes* (London: M. O'Mara, 1997).

3. For instance, P. Dickens *SAS: the jungle frontier* (London: Fontana, 1983); R. Fiennes *Where soldiers fear to tread* (London: NEL, 1975); M. Urban *Big boys' rules* (London: Faber & Faber, 1992); B. Davies *Assault on LH-101* (London: Bloomsbury, 1994). Also on the SAS in Aden, Col. Sir *David Stirling*, cited in A. Hoe David Stirling (London: Warner, 1994) p.474. The SAS has been involved in over 200 military commitments since the Falklands in 1982 - personal information, MoD, 2004.

4. P. Warner *The SAS* (London: Warner, 1971). Ex-SAS men were widely quoted in newspaper coverage of the Beslan siege, 2004.

5. Maj.-Gen. J. Strawson *A history of the SAS Regiment* (London: Grafton, 1986); T. Geraghty *Who Dares Wins* (London: Fontana, 1981/92).

6. Strawson p.13.

7. J.D. Ladd *SAS operations* (London: R. Hale, 1986/99); J. Ramsay *SAS- the soldiers' story* (London: MacMillan, 1996); A. Kemp *The SAS at war, 1941-45* (London: Signet, 1993); *SAS- the savage wars of peace, 1947 to the present* (London: John Murray, 1994).

8. Such as S. Crawford *The SAS Encyclopedia* (London: Simon & Schuster, 1996); B. Davies *The SAS- an illustrated history* (London: Virgin, 1996).

9. Kemp *Savage* p.xi.

10. From the SAS Regimental Collect (prayer).

11. Warner pp.xiv,190.

12. See, Strawson p.219; C. Philip/A. Taylor *Inside the SAS* (London: Bloomsbury, 1992) p.217; Hoe p.263; K. Connor *Ghost force* (London: Weidenfeld & Nicolson, 1998) pp.4-24; A. Weale *The real SAS* (London: Sidgwick & Jackson, 1998) pp.51-81; and also on the supposed date of the Regiments' disbandment, Ladd (1986) *Operations* p.103; P. Darman *A to Z of the SAS* (London: Brown Packaging, 1993) pp.32,168; Davies *Illustrated* p.214; R. Hunter *True stories of the SAS* (London: Virgin, 1995) pp.xi,83; W. Seymour *British special forces* (London: Sidgwick & Jackson, 1985) p.267; A. Hoe/E. Morris *Re-enter the SAS* (London: Leo Cooper, 1994) p.210; D. Rooney *Mad Mike* (London: Pen & Sword, 1997) pp.1,120; A. Weale *Secret warfare* (London: Hodder & Stoughton, 1997) p.137; J.G. Shortt *The SAS* (London: Osprey, 1981) p.16; J.D. Leary 'Searching for a role: the SAS in the Malayan Emergency' *Journal of the Society for Army Historical Research* 73[296] (Winter 1995) p.251; R.J. Aldrich 'Secret intelligence for a post-war world: reshaping the British intelligence community, 1944-51' in (ed.) *British intelligence, strategy, and the Cold War, 1945-51* (London: Routledge, 1992) p.26; P. Harclerode *Fighting Dirty* (London: Cassell, 2001) pp.ix,2.

13. Kemp *War* p.228; *Savage* p.3. Geraghty (1981) pp.18,22; D. Buxton *Sword of Honour* (Solihull: Elmdon, 1985) pp.15,38; and re 1946, L. Whittaker *Some talk of private armies* (Harpenden, Herts.: Albanium, 1984) pp.33,87,88.

14. For instance, Ramsay p.8; J. Adams *Secret Armies* (London: Pan, 1989) p.31; Adams *et al* p.47; Stewart pp.56-57; T. White *The making of the SAS and the world's elite forces* (London: Brown Packaging, 1992) p.136.

15. Also see Adams p.33.

16. Warner p.218; Kemp *Savage* p.18.

17. Warner p.218.

18. T.L. Jones *The development of British COIN policies and doctrine, 1945-52* (PhD, Univ. of London, 1992). Kemp *War* p.229.

19. This British COIN effort has been ignored by historians, but see T.L. Jones 'The British Army, and counter-guerilla warfare in transition, 1944-52' *Small Wars & Insurgencies* 7/3 (Winter 1996) p.274; 'The British Army and counter-guerilla warfare in Greece, 1945-49' *Small Wars & Insurgencies* 8/1 (Spring 1997); *Postwar Counterinsurgency and the SAS, 1945-52 — A Special Type of Warfare* (London: Frank Cass, 2001).

20. On the re-formation of the regular (as opposed to Territorial) SAS - initially 22 SAS (as opposed to 21 SAS) - for instance, Hoe/Morris Introduction.

21. Cited in Kemp *Savage* p.xi.

22. *Ibid* p.v.

Chapter 1- Towards a new beginning
1. Ladd *Operations* p.68.

2. Kemp *War* p.121; Philip/Taylor p.18.

3. Hoe p.265; Darman p.37; Kemp *War* p.122.

4. Warner p.136; Ladd *Operations* pp.75-76; Seymour p.252; M.R.D. Foot *SOE* (New York: University Publications of America, 1986) *passim*.

5. M. Bennett 'The German experience' in I.F.W. Beckett (ed.) *The roots of counter-insurgency* (London: Blandford Press Ltd., 1988) pp.66-80; Kemp *War* p.182.

6. Warner p.176; Darman p.37; Kemp *War* pp.137,194-96,202.

7. T.L. Jones *Small Wars* 7/3, p.268.

8. Regarding SBS actions in Greece, Warner p.111; Strawson p.174; Kemp *War* p.203; Maj. R. Farran *Winged Dagger* (London: Collins, 1948) pp.252-54; J.D. Ladd *SBS — the invisible raiders* (Newton Abbot, Dorset: David & Charles, 1989) p.125. Until mid-December 1944 the SBS were commanded by Lt.-Col. George (the Earl) Jellicoe, at which point Lt.-Col. Sutherland took over. Former SAS personnel informed me that Jellicoe knew "all about what went on in Greece", but he has not published an account. For more details on Athens see, for example, Brig. E.D. Smith *Victory of a sort* (London: R. Hale, 1986) *passim*.

9. On Farran, Warner p.159; Ladd *Operations* pp.67,99; Kemp *War* p.203; Darman p.58; Philip/Taylor p.29.

10. Re 1944, Hoe p.473; Kemp *Savage* p.18. Re 1945, Strawson p.213; Shortt p.15; Seymour p.262; Darman p.109. Rooney p.114.

11. Kemp *War* p.213; Warner pp.144,175; Philip/Taylor p.217; Darman p.32; and for more about his background, Brig. J.M. Calvert *Prisoners of hope* (London: Corgi, 1973); *Fighting Mad* (London: Airlife Publishing, 1996); Rooney pp.20-56; Weale *Real* p.71.

12. Ladd *Operations* p.103; Warner p.188; and especially J.E. Lewis *The handbook of the SAS and elite forces* (London: Magpie, 1997) p.13. On the letter to the War Office [WO], Lt.-Col. I.G. Collins, "Unofficial memo", 7 May 1945, Brig. R.W. McLeod Papers, 2/1, Liddell Hart Centre for Military Archives, London, [LHC].

13. Kemp *War* pp.199,224-25; *Savage* p.2; Darman p.37; Rooney pp.118-20.

14. Lt.-Col. Collins memo, "Note on future of SAS", / May 1945, Brig. R.W. McLeod Papers, 2/1, LHC; Brig. J.M. Calvert, interview at the Special Forces Club, London, 10 Apr. 1991.

15. Darman p.59.

16. A. Kemp *The secret hunters* (London: M. O'Mara, 1986); *War* p.229; *Savage* pp.3-5; Hoe p.416.

17. Brig. J.M. Calvert 'COIN policies', unpublished paper written for the author, 20 March 1991, Author's Collection; Kemp *War* pp.138,226; *Savage* p.1; Darman p.175; especially on Winston Churchill, Ladd *Operations* p.41.

18. Ladd *Operations* p.103; Philip/Taylor p.29.

19. Calvert, paper.

20. For instance, Kemp *War* p.230; *Savage* p.5; Weale *Secret* p.137, who asserts that "the established view was that the SAS had made a valuable contribution and that similar units might do so again"; Rooney p.122.

21. Calvert paper. British and Allied special forces included dozens of different units and organisations, ranging from the Small Scale Raiding Force, Royal Marine Boom Patrol Detachment, Small Operations Group and Combined Operations Assault Pilotage Parties to Kalpaks, 'Y' Force, 'D' Force and other little known bodies. See, for example, J.D. Ladd *Commandos and Rangers of World War Two* (Newton Abbot, Devon: David & Charles, 1989) pp.329-37,352-93.

22. 2 i/c, (Maj. Hart), to C.O. 21 SAS, (Lt.-Col. Franks), 10 May 1949, WO32/13867.

23. Calvert, paper; interview.

24. Calvert, paper.

25. Calvert, paper. On Alex and Monty, Ladd *Operations* p.111; Rooney p.23; B. Pitt *Special Boat Squadron* (London: Corgi, 1985) p.63. Monty's views in, Seymour p.164; E. Morris *Guerillas in uniform* (London: Hutchison, 1989) pp.133,135,138; and also on others, p.6; Warner p.66; Strawson pp.68,76.

26. Calvert, paper.

27. Calvert, paper; WO SCAPP memo, n.d. (probably Aug. 1945), WO32/11538. On the SAS subsequently, Lt.-Col. K.S. Beale, letter, 23 July 1973, WO32/10921.

28. On the WO's October 1945 enquiry, for instance, Kemp *War* pp.246-47.

29. Calvert, paper.

30. Kemp *War* p.194; *Savage* p.1. US Team in, Maj. W.B. Kennedy-Shaw, HQ SAS Troops, to Brig. J.M. Calvert, 1 August 1945, Box 6, Calvert Papers, IWM.

31. On the Army's heritage and its views, Gen. Sir J. Thompson *The Imperial War Museum book of warfare behind the lines* (London: Sidgwick & Jackson, 1998) pp.7-8,417; J. Parker *SBS* (London: Headline, 1997) p.106; Weale *Secret* pp.138-42; T.L. Jones *Postwar counterinsurgency, passim*; and on the WO, Kemp *War* pp.xi,2,7,227,247-51; Ladd *Commandos* p.169; Seymour pp.64,68; Morris *Guerillas* p.53, and re Brooke/Dill pp.59,141; for views on Wingate, pp.193-94; O. Heilbrunn *Warfare in the enemy's rear* (London: George, Allen & Unwin, 1963) p.44. Also see, for instance, Sir W. Slim's *Defeat into victory* (London: Corgi, 1971) pp.548-49.

32. Warner pp.176-77,189-90; Hoe p.263; Adams *et al* p.46.

33. On Gen. Dempsey's connections with the SAS, Warner p.129; Strawson pp.153-55; Ladd *Operations* p.67; Kemp *War* pp.87-88,96; T.L. Jones *Origins*. For Dempsey's views about the Colonel Commandancy, Maj. L.E.O.T. Hart, to Lt.-Col. B.M.F. Franks, 10 May 1949, WO32/13867. Philip Warner, p.78, has noted that the SAS's first Colonel Commandant was Commando Gen. Robert E. Laycock, in 1960. But *Who Was Who* (London: A. &. C. Black, 1960) says Gen. Dempsey held this post, 1951-60. In fact, Dempsey took up the post in 1949.

34. Maj. Hart, to Lt.-Col. Franks, 10 May 1949, WO32/13867. Maj.-Gen. M.C. Dempsey, to Brig. J.M. Calvert, 23 July 1945, Box 6, Calvert Papers, IWM.

35. DAW, "Post-war Airborne Forces", to SCAPP, 13 Aug. 1945, WO32/11538.

36. On disbandment, WO Minute, 4 Oct., and WO Adjutant General (2B), to HQ Eastern Command, O i/c [Officer-in-charge] AAC Records, 12 Nov. 1945, WO32/10921. Also see Kemp *War* pp.227-28.

37. Lt.-Col. K.S. Beale, HQ, Director SAS & SAS Group, letter, 23 July 1973, WO32/10921; Kemp *War* pp.246-47; Strawson p.393; Weale *Secret* pp.137-42.

It's interesting to note that Lt.-Col. Wigham was appointed shortly after to co-write a revised WO doctrine on Internal Security policy and, when drafts of this appeared by 1947, they were traditionalist in tone, omitting the idea of special forces or techniques such as air-supplying. Hence, it's unlikely that Wigham was very favourably disposed to an SAS COIN role as proffered by Brig. Calvert. Refer to T.L. Jones *Small Wars* 7/3 pp.272-73.

38. Kemp *War* pp.246-47; Strawson p.393; P. Wilkinson/J.B. Astley *Gubbins and SOE* (London: Leo Cooper, 1993) pp.218-19,236.

39. Regarding Stirling and Mayne, see R. Bradford/M. Dillon *Rogue warrior of the SAS* (London: J. Murray, 1987) p.212. On the others, Calvert, interview; and especially re air support/helicopters, Rooney p.121.

40. Strawson pp.133,219-20; Kemp *War* p.207; Hunter p.52.

41. Warner pp.134,140,142; Hoe p.260; Strawson pp.63-64,147,200; Kemp *War* p.191; Darman p.59. For other leading thinkers in the SAS see, T.L. Jones *Origins, passim*.

42. Calvert, interview; Rooney pp.123-25. On Paddy Mayne, Warner p.188; and on Brian Franks, p.191; David Stirling cited in Hoe pp.260,357,473; Kemp *War* p.232; *Savage* p.ix; Darman p.59. Minutes of 1st. Meeting of the SAS Regimental Association, 12 Oct. 1945, WO218/118. Cf. Warner, (November).

Chapter 2- A life-line: Greece
1. Warner p.191; Seymour p.252; Kemp *War* pp.93,232; *Savage* p.ix.

2. Farran pp.252-58; Weale *Secret* p.136; Ladd *Operations* pp.58-59; *Commandos* pp.365-66; Hunter *SAS* p.45; Warner pp.9,80,120,137; Strawson pp.167-68,174; Kemp *War* p.78. Also, X. Fielding *Hide and seek* (London: Secker & Warburg, 1954) pp.253-54; who went on, with the SIS, to Indo-China/Germany, N. West *Secret war* (London: J. Curtis, 1992) p.170. On GSS, Whittaker p.87.

3. On Hart, Kemp *War* p.231; Warner p.192. Stirling, quoted in Hoe, p.473. On Mayne, for example, Philip/Taylor p.126.

4. Warner p.188; Kemp *War* p.228. Further to Mayne and the SAS Regimental Association, SAS Regimental Association Minutes, 12 Oct. 1945, WO218/118.

5. Kemp *War* pp.74,86,93,217,228; Darman pp.11-12,144.

6. For more on Greece see, for example, G.M. Alexander *Prelude to the Truman Doctrine* (Oxford: Clarendon Press, 1982) pp.6-12; D.H. Close *The origins of the Greek Civil War* (Harlow, Essex: Longman, 1996) *passim*.

7. Churchill note, 3 April 1945, R6104/FO371/48264.

8. For instance, Close pp.155,177.

9. Personal information, 14 Nov. 1996.

10. Lt.-Col. B. Franks, to WO AG 2(B), 6 Nov.; WO AG 2(B) to HQ SAS Troops, n.d., (Nov. 1945); to HQ Eastern Command/Officer-in-charge [O-i-c] AAC Records, 12 Nov. 1945, WO32/10921. Also on SAS HQs, Eastern Cmd. Location Statement & Orbat, Amendment #32, 3 Sept. 1945, WO166/16366. And on Spanish members of the SAS also see Kemp *War* p.232; personal information, 1996.

11. 2 Para. Roll of Officers, in War Diary [WD], 31 Dec. 1945, WO166/17184.

12. Maj. H. Poat, C.O. 1 SAS, to Under-Sec. of State for War, WO AG 2 (B), 13 Nov. 1945, WO32/10921.

13. FORCE DLY 2(B) [AG], to Eastern Cmd. HQ, n.d., (14 Nov. 1945 according to WO Minute Sheet), WO32/10921. Maj. H.W. Poat, to Brig. J.M. Calvert, 21 Dec. 1945, Box 6, Calvert Papers, IWM.

14. Stirling's recollections in Hoe p.416.

15. Philip/Taylor p.29.

16. Warner p.81; Kemp *War* pp.138,199-200.

17. Kemp *War* p.40; Stirling in Hoe, *passim*.

18. ASC(G) WDs, July-Dec. 1945, Operational Instructions [OI], 19 Oct., 28 Dec., Directive, 12 Dec., Field Returns, 1-29 Dec. 1945, WO170/7558; WD, Jan. 1946, WO170/7654; Capt. (later Maj.) M. Ward *Greek assignments, 1943-48* (Athens: Lycabettus Press, 1992) pp.227,256-57. On MI9, M.R.D. Foot/J.M. Langley *MI9* (London: Futura, 1979) *passim*. Social conditions in, for instance, N. Gage *Eleni* (New York: Ballantine, 1983) *passim*; which was also made into a movie in 1986 (and is available on Columbia Tristar video). Re the WO study, G.W. Lambert, WO memo, 16 Jan. 1946, L/WS/1/1485, India Office Library and Records, British Museum, London, [IOLR].

19. Hoe pp.75,111; Philip/Taylor p.18; White p.130.

20. Kemp *War* pp.11,228; *Savage* p.3; interview, 16 May 1996; Anonymous (Philip Warner) 'Bob Bennett' [Obituary] *Daily Telegraph* 7 Feb. 1996; SAS Regimental Association *Newsletter* 33 (Apr. 1958); J. Thomas (Hyde Park Hotel historian), interview, 10 July 1996 - unfortunately no written records for the 1940s remain at the Hotel, as they were retained by the owners, (coincidentally) the Bennett family.

21. Kemp *War* p.229.

22. Kemp *War* p.229; *Savage* p.3; interview, 16 May 1996.

23. On the WO DMO and the G(Raiding Forces) HQ, (which was commanded by Col. J. 'Shan' Hackett), Kemp *War* p.73; interview, 16 May 1996; Maj. A. McGregor, interview, 19 May 1996; and on subsequent SAS action, Hoe p.364.

24. Kemp War pp.229-30; *Savage* pp.3-4; *Secret, passim*; W. Fowler *SAS- behind enemy lines* (London: Harper Collins, 1997) p.75.

25. Bob Bennett seems to have been listed first with the Royal Artillery, which had many personnel in Greece during 1945/46, assisting in the training of the GNA through British Liaison Units [BLU]. He was then likely listed under his parent regiment, the Grenadier Guards, in 1948. On the SAS War Crimes Teams, Kemp *War*

p.228; *Savage* p.3. On Bob Bennett, Obituary; Lt.-Col. D.G.C. Sutherland, letter, - May 1996; Kemp, interview, 16 May 1996; BMM(G) Postings of Officers, 1 Nov. 1945- 20 Jan. 1946, and Staff List, Jan. 1946, WO202/893.

26. Kemp *War* p.230; T.L. Jones *Small Wars* 7/3, pp.273-74.

27. Kemp *War* pp.39,229-32; *Savage* pp.3-5; J. Simpson *The quiet operator* (London: Leo Cooper, 1993) p.127.

28. Also see T.L. Jones *Small Wars* 8/1, pp.90-91.

29. ASC(G) WD Jan. 1946, OI, 5 Jan. 1946, WO170/7654.

30. ASC(G) WD, Feb. 1946, OI8, 7 Feb. 1946, WO170/7654. On the SAS, Regimental Association *Newsletter* 1, March 1946, Box 6, Calvert Papers, IWM; M.R.D. Foot *SOE* (London: Mandarin, 1990) p.28.

31. On possible GSS action, Col. the Hon. C.M. Woodhouse, letter, 25 July 1996; J. Mavrikis, interview, 16 May 1996. Regarding the SOE, "Report on SOE activities in Greece and the Isles of the Aegean Sea", 27 June 1945, Count J.A. Dobrski Papers, 28, LHC.

32. R.J. Aldrich in (ed.) p.26; 'Unquiet in death: the post-war survival of the SOE, 1945-51' in A. Gorst/L. Johnman/W.S. Lucas (eds.) *Contemporary British history, 1931-61* (London: Pinter, 1991) p.201. Certainly ex-SOE officers such as Brian Dillon were fighting against the DSE for the SIS in 1948.

33. WO DAAG Minute, to WO Air 2, 21 Feb., and Maj. G.S. Stockwell, Air 2, to DAAG, 28 Feb. 1946, WO32/10921. COS In, FO Permt. Sec., O. Sargent, memo, 20 Feb. 1946, R1992/FO371/58673.

34. WO Directorate of Organisation to O-i-c, AAC/ACC/GSC Records Office, 8 Feb., and Minute Sheet, 8 Feb. 1946, WO32/10921.

35. Maj. B.K. Smith, AAC/ACC/GSC Record Office, to WO Under-Sec. of State, AG 2(B), "Disbandment of SAS Regiment", 13 Feb. 1946, WO32/10921. On SAS

wartime moves and locations, Eastern Cmd. Location Statement & Orbat, Amendment #5, 29 Nov. 1945, WO166/16366; Ladd *Operations* p.69; Warner p.135; Kemp *War* pp.120,122. For a parallel with the SAS Greek unit, see chapter 8 on Korea, when an 'independent squadron' was prepared for use there in 1950. Its manpower included Bob Bennett and others who had served in a similar fashion in Greece, "22 SAS Regiment in Malaya", n.d. (drafts), Harry Miller Papers, 67/194/3, IWM.

36. Kemp *War* p.229; *Savage* p.3; interviews, 16,26 May 1996.

37. GRCC public statement in, GRCC Poster, 27 March 1946, R-/FO371/58884.

38. ASC(G) WDs, Jan.-May 1946, Admin. Instruction #1, 28 May 1946, WO170/7654; Ward pp.227,256-57; interview, 31 May 1996. Maj. Ward noted that the ASC(G) ceased functioning early in July 1946, and he handed over its documentation to the Embassy in Sept. 1946.

39. ASC(G) WDs, Mar.-Apr., Release Returns, 6-27 Apr. 1946, WO170/7654.

40. WO OT "Paramil. Establishments", Amendt. #1, 16 March 1946, WO33/2501.

41. WO Organisation Table [OT], "Paramil. Establishments", 5 Jan., and Amendment #1, 16 March 1946, WO33/2501; WO OT "SOE", Amendment #2, 5 May 1946, WO212/213; H. Caccia, Athens Embassy staff, to Foreign Office [FO], 27 June 1945, R11283/FO371/48273, (incidentally the same date as the SOE Greek report in the Dobrski Papers, LHC); Ward pp.179-80,209-10,223-24; J.H. Pederson *Focal point of conflict* (PhD, Univ. of Michigan, 1974) p.200.

42. BMM(G) Monthly Progress Report on the GNA [MPR], to 20 May 1949, WO202/952; MoD, to GHQ Middle East Forces [MEF], 16 July 1947, WO32/11436.

43. T.L. Jones *Small Wars* 7/3, pp.273-74.

44. FO view in note, R. Selby, 19 Sept. 1946, R13589/FO371/ 58708; Pederson pp.207-08. Re Bob Bennett, Obituary; Kemp *War* p.229; Savage p.3; interview,

16 May 1996; Gordon Stevens, interview, 9 June 1996; J. Mavrikis, interview, 16 May 1996. Also refer to chapter 5 on 'The International Squadron' for details about Bennett's activities in 1948-49. For more on the GSS, Lt.-Col. D. Stirling, "On the origins of the SAS", 8 Nov. 1948, WO218/223; Ladd *Operations* p.58; Hoe pp.220,474; Seymour p.217. 'Bennett' incident in, Capt. T.T. Doonan, Report, 13 Oct. 1946, WO261/772. Mr. Dougan, Museum of Army Transport, interview, 15 Aug. 1996.

45. For example, 1st. Field Regt. R.A., Quarterly Historical Report [QHR], 30 Sept. 1946, WO261/715- possibly Bob Bennett's unit?; 2nd. Beds. & Herts. Regt. QHRs, 30 Sept., 31 Dec. 1946, WO261/774, WO261/761 [closed till 2022].

46. WO DAAG, to Air 2/C3, 18 June 1946, WO32/10921.

47. Army Council Secretariat/WO SCAPP, "Re-formation of the SAS Regiment", 21 Apr. 1947, and Memo by the WO Dir. of Air, n.d., (Apr. 1947), WO32/10921. Also on the SAS see, Whittaker pp.33,87-89; I.S. Hallows *Regiments and Corps of the British Army* (London: New Orchard, 1994) p.237.

48. SCAPP report, *ibid*; Whittaker *ibid*. Also on the SOE's activities from 1946, Aldrich in (ed.) pp.15-35; in Gorst/Johnman/Lucas (eds.) pp.193-209.

49. WO Air C/3, to WO AG 2, memo, 29 July, and Army Order #128, with file reference, Aug. 1946, WO32/10921.

50. T.L. Jones *Small Wars* 7/3, pp.269-78.

51. On Gen. Dempsey, Strawson pp.102-05; Hunter *SAS* p.19; Kemp *War* p.96; Calvert, interview; S. Dorril *MI6* (London, 2000) p.33; letter, 10 July 2006.

Chapter 3- Fighting for survival on two fronts
1. On the Territorial Army, WO *Report of the Accounts of Army Expenditure, 1946/47 to 1948/49* (London: 1949), WO350/3. On the War Office's studies see, WO DTI Working Party Report, "Control of Special Units and Organisations", 20 Sept. 1946, and file minutes, 18 Apr.-22 Aug. 1946, WO232/10B, WO106/6024.

2. WO DTI Report, *ibid*. On studies, Dirve., 6 May 1946, L/WS/1/1485, IOLR.

3. On CMSWC, A.R. McGeorge for Ch. Comb. Ops, to O.C., Commando & Mountain Warfare Training Centre (sic.), 12 June 1946, DEFE2/1143. On the Royal Marines Commandos, Ladd *Commandos* pp.357-71. On Gen. Laycock, and Brig. Fergusson, (who later went to the PPF as Maj./Col.), B.E. Fergusson *The trumpet in the hall* (London: Collins, 1970) p.72; Rooney pp.48-49,68; Calvert, interview.

4. WO DTI Report, *ibid*. In an intriguing parallel with the SAS's actions, Brian Franks' former unit, Phantom, lobbied the WO for a post-war role after disband-ment in spring 1946, with similar results (refer to ff. 17). See, for instance, R.J.T. Hills *Phantom was there* (London: E. Arnold, 1951) pp.329-30. Brig. R.W. McLeod, GHQ New Delhi, to Brig. J.M. Calvert, HQ Northern Command, India (his current posting), 10 June 1946, Box 3, Calvert Papers, IWM.

5. T.L. Jones *Small Wars* 8/1, p.90.

6. Sir C. Norton, to FO, 20 Oct. 1946, R14782/FO371/58759. For details of the September vote arrangements, Air Min. A.L.M. Cary, to S.N. Hampshire, FO, 28 Aug., and FO Minute, 30 Aug. 1946, R12828,R12841/FO371/58705; LFG OI32, 22 Aug. 1946, WO261/771. Re the Greek village Home Guard and British assis-tance, "Note on C.S.S.U.s", 7 Oct. 1946, R9984/FO371/67005.

7. Stellin *et al* in, Pitt pp.101,116-17,163; J. Lodwick *The filibusters* (London: Methuen, 1947) pp.39,118,133; and on SBS links with the Greeks, p.152; person-al information, 14 Nov. 1996. SAS Regimental Association *Newsletter* 3, Nov. 1946, Churchill Archive, Cambridge [CAC], 2/309.

8. Gen. K. Crawford, HQLFG note, 4 Oct. 1946, R15192/FO371/58852. Gen. S. Rawlins, in C. Norton, to FO, 14 Nov. 1946, R16717/FO371/58759. Crawford and the SAS in, Lt.-Col. I.G. Collins, HQ 1 Airbne. Corps, to Maj.-Gen. Crawford, WO Dir. Air/DMI/DMO, 8 Aug. 1945, Box 6, Calvert Papers, IWM.

9. LFG to WO, 29 Dec., WO32/11436; GREEKMIL. (LFG), to TROOPERS (WO), 24 Dec., WO261/772; and on German failures, C. Norton, note, 23 Aug. 1946, R12925/FO371/58705.

10. Maj. M. Ward, (BMM(G) Staff Liaison Officer), interview, 31 July 1996; Alex J. Kellar, (MI5 'E' Overseas Dept.), in FO minute, 18 Feb. 1949, R2164/FO371/78456. Also see T.L. Jones *Small Wars* 7/3, p.274.

11. C.M. Woodhouse *The struggle for Greece* (London: Granada, 1976) p.213; Col. J.C. Murray 'The anti-bandit war' in T. Greene (ed.) *The guerilla and how to fight him* (New York: Praeger, 1962) p.83.

12. Greek Gen. Staff in BMM(G) MPR to 20 Nov. 1946, R34/FO371/67028, WO202/946. This would give a total of 3000 men, with 1500 to be assigned to GNA 'B' Corps area (Thessaly) and 1500 to 'C' Corps (Macedonia and Thrace).

13. On the Commandos, Murray *ibid*. Reference to the JPS report, 6 Nov. 1946, R16360/FO371/58714. No more detail is in this or in a copy file in CAB80/103.

14. Woodhouse *ibid* p.199; S.G. Xydis *Greece and the Great Powers, 1944-47* (Thessaloniki: Institute for Balkan Studies, 1963) pp.361,432-36; Gen. E. Averoff-Tossizza *By fire and axe* (New York: Caratzas Bros., 1978) p.190; J.R. Colville, FO notes, 22 Nov. 1946, R16572/FO371/58714; Murray p.109.

15. T.L. Jones *Small Wars* 8/1, pp.93-94, and especially refer to, WO to CINCME, 17 Dec., and LFG to WO, 29 Dec., WO32/11436; BMM(G) MPR to 20 Dec., WO202/946; Athens telegram, 3 Dec. 1946, R17424/FO371/58716; DO(47)1, 1 Jan. 1947, CAB131/4.

16. WO support for a TA Unit, Warner p.195. Opposition to it, J.G. Shortt pp.17-18. On the WO decision itself, B.A. Young *The Artists and the SAS* (London: 21 SAS (Artists' Rifles) TA, 1960) p.53; Kemp *War* pp.231-32; *Savage* pp.5-6. Re Brian Franks, Hoe p.473.

17. For example, Adams *et al* p.47; Hunter *SAS* p.xi. In an interesting parallel to this decision and the events that led up to it, the Phantom signals organisation (in which Lt.-Col. Franks had served during the War at a senior level), lobbied the WO for a post-war role. The WO granted it Territorial status in 1947, with the formation of the Army Phantom Signals Section (Princess Louise's Kensington Regiment, TA), Whittaker p.13; cf. Hills, who dates this to 1950, pp.329-30.

18. WO SCAPP, "Future of the Airborne Forces", 14 Oct. 1946, WO32/11538.

19. Adams p.27. Warner pp.191-92; Kemp *War* p.231; Ladd *Operations* p.104; Seymour p.268; Lt.-Col. L.E.O.T. Hart, "The SAS", (n.d.- the LHC Catalogue suggests that this was written in the 1940s, but judging by references made in it, this paper was written in the 1960s), Brig. R.W. McLeod Papers, 1/1, LHC.

20. Kemp *Savage* p.6.

21. Warner pp.123,177.

22. CIGS in LFGHQ QHR, 31 March 1947, WO261/637.

23. CIGS Meeting notes, 3 Dec. 1946, Montgomery Papers, 117/4, IWM.

24. BMM(G) Revised War Establishment [WE], Dec. 1946, and Brig. C.D. Steel, Dep.-Cdr. BMM(G), WE, 30 Jan. 1947, WO261/637. Also refer to p.172, ff.40.

25. LFG Minutes of Conference, 4 Dec. 1946, WO261/771.

26. WO to CINCME, 17 Dec., and LFG to WO, 29 Dec. 1946, 12 Jan. 1947, WO32/11436.

27. Maj. R.E. Austin, WO MO3, "Official History of BMM(G) 1945-52", (1952), WO202/908; J. Mavrikis, letter, 30 Apr. 1996.

28. BMM(G) G(Ops & Trg) QHR, 31 Dec. 1946, WO202/946. Like so many other British soldiers involved in the COIN campaign in Greece (including Bob Bennett), Lt.-Col. Fitzgerald was (or at least was listed as) an RA officer.

Chapter 4- Fighting insurgency on two fronts

1. T.L. Jones *Small Wars* 7/3, p.276.

2. BMM(G) MPRs, to 20 Jan., WO202/946; 20 Feb., 20 Mar., WO202/947; GHQMELF to MoD/COS, 12 Jan., 15 Jan. 1947, WO32/11436. At that time, BTG had about 16,000 men at its disposal in Greece, C. Chiclet 'The Greek Civil War'

in M. Sarafis/M. Eve (eds.) *Background to contemporary Greece* (London: MacMillan, 1990) p.210.

3. Lt.-Col. G.A. Fitzgerald, "Combined Operations Training", to BLUs, 28 Jan., and "GGS Training", 17 Jan. 1947, WO202/947.

4. BMM(G) G(Ops & Trg) QHR, 31 Mar. 1947, WO202/947. On Ray Keep's wartime service, Kemp interview, 16 May 1996.

5. Although figures for the total number of SAS reinforcements are unavailable, it's worth pondering the exisiting evidence that might have a bearing on this. There's an apparent discrepancy in official Tables for the BMM(G)'s WE: This was revised on 30 Jan. 1947 (WO261/637) as 341 officers and 1524 ORs, which was an increase of 73 officers and 340 ORs (from 268 officers and 1184 ORs). Yet on 7 Feb. 1947, the WO Orbat for "Miscell. Secret and Special Establishments" omitted any such increase in the BMM(G), WO33/2608, WO33/2628. In time, the planned increase was prevented because of political developments, but the War Office's failure to raise the BMM(G)'s official WE in February 1947 raises questions about whether it was trying to conceal reinforcements that consisted at least in part of "unofficial" SAS manpower.

6. D.A. Charters *The British Army and the Jewish insurgency in Palestine, 1945-47* (London: MacMillan, 1989) pp.43-48.

7. High Commissioner [HC], to Secretary of State for the Colonies, [SSC], 1 Aug. 1946, CO537/3847.

8. Colonial Office [CO] Minute, 5 Aug., SSC to HC, 7 Aug., and R.W. Selby, CO note, 20 Dec. 1946, CO537/3847.

9. C. Smith 'Communal conflict and insurrection in Palestine, 1936-48' in D.M. Anderson/D. Killingray (eds.) *Policing and decolonisation* (Manchester: Manchester Univ. Press, 1992) pp.76-77. Cf. Charters Jewish p.150; E.P. Horne BEM (Palestine Police Force Association), letter, 19 Aug. 1997.

10. On Col. Gray, Brig. J.M. Rymer-Jones "Memoirs", (Unpublished typescript,

n.d.) pp.145-46, Rymer-Jones Papers, IWM; and on Fergusson and his background, Fergusson pp.199,201; D.J. Clark *The Colonial police and anti-terrorism:
Bengal, 1930-36, Palestine, 1937-47, Cyprus, 1955-59* (D.Phil., Univ. of Oxford,
1978) p.234. On Fergusson's tasks, D.A. Charters *Insurgency and counter-insurgency in Palestine, 1945-47* (PhD, London, 1980) p.131; Col. Fergusson, to CO,
12 Feb. 1947, CO537/2270.

11. Rymer-Jones p.151; Fergusson pp.199-201; Horne letter, *ibid*.

12. Rymer-Jones pp.145-46,151; Fergusson pp.72,142,161,184,194, 201; Ladd
Operations p.372. On the SNS, C. Sykes *Orde Wingate* (London: Collins, 1959)
pp.141,147,152,156,170,172.

13. Fergusson pp.210-11.

14. CM(47)6, 15 Jan. 1947, CAB128/9.

15. On the talks in London, HC, to SSC, 5 Feb., 11 Feb., Fergusson to CO, 12
Feb., W.W. Clark, CO note, 12 Feb. 1947, CO537/2270; Fergusson pp.210-11,
and on air support, pp.221-25; N. Bethell *The Palestine triangle* (London: Andre
Deutsch, 1979) p.302. Re contacts between Calvert and Fergusson, Col. R.E.
Strong, Mil. Operational Research Unit, West Byfleet, to Lt.-Col. Calvert, 1 Armd.
Div., India, 15 Oct. 1946, Box 7; Maj. H.J. Lord, WO Q(Ops)3, to Calvert, Feb.
1947, Box 12, Calvert Papers, IWM. Also on the SNS, G.J.L. Hall *The guerilla as
mid-wife* (PhD, Univ. of Alabama, 1987) p.348.

16. Rymer-Jones p.151, IWM; cf. Calvert interview on Monty's "ambivalence". On
Perkins, Harclerode *Dirty* p.48.

17. Cunningham in, W.W. Clark, CO note, 12 Feb. 1947, CO537/2270.

18. Regarding Antrim and Smiley, Bethell p.302; and on Farran and McGregor,
Farran pp.345-48; Fergusson pp.225-40; 3rd. Hussars Summary of Regt.
Moves/Personnel, 1945-46, Queen's Own Hussars Regiment Museum, Warwick;
R. Farran, 3 KOH, MEF, to Brig. J. Calvert, HQ SAS, Essex, 10 Sept. 1945, Box
12; B. Franks, to J. Calvert, 3 Feb. 1947, Box 7, Calvert Papers, IWM. Farran was

2 i/c and Major, Oct.-Nov. 1945, then Adjutant to Mar. 1946. Also Kemp *War* pp.104-14,185-86,190; Warner p.97; Major Alastair McGregor, interview, 19 May 1996. Rupert Allason asserts that McGregor was nominated by the SIS - (as) N. West *The Friends* (London: Weidenfeld & Nicolson, 1988) p.37. Pte. L. Roche, YMCA London SW1, to Calvert, 4 Feb. 1947, Box 6, Calvert Papers, IWM.

19. Other accounts state that there were two police squads, for example, Charters PhD pp.131-35; Horne letter, *ibid*, who states that one squad was led by "Reilly". But cf. McGregor interviews, 19 May, 2 Sept. 1996.

20. For instance, Charters *Jewish* p.151. Cf. Rymer-Jones p.151, IWM.

21. Re the CO, Clark PhD, pp.234-39. On Farran and McGregor and their actions, Farran pp.347-48; Fergusson pp.221-22,226; McGregor, interviews; Charters *Jewish* p.123.

22. On the squads, D.A. Charters/M. Tugwell 'From Palestine to Northern Ireland' in (eds.) *Armies in low-intensity conflicts* (London: Brassey's, 1989) p.208. On the SAS in Palestine, Warner pp.76,82; Kemp *War* pp.86,88; Darman pp.45-46. On ME Raiding Forces and Col. Hackett, Whittaker p.52; D. Brutton *A captain's mandate* (London: Leo Cooper, 1996) p.23; Weale *Secret* p.115.

23. On Germany, Warner p.178; Kemp *War* pp.219-20. On Palestine, Buxton p.15. Re Lt. McGonigal, Pitt pp.181-82,226; Lodwick pp.134-35,169-72.

24. McGregor interview, 2 Sept. 1996; Farran p.348; Fergusson p.226; D.A. Charters 'Special ops in counter-insurgency: The Farran case, Palestine, 1947' *Journal of the RUSI* 124/2 (June 1979) p.60. Horne *ibid* asserts that up to 24 men served In the squads, including W. Abraham; Birch; Burke; Cade; Carson; Carter; Clarke; J. Faulkner; R. Long; Murphy; Brian O'Dell; O'Regan; W. Pilkington; Thompson; and Tomkins. SAS Regimental Association *Newsletter* 3, Nov. 1946, Churchill, 2/309, CAC, and *Newsletter* 1, March 1946, Box 6, Calvert Papers, IWM.

25. Regarding Farran's actions in France, Kemp *War* p.175; and on police operations and training, Farran pp.348-51,370-71; Fergusson p.226; Charters *Jewish* p.151. For the incident cited, personal information, 25 June 1996.

26. On tactics, C.J. McInnes *Hot war, Cold war* (London: Brassey's, 1996) p.120. Cf. T.L. Jones *Small Wars* 7/3, p.272; re Gale, Brutton p.64; Kemp *War* p.231.

27. CID view in, HC to SSC, 5 Jan. 1948, CO537/3872. For details about the abduction, HQ Pal. Diary of Events, 5 Apr. 1948, Airborne Forces Museum, Aldershot, Hampshire, [AFM]; Farran pp.348,351-53. Accusations against Farran are made in B. Lapping *End of Empire* (London: Granada, 1985) p.129; Col. R.L. Clutterbuck 'Bertrand Stewart Prize Essay' *Army Quarterly* 81/1 (Oct. 1960) p.167; and especially, S. Tsadka (or Zadka) *Guerilla warfare in Palestine, 1944-47: the role of the Irgun* (PhD, London, 1992) p.133, though this is omitted from his *Blood in Zion* (London: Brassey's, 1995).

28. Re LHI, Z. Eytan, letter, 14 Sept. 1990; Bethell p.318; Brutton p.82.

29. HQ Pal. Diary of Events, AFM; cf. Farran p.368, who wrote that he actually surrendered to the authorities on 19th. June 1947.

30. H. Gurney to SSC, 25 June 1947, Gen. Sir A. Cunningham Papers, 2/1, Middle East Centre, Oxford, [MEC]; Charters *Jewish* p.151; PhD pp.200-01.

31. Rymer-Jones p.151, IWM; GOC to Commanders, 23 Jan. 1947, Maj.-Gen. Sir H. Stockwell Papers, 6/2, LHC.

32. On Farran and Fergusson, Bethell p.318; Diary of Events, AFM; Horne *ibid*, notes that the squad leaders were only "attached" to the PPF.

33. This was the first and a most graphic demonstration of the need for complete anonymity for SAS witnesses in I.S.-related trials, and Capt. McGregor's treatment compares most unfavourably with the procedures devised later, such as in Northern Ireland, Gibraltar, etc.. On Farran, Fergusson and McGregor, Bethell pp.347-48; Farran p.382; McGregor, interviews.

34. Farran p.382.

Chapter 5- The International Squadron- bending the rules in Greece
1. T.L. Jones *Small Wars* 7/3, p.276; 8/1, p.95.

2. On the British advisors and their role, BMM(G) to BLUs, 28 Jan., and BMM(G) QHR, Appendix 'C'- Personnel: Officers, Apr. 1947, WO202/947; and on their activities, BMM(G) MPRs, to 20 Apr., 20 May, and G(Ops & Trg) QHR, 30 June 1947, WO202/948. For more details about Britons in Greece avoiding the new government I.S. directive, T.L. Jones *Small Wars* 8/1, p.95.

3. BMM(G) MPRs, to 20 Jan., 20 Feb., 20 Mar. 1947, WO202/947.

4. BTG QHR, 30 June, WO261/759; GHQMEF note, 5 May 1947, WO202/947. By mid-1947, BTG had around 6000 men in Greece, COS(47)95, 28 July 1947, DEFE5/11. And see, J. Cooper (with A. Kemp) *One of the Originals* (London: Pan, 1991) p.168.

5. On the SAS's organisation, for instance, Kemp *War* p.73. It should be noted, though, that the wartime SAS Regiments had four Squadrons, while the Greek Commandos initially operated with five.

6. Wg.-Cdr. P. Broad, Loose minute, 21 June 1947, AIR 46/30.

7. Sir C. Wickham in, BPPM Monthly Report, 26 June 1947, R8890/FO371/ 67031. Re the BMM(G) and training matters, GHQMEF QHR, 20 Sept., WO261/547; BMM(G) QHR, 30 Sept., Formation of Inf. Branch, 4 July, and WE, 23 July 1947, WO202/949.

8. D. Reilly, Embassy, to FO, 21 Aug. 1947, R11758/FO371/67031.

9. BMM(G) WE, Personnel: Officers, 23 July 1947, WO202/949.

10. Sec. of State for War [SSW] Written Answer, 22 July 1947, Parliamentary Debates 5th. Series, (1946-50) Vol. 440. Also, T.L. Jones *Small Wars* 8/1, p.96.

11. BMM(G) G(Ops & Trg) QHR, 30 Sept. 1947, WO202/949; Maj. McGregor interview, 16 May 1996.

12. BMM(G) Command/Maj.-Gen. S.B. Rawlins, "Review of the Anti-bandit campaign", 22 Oct. 1947, WO202/893.

13. Calvert, interview.

14. McGregor, interviews.

15. On the WO and advisors, T.L. Jones *Small Wars* 7/3, pp.277-78. Maj. B. Dillon, interview, 10 May 1998; Dillon Obituary, Aug. 2003, by Gen. Jack. B. Dye, who notes that Dillon should have been given a medal for "individual bravery" during his 18 months fighting the Communists - www.norfolkbc.fsnet.co.uk; SAS Regt. Assoc. *Newsletters* 8 (Apr. 1948), 10 (Dec. 1948), 11 (Apr. 1949), National Army Museum, London [NAM].

16. WO to GHQMELF/16 Abne. Div. HQ/2 Para./CAE/AAC Records, Apr. 1947, WO32/10921. Also on the TA see, Ladd *Operations* p.104; Kemp *War* p.231; P. Harclerode *Para!* (London: Orion, 1996) p.210. Maj. L.E.O.T. Hart, HQ BTE, MELF, 21 May, to Maj. Calvert, Camberley, Box 12; Lt.-Col. B.M.F. Franks, Hyde Park Hotel, to Calvert, 22 May 1947, Box 6, Calvert Papers, IWM; Harclerode *Dirty* p.48.

17. Memo by the Army Council Secretariat/WO DAW, "Re-formation of SAS Regiment", 21 Apr. 1947, and ACS minute, 5 May 1947, WO32/10921.

18. WO DAAG to Air C3, 28 May, and WO Directorate of Land/Air Warfare [DL/AW] 2, to C3, 3 June 1947, WO32/10921.

19. WO Directorate of Personnel Administration [DPA], to Col. the Lord Strathcona and Mount Royal, 19 June 1947, WO32/10921.

20. For example, Kemp *Savage* p.6.

21. 21 SAS Royal Warrant, 20 June, and "Explanatory Memorandum", (n.d.-June), and notes, 7-8 July 1947, WO32/10921.

22. WO DPA, to 16 Abne. Div. (TA) HQ, 18 June 1947, WO32/10921.

23. Lt.-Col. B.M.F. Franks, "Annual Report of 21 SAS Regiment (Artists) TA", 31 Oct. 1948, Brig. R.W. McLeod Papers, 2/1, LHC. Also refer to Ladd *Operations*

p.104; Kemp *Savage* p.6; Harclerode *Para* p.210.

24. Franks *ibid*; Young p.56. Also see SAS Regt. Assoc. *Newsletter* 1 (Nov. 1946), Churchill, 2/309, CAC.

25. Kemp *Savage* p.6.

26. For instance, Warner p.75; Ladd *Operations* p.43; Kemp *War* p.97; Farran p.256; Seymour pp.40,44; Lt.-Col. D.G.C. Sutherland, letter, 8 May 1996; and on the British Commandos and their operations in general, C. Messenger *The Commandos, 1940-46* (London: Granada, 1988) *passim*; T.L. Jones *Small Wars* 8/1, pp.98-99; *Origins*, *passim*.

27. Lt.-Col. D.G.C. Sutherland *He who dares* (London: Leo Cooper, 1998) pp.177-82; letter, 8 May 1996; J. Mavrikis, letter, 30 Apr. 1996; BMM(G) MPR, to 20 Feb., WO202/950; to 20 Nov. 1948, WO202/988; Lt.-Col. R.W. Selby 'The cradle of US Cold War strategy' *Military Review* 46/8 (Aug. 1966) p.52; Parker pp.116-17. Also on Sutherland's training methods, Pitt p.64.

28. Col. J. Waddy, letter, 24 Sept. 1996.

29. Maj. A. McGregor interview, 19 May 1996; BMM(G) MPR, to 20 Nov. 1948, WO202/908. And on arrangements in World War Two, for example, Seymour pp.212-13; Kemp *War* p.73.

30. Col. A.C. Shortt, to Col. Price, WO MI3, Feb. 1948, R1257/, and Shortt, Monthly Defence Review, Apr. 1948, R6329/FO371/72207; 15 May, R6706/FO371/72212; 15 June, R7618/FO371/72213; RAFDG Progress Report [Progrep.] to 30 Apr. 1948, AIR24/760.

31. FO note, 25 Dec. 1948, R13373/FO371/72332; Lt.-Col. Sutherland, letter, 8 May 1996.

32. Maj. C.L.D. Newell 'SAS warfare in the jungle' *The Sphere* 11 Aug. 1956.

33. Kemp *Secret*; Kemp *War* pp.229-30,254; *Savage* pp.4-5; Fowler p.75.

34. "22 SAS Regt. in Malaya" Drafts, (n.d.), Harry Miller Papers, 67/194/3, IWM.

35. Aldrich in (ed.) p.26; especially on Burma, in Gorst/Johnman/Lucas (eds.) pp.201-06. Further details of the Burma episode were revealed in a BBC TV *Timewatch* documentary (1997). Burma was just one of the several countries where British military personnel offered I.S. assistance/advice at this juncture, e.g. Siam, the Phillipines, Indo-China.

36. For details see T.L. Jones *Small Wars* 7/3, pp.280-82. And especially on the Greek Commandos' training role in 1948, Murray p.83. On Whinney, Harclerode *Dirty* pp.53-56. The timing of the curtailment of his activities may also be significant, given other concurrent developments in Greece. Julian Amery of the SIS/SOE was also there in mid-1948, planning subversion against Albania - *ibid* p.46.

37. Maj.-Gen. A.J.H. Cassels, WO DL/AW, "Disbandment of the Army Air Corps", 29 July, to WO DPA; DPA minutes, 23 Aug. 1948, WO32/13382. For details of Maj.-Gen. Cassels in Palestine, for instance, Charters *Jewish* pp.56,88.

38. Lt.-Col. B. Franks, 21 *Annual Report*, 31 Oct. 1948, McLeod Papers, 2/7, LHC.

39. On American opposition to the use of the Commandos, M. McClintock *Instruments of statecraft* (New York: Pantheon, 1992) pp.13,466; L. Cable *A conflict of myths* (New York: New York Univ. Press, 1986) p.19. Regarding the British/American domestic and international political position over Greece, the two governments' public relations policies, and their COIN efforts there, T.L. Jones *Small Wars* 7/3, pp.277-78; 8/1, pp.98-100; and H. McNeil, FO statement, 23 Feb. 1948, *Hansard* Vol.447. Also see ff.40, dating from the same time, indicating that, by Feb. 1948, events had led to the subject of Britons receiving Greek war medals being broached.

40. HMG policy in, FO, to Athens, 26 Feb. 1948, T303/4; and see awards file, T303/1.

41. Gen. Sir J.T. Crocker, to D.A.P. Reilly, *chargé d'affaires*, Athens Chancery, Aug. 1948; Maj.-Gen. Sir R. Mansergh, to E.W. Light, FO, 17 Aug.; E.W. Light, to Mansergh, 25 Aug. 1948, T303/4.

42. On Meynell and FO, Lt.-Col. A.F.S.A. Turner, WO, to E.W. Light, FO, 11 Mar. 1949, T303/4; Lt.-Col. C.H.T. MacFetridge [BLO], letter, 5 May 1998. Re O'Connor, Maj.-Gen. H. Pyman, chief of staff MELF HQ, to Gen. E.E. Down, Head of BMM(G), 3 Jan. 1949, Maj.-Gen. Sir H. Pyman Papers, 6/1/23, LHC.

43. Lt.-Col. D.G.C. Sutherland, letter, - May 1996. On Bennett's award, see ff.45.

44. Quoted in *Hansard* Vol.462; and extracts and official report, 2 Mar. 1949, T303/4. On the BMM(G)'s role see, T.L. Jones *Small Wars* 8/1, pp.99-100.

45. WO Official Report, E. Shinwell, "Written Reply", 8 Mar. 1949, T303/4. Reference to Bob Bennett's award in Buxton p.18. He notes that Bennett received his medal in 1950 through the BMM(G), and that this was the Greek War Cross (actually Greek Military Cross).

46. On the BMM(G)'s position and its role in GNA training, BMM(G) MPR, to 20 Nov., QHR, 31 Dec. 1948, WO202/898; Col. Shortt, note, 13 Dec. 1948, R14354/FO371/72252. Also for details of the position in 1949, T.L. Jones *Small Wars* 8/1, pp.99-100. SIS, Harclerode *Dirty* pp.47-49-50,52.

47. Maj. MacGregor interview, 19 May 1996; obituary, *Daily Telegraph*, 10 Oct. 2002 - he was awarded the Greek Military Cross. Hoe/Morris pp.63-64.

Chapters 6- "Too funny to be true!"- the Middle East Rangers (SAS)
1. This designation for the SAS's Middle East Unit was used by Maj. Hart in a letter to C.O., 21 SAS, (Col. A.C. Newman), 23 May 1951, WO218/223. Also see ff.2.

2. The whole scheme was known only to a small group of people, so that even senior SAS officers were kept in the dark about it. Maj. McGregor in fact thought that the very idea of a "Middle East Rangers (SAS)" sounded "almost too funny to be true!", and he greeted it with great mirth. Similarly, Col. Waddy had "certainly" never heard anything about the Unit, and he added that "it sounds like an American outfit!" Maj. McGregor interview, 2 Sept. 1996; Col. Waddy letter, 24 Sept. 1996.

3. COS paper, "The Organisation of Command in the Middle East", 6 Dec. 1948, Pyman Papers, 6/1/22, LHC; JPS in, JP(48)50, 30 Apr. 1948, DEFE4/13. Also see,

R.J. Aldrich/J. Zametica 'The rise and decline of a strategic concept: the Middle East, 1945-51' in Aldrich (ed.) p.254.

4. Maj.-Gen. Pyman, memo, 4 Nov. 1948, Papers, 6/1/21, LHC.

5. ME chief of staff's committee, "Review of Mobilisation Situation", 15 Nov., and GHQMEF note, 7 Nov. 1948, Pyman Papers, 6/1/21, LHC; Lt.-Col. Franks, 21 SAS *Annual Report*, Brig. McLeod Papers, 2/1, LHC; Young p.60; Kemp *Savage* p.6; WO DMT memo, 2 Jan. 1950, DEFE2/1621.

6. Maj.-Gen. Pyman, note, 25 Nov. 1948, Papers, 6/1/21, LHC.

7. "Points for chief of staff", Maj.-Gen. Pyman, 16 Feb., and Pyman, note, 17 Feb. 1949, Papers, 6/1/24, LHC. Slim/Calvert in Burma, Rooney pp.31-34.

8. Chief of staff committee, notes, 14 Feb. 1949, Pyman Papers, 6/1/24, LHC.

9. Chief of staff committee notes, 2 Mar. 1949, Pyman Papers, 6/1/25, LHC.

10. Maj.-Gen. Pyman note, "Formation of SAS Unit", 18 Feb. 1949, and note, 7 Mar. 1949, Papers, 6/1/24, LHC. Also on Cyrenaica see, Aldrich/Zametica in Aldrich (ed.) pp.254-56; and on the Second World War, Ladd *Operations* pp.27-28,33-34,40-41; Strawson pp.58-59,65,87-91,100-04; Warner pp.24-27; Hoe pp.58-59; Kemp *War* p.16; Darman pp.127-28.

11. Maj.-Gen. Pyman, note, 18 Feb. 1948, Papers, 6/1/24, LHC. On the wartime SAS/SBS and Iraq, Ladd *Operations* p.42; Warner p.81; Strawson pp.164-68. Re bases, R. Ovendale *The origins of the Arab-Israeli wars* (Harlow, Essex: Longman, 1986) p.136; *Special Report by HMG to the Council of the League of Nations on the progress of Iraq during the period 1920-31* (London: HMSO, 1931) *passim*.

12. Chief of staff committee, memo, 2 Mar., and Pyman note, 11 Apr. 1949, Pyman Papers, 6/1/25, 6/1/26, LHC.

13. See T.L. Jones *Small Wars* 7/3, p.286; Field-Marshal Slim Report, 22 Mar. 1949, R2119/FO371/78348.

14. J. Paskin, CO, draft memo, to WO, n.d., and CO draft letter, to WO, 2 Apr. 1949; W. Geraghty, WO DMO, to W.F. Dawson, CO Private Sec., 4 Apr. 1949, CO537/4751; T.L. Jones *Small Wars* 7/3, p.286.

15. Maj.-Gen. Pyman, note, 15 Apr. 1949, Papers, 6/1/26; GHQMEF Coordination Branch, "Redeployment of MELF", 20 May 1949, Pyman Papers, 6/1/27, LHC.

16. GHQMELF, BGS(SD), "Demolitions Training", Pyman Papers, 6/1/27, LHC.

17. Chief of staff, MELF Conf. notes, 4 July 1949, Pyman Papers, 6/1/29, LHC.

18. In May 1950 the WO noted that "the SAS Regiment consists, at present, of one unit only", indicating possible future expansion beyond 21 SAS. See SAS Corps Warrant "Explanatory Memorandum", n.d. (May 1950), WO32/13867.

Chapter 7- Fighting for Corps status
1. Lt.-Col. B. Franks, to Gen. Sir M.C. Dempsey, 11 May 1949, WO32/13867. He was apparently made Hon. Col. of 21 SAS on 29 Jan. 1948, according to www.regiments.org.

2. Lt.-Col. B. Franks, to Gen. Sir M.C. Dempsey, 11 May 1949; 2-i-c, 21 SAS, (Maj. Hart), to C.O. 21 SAS, (Franks), 10 May 1949, WO32/13867. Weale p.144 says the Winged Dagger replaced Mars & Minerva for 21 in 1949 (possibly after the Greek effort).

3. Kemp *Savage* p.9.

4. 2-i-c, 21 SAS, to C.O., 10 May 1949, WO32/13867. On Maj.-Gen. Cassels, Staff List, 1949, WO32/13824, Charters *Jewish* pp.56,88. For Montgomery's actions, WO Assistant-AG (2), minute, 26 Apr.; WO, to GOC 16 Abne. Div. (TA), in DL/AW minute, 20 May 1949, WO32/13382; Harclerode *Para* p.211.

5. Maj. Hart, to Lt.-Col. Franks, 10 May 1949, WO32/13867; WO DL/AW, minute, 5 May 1949, WO32/13382.

6. Maj. Hart, to Lt.-Col. Franks, 10 May 1949, WO32/13867. On SAS records in

1945 see, Kemp *War* p.xiii.

7. Lt.-Col. B. Franks, to Gen. Sir M.C. Dempsey, 11 May 1949, WO32/13867.

8. Maj.-Gen. A.J.H. Cassels, to 16 Abne. Div. (TA), memo, 20 June 1949, WO32/13882.

9. 21 SAS (TA) HQ, London, to Gen. Dempsey, 7 July 1949, WO32/13867. On Col. Newman, *Combined operations, 1940-42* (London: HMSO, 1943) pp.72-94.

10. Head of WO Directorate of Personnel Administration [DPA], Maj.-Gen. J.E.C. McCandlish, minute, 28 July, note, 13 Sept. 1949; Anonymous notes (by Franks?), 15 July 1949; Gen. Sir J.S. Steele, AG to the Forces, to Gen. Sir M. Dempsey, Hon. Col. SAS Regiment, 24 May 1950; C.S. Sugden, WO DPA minute, 27 Feb., and "Abolition of the AAC", 19 May 1950, WO32/13867.

11. Anon. Notes, 15 July 1949, *ibid*. Ramsay pp.7-8; Kemp *Savage* pp.7-8.

12. Kemp *Savage* p.8.

13. WO DL/AW, to WO DPA, 9 Aug. 1949, WO32/13867.

14. P.H. Man, WO AAG minutes, 7 Sept. 1949, WO32/13867.

15. WO DPA minute, 2 Nov. 1949, WO32/13867.

16. Maj.-Gen. McCandlish, WO DPA, notes and minutes, 13 Sept. 1949- "The organisation of the SAS Regiment at the present", "Present composition", "Recommendations"; C.S. Sugden, DPA minutes, 27 Feb. 1950, WO32/13867. On the SAS/Paras, for example, Ramsay p.8, and also cf. Ladd *Operations* p.105.

17. Maj.-Gen. McCandlish, DPA notes and minutes, "Advantages", "Disadvantages", (drafts), 13 Sept. 1949, WO32/13867.

18. Minutes of Meeting of 20 Sept., Maj. W. Bevan, Sec. DAAG 2(B), 23 Sept. 1949, WO32/13382, WO32/13867. Also regarding Dempsey's appointment as

SAS Colonel Commandant by the 1950s, Hoe/Morris p.162.

19. Gen. Sir J.S. Steele, WO AG, to Field-Marshal Alanbrooke, 17 Oct. 1949; Maj. W. Bevan, DAAG note, 27 Sept. 1949, WO32/13867.

20. Ladd *Operations* p.105.

21. Col. R.C. Elstone, WO DL/AW loose minutes, "Orbat of an Airborne Division"; "The organisation of an Airborne Division", 9 Jan. 1950, WO32/13868. WO DMT directive, 2 Jan. 1950, DEFE2/1621. J. Parker *SBS* (London: Headstone, 1997) pp.116-17.

22. WO AAG, "Title of new Corps- Glider Pilot and Parachute Regiment", 24 Jan. 1950, WO32/13867.

23. Brig. Calvert interview, paper.

24. WO Notes of Meeting, 14 Feb. 1950, WO32/13867.

25. Capt. C.W. Weston, WO AG1, loose minute, 20 Feb. 1950, WO32/13867.

26. C.S. Sugden, WO DPA, minutes, 27 Feb. 1950, WO32/13867.

27. Maj. W. Bevan, AAG Sec., note, 28 Mar.; Anonymous memo, 24 Apr.; J.H. Cresswell, AAG Explanatory Memo, 26 Apr.; Anon. draft memo, c. May 1950; Proofs for Army Orders- "Corps Warrant Amendments", 13 May; G.W. Lambert, WO Circular Letter, 15 June; Gen. Sir J.S. Steele, WO AG, to Field-Marshal Viscount Montgomery, Colonel Commandant of the Parachute Regiment, 24 May 1950, WO32/13867. On the SAS Corps' dating, for instance, Kemp *Savage* p.11. Re the SBS and Malaya, for instance, R. Hunter *True stories of the SBS* (London: Virgin, 1998) p.224.

28. C.M.B. Howard, WO DPA, memo, 3 July; DAAG notes, 26 June 1950, WO32/13867. Re the JPS, Warner p.287; Ladd *Operations* p.105; Hoe/Morris p.61.

29. Corps Warrant Explanatory Memorandum, n.d. (May 1950), WO32/13867. Cf.

Kemp *Savage* pp.7-8; Ramsay p.8.

30. Explanatory Memorandum, n.d. (May 1950), *ibid*.

31. WO DMT, Training Memorandum, 14 July 1950, WO32/13868.

Chapter 8- Korea: the war that never was?
1. For instance, P. Lowe *The origins of the Korean War* (Harlow, Essex: Longman, 1986) pp.150-170.

2. Warner p.201; Ladd *Operations* p.105; Maj. McGregor interview, 19 May 1996; Rooney pp.145-46; Weale p.147 asserts that MacArthur requested two SAS regiments; and re US special forces, p.155; Adams p.39. Maj. W.B Kennedy-Shaw, to Brig. J. Calvert, 1 Aug. 1945, Box 6, Calvert Papers, IWM.

3. "22 SAS Regiment in Malaya", n.d., (drafts); "John Cooper", n.d., Harry Miller Papers, 67/194/3, IWM; Kemp *Savage* pp.9-10; Strawson p.139; Darman p.69.

4. "22 SAS Regiment in Malaya"; "John Cooper", *ibid*; McGregor interviews; Kemp *War* pp.104-09,113-14; Savage pp.9-10,19-20; Geraghty p.19; Warner p.201; Hoe/Morris pp.63-64.

5. "22 SAS Regiment in Malaya" *ibid*; L. Thompson *SAS* (Osceola, Wisconsin: Motorbooks International, 1994) p.65; Hoe/Morris pp.62-64; Kemp *Savage*, p.6, wherein the SAS troop is called the 10th. Yorkshire Parachute Battalion.

6. Kemp *Savage* pp.9-10.

7. For details of SAS preparations, McGregor interviews; and decisions taken by MacArthur, "22 SAS Regiment in Malaya" *ibid*; Warner p.201. Cf. the British government's purported thinking as per Ladd *Operations* p.105; Philip/Taylor p.32; Darman p.96.

8. Kemp *Savage* p.10; R. Neillands *In the combat zone* (London: Weidenfeld & Nicolson, 1997) p.103.

Chapter 9- Hearts, minds and winged dagger

1. Warner p.218; and also on the importance of the Malaya enterprise, for example, White p.137; S. Crawford *The SAS at close quarters* (London: Brown Packaging, 1993) p.26. On the SAS commitment there, Strawson p.224. Regarding the formation of a special force for Malaya, Geraghty, pp.11,18.

2. T.L. Jones *Small Wars* 7/3, pp.280-82,301.

3. Re JGF and Ritchie, Gen. Sir N.M. Ritchie, "CINCFELF's Report on Operations in Malaya, 1948-49", 6 Sept. 1949, WO106/5884. On the JGF leaders, J.C. Litton, (civil government officer), Circular Letter #3, 27 Feb. 1949, J.C. Litton Papers, Ms.Ind.Ocn.s.113, Rhodes House Library, Oxford, [RHO]; A. Short *The Communist insurrection in Malaya, 1948-60* (London: F. Muller, 1975) p.132. Re Maj.-Gen. Boucher, Sir R.G.K. Thompson *Make for the hills* (London: Leo Cooper, 1989) p.88; Rooney p.51; A.H.P. Humphrey "Talk to the Far East Centre, Oxford" (Unpublished typescript, 22 May 1979), p.7, Mss.Pac.s.115, RHO; Anon.- Weasal 'Ferret Force' Malaya 1 (Sept. 1952) p.21; Gen. J. Coates *Suppressing insurgency* (Boulder, Colorado: Westview Press, 1992) pp.46-47.

4. On Greece, T.L. Jones *Small Wars* 7/3, pp.274-75; Murray p.83. Cf. Rooney p.136. For the JGF, GHQFELF, to Under-Sec. of State, WO, 18 Aug.; FELF, to TROOPERS [WO], 9 Aug. 1948, WO268/8.

5. Boucher and FELF's action in, Weasal *ibid* p.21; Short pp.132-33; FELF G(Ops) QHR, 30 Sept. 1948; and re FELF on the JGF's code-name, FELF, to Singapore HQ, 19 July 1948, WO268/8.

6. FELF G(Ops) QHR, 30 Sept. 1948; 21 Sept. Conf., notes, 28 Sept. 1948, WO268/8.

7. J.C. Litton *ibid*; "Future Ferret policy", 20 Sept., FELF G(Ops) QHR, 30 Sept., WO268/8; FELF, to WO, 9 Aug. 1948, L/WS/1/1498, IOLR; Weasal *ibid* pp.21-22; Coates pp.146-47.

8. FELF G(Ops) QHR, 30 Sept.; CINCFELF "Agenda for District Commanders' Conference", 19 Aug.; CINC's Conference, notes, 23 Aug.; GOC Malaya, "Outline" notes, 23 Aug.; "Future Ferret policy" memo, 20 Sept. 1948, WO268/8.

9. WO, FELF Sitrep [Situation Report] #23, 22 Dec. 1948, L/WS/1/1514, IOLR.

10. J.C. Litton, Circ. Letter #3, 27 Feb.; "Chuk Pa Operation" notes, 19-22 Feb. 1949; "Chinese Assault Team Diary, 1949", Litton Papers, RHO; on Dalley, D. Mackay *The Malaya Emergency* (London: Brassey's, 1997) p.31.

11. H. Andrew *Who won the Malaya Emergency?* (Singapore: Graham Brash, 1995) pp.103-04; Suff. Regt. WD, 20 Jan. 1951, B1/24, Suff. Regt. Museum, Bury St. Edmunds [SRM]. See J. Latimer *Deception In War* (London: J. Murray, 2001) p.279; L. Spicer *The Suffolks in Malaya* (Peterborough: Lawton Phelps, 1998) pp.1,39.

12. For details see, T.L. Jones *Small Wars* 7/3, p.286.

13. Gen. Ritchie Report, 1949, WO106/5884; W.F. Dawson, CO Private Sec., to W. Geraghty, WO, 2 Apr.; J. Paskin/T. Lloyd, CO, draft for WO DMO, (for despatch to HC/Commissioner Gen.); W. Geraghty, to W.F. Dawson, 4 Apr.; M. MacDonald, to SSC, 20 Apr. 1949, CO537/4751; GHQFELF Command Conference, Apr. 1949, notes, 3 May 1949, WO268/10; T.L. Jones *Small Wars* 7/3, pp.285-88.

14. For more details see, T.L. Jones *Small Wars* 7/3, pp.288-89; J.B.P. Robinson "History of the Malaya Emergency", (Unpublished report, 31 July 1954), CAB103/532.

15. Coates p.147; and he was unsure about 'LRP' operations, Rooney p.91.

16. T.L. Jones *Small Wars* 7/3, p.286. Re Slim in 1946, Parker p.100.

17. On Gen. Harding, Strawson p.229; Ramsay p.9; Shortt p.18; Buxton p.39; Ladd *Operations* p.106; Philip/Taylor p.30; Darman p.32; Seymour p.270; Kemp *Savage* p.17. Re Maj. Calvert, Warner p.201; White p.136. Reference to the Ferret example in, T. Pocock *Fighting General* (London: Collins, 1973) p.88.

18. Brig. Calvert in, paper, interview. On Harding's views, Hoe/Morris p.42. Also on Slim's initiative, Rooney p.135; Weale p.152. And on his uncanny ability to choose the most "qualified individuals" for particular military tasks, especially COIN, see, D.D. Avant *Political institutions and military change* (London: Cornell Univ. Press, 1994) p.126.

19. Calvert, paper; his medals, incidentally, came up for auction in mid-1997, when the Brigadier was obliged to sell them off for a paltry sum; Hoe/Morris p.42; Rooney pp.130-31,135; and on Brig. Calvert himself, Kemp *Savage* pp.17-18; Shortt p.18; Geraghty p.22; Strawson p.230; Warner pp.201-02; Ladd *Operations* p.106; "22 SAS Regiment in Malaya", Miller Papers, IWM.

20. Calvert paper; Hoe/Morris pp.42,44.

21. Calvert paper; CO note, 16 Feb. 1950, CO537/5974.

22. Calvert paper; D.A. Charters/M. Tugwell in (eds.) p.208; Rooney p.137; Weale pp.154,157; FELF, to WO, 17 May 1950, DEFE11/36.

23. Calvert paper; T.L. Jones *Small Wars* 7/3, p.267.

24. Calvert paper.

25. Calvert paper; W. Elliot, Sec. COS C'ttee, note, 13 June 1950, DEFE11/37.

26. J.H. Cresswell, WO AAG, memo, "Separate B.M.", 19 June; DAAG minute, 26 June 1950, WO32/13867.

27. Calvert paper; Hoe/Morris p.47; Ladd Operations p.107; Geraghty p.25. On the ME Rangers, Maj. L.E.O.T. Hart, to C.O. 21 SAS, (Lt.-Col. A.C. Newman), 23 May 1951, WO218/223. Forty years later, the SAS returned to Iraq during the 1991 Gulf War, when SAS patrols such as Bravo Two Zero were given maps prepared in 1951! See *The Real Bravo Two Zero* (Channel 5 TV, 17 April 2003). The SAS has also been committed there since 2003. It is worth noting too re the nomenclature of 'Rangers' that the Greek Commandos became the "1st Commandos, Special Operations Regiment (Rangers)", and some 'Q' squads in Malaya adopted this same Ranger designation in 1952: T.L. Jones *Postwar* p.132.

28. Calvert paper; Rooney p.137. Similarly, Pitt p.214 overestimates Calvert's role and asserts that he was a member of the 1946 DTI Committee.

29. Calvert paper; J.H. Cresswell, WO AAG, memo, 19 June 1950, WO32/13867.

Calvert, to FTC, June 1950, Box 3, Calvert Papers, IWM.

30. Geraghty p.23.

31. Maj.-Gen. R.E. Urquhart, "Notes of Conference", 11 July 1950, WO231/38.

32. Calvert paper; Gen. A.F.J. Harding, to WO, 23 Aug. 1950, DEFE11/37. Templer also had experience of unconventional warfare as temporary head of SOE Germany during the War. See Mackay p.122. Also on the other candidates for the supremo's job, Hoe/Morris pp.46,56; and on the likes of Sir William Battershill (governor of Cyprus in 1941), T.L. Jones *Small Wars* 7/3, pp.292,306. In Oct. 1950, Harding proposed Mountbatten for the post (given his wartime example of SE Asia Command); and also see List by VCIGS, Lt.-Gen. Neville C.D. Brownjohn, Feb. 1951, WO216/835.

33. Calvert paper. For claims about Calvert and resettlement, for example, Rooney pp.136,138; Warner p.203; Strawson p.230; Ladd *Operations* p.106. Cf. T.L. Jones *Small Wars* 7/3, p.305.

34. T.L. Jones *ibid* pp.288-89.

35. Calvert paper. Also see, Hoe/Morris pp.46,56; Adams *et al* p.48; Kemp Savage pp.18,20; Strawson p.230; Philip/Taylor p.32.

36. Calvert paper; Hoe/Morris pp.53,56.

37. Calvert paper; "22 SAS Regiment in Malaya", Miller Papers, IWM. Also on the Bridgeford Mission, P. Dennis/J. Grey *Emergency and Confrontation* (St. Leonard's, Australia: Allen & Unwin, 1996) pp.25,45-46.

38. Hoe/Morris p.57.

39. Kemp *Savage* p.19; T.L. Jones *Small Wars* 7/3, p.272.

40. Charters/Tugwell in (eds.) p.210; Strawson pp.230-31; Hoe/Morris pp.51,54-56,58; J.D. Leary p.253; Rooney pp.139,141.

41. Calvert interview. On the Rhodesian government, Hoe/Morris pp.68-69.

42. Calvert paper.

43. Calvert paper; Seymour p.270; Ladd *Operations* p.201; Kemp *Savage* p.18.

44. McGregor interview, 19 May 1996; Hoe/Morris pp.53, and cf. p.64, citing Bob Bennett that 30-40 of the 'M' Squadron went on to Malaya; Hoe p.265; Ladd *Operations* pp.106-07; "22 SAS Regiment in Malaya", Miller Papers, IWM; Maj. C.L.D. Newell *The Sphere*, who has been called 'Mr. SAS'; Darman p.190, who referred to Woodhouse as "the father of the modern SAS", though step-father is probably a more accurate description! Airbne. Forces notes, n.d. (1950), Box 4, Calvert Papers, IWM.

45. Calvert paper; Rooney pp.146,151; Weale p.156. Maj. T. Greville-Bell, to Lt.-Col. J.M. Calvert, 14 Jan. 1951, Box 4, Calvert Papers, IWM.

46. Hoe/Morris p.83; Ladd *Operations* p.201; Strawson pp.230-31; Seymour p.270.

47. Kemp *Savage* p.19; Hoe/Morris p.71; Hoe p.473; Strawson p.231; Col. J.M. Woodhouse 'Some personal observations on the campaign in Malaya' *Army Quarterly* 66 (Apr. 1953) pp.69-74; White p.136; Warner p.201, though he also refers to 1952 as the 'official date' of the regular SAS's establishment, pp.7-8. 'D' Squadron training in, Weale *Secret* pp.156-57.

48. For instance, Hoe/Morris *passim*.

Chapter 10- The SAS family

1. Will Fowler's *SAS- behind the lines* was said to "bring together in one book the story of the world-wide Regimental family", pp.11-12, but there's no mention of the International Squadron or the ME Rangers. GHQFELF, "Report on the Malayan Scouts (SAS Regt)", to WO, 22 Dec. 1951, WO216/494; Hoe/Morris p.105; Darman p.163.

2. Maj. Hart to C.O. 21 SAS, 23 May 1951, WO218/223. It's possible that Hart was referring to other former units such as the War Crimes Organisation or 'M'

Squadron, though, equally, he appears to have been looking to future additions as well. Re SAS Middle Eastern arrangements, Amphibious Warfare HQ Staff Meeting, notes, 13 Mar. 1952, DEFE2/1798.

3. Kemp *Savage* p.10; Hoe/Morris pp.71-72. On exercises, 21 SAS HQ, to Combined Operations HQ, 2 Mar. 1950, DEFE2/1621.

4. Kemp *Savage* p.12. Re 21 and 22 SAS, MoD, to Brig. F. MacLean, 24 Sept. 1952, PREM11/47 (with thanks to Dr. R. Aldrich).

5. For some of these cases and the background to them see, P. Brogan *World conflicts* (London: Bloomsbury, 1992) pp.621-26.

6. For instance, Hoe/Morris, Introduction; *SAS- Britain's Secret Warriors* (Chester: DD Video, 1994).

7. Aldrich in Gorst/Johnman/Lucas (eds.) p.209.

Appendix
1. T.L. Jones *Postwar* pp.119,133; Brig. C.R. Price, VCOS Paper, 'Deception in Malaya', 13 June; Note by Commandant, VISTRE, 21 June; GHQFELF, to MoD, 21 June; COS(50)95, 26 June; J.A. Drew, London Controlling Section, to Air Marshal Elliot, 27 June; MoD, to GHQFELF, 29 June; Col. Wild, 'Deception: Singapore and Malaya', 19 July; COS Paper, 'Deception in Malaya and the Far East', 20 July; GHQFELF, to MoD, 25 July; GHQFELF, to MoD, 2 Aug.; Lt.-Gen. Brownjohn also proposed Col. E.H.L. Jacobs-Larkcom, who was on special duties from 1940 - Gen. Brownjohn, to Col. Wild, 31 Aug. - other candidates were Lt.-Col. M.H.F. Waring, who was in Rhodesia - COS(50)180, 28 July - and Col. Koch de Gooreynd, COS(50)175, 6 Nov. 1950; MoD, to GHQFELF, 19 Jan. 1951, DEFE28/189. On Clarke, see T.L. Jones *Origins, passim.*

Bibliography

Primary sources:
a) **Unpublished official records-**

Airborne Forces Museum, Aldershot.
HQ Palestine Diary of Events, 1945-48.

Churchill College Archives, Cambridge.
Sir W.S. Churchill Papers.

Imperial War Museum, London.
H. Miller Papers.
Field-Marshal B. Montgomery Papers.
J. Rymer-Jones Memoir.
Brig. Calvert Papers. [privileged access to uncatalogued collection, 2001]

India Office Library and Records, British Library, London.
War Staff Papers.

Liddell Hart Centre for Military Archives, London.
Count J.A. Dobrski Papers.
Brig. R.W. McLeod Papers.
Maj.-Gen. Sir H. Pyman Papers.
Maj.-Gen. Sir H. Stockwell Papers.

Middle East Centre, Oxford.
Gen. Sir A. Cunningham Papers.

Public Record Office of England & Wales, Kew.
Air Ministry, AIR24/760, AIR46/30.
Cabinet Papers, CAB80/103, CAB131/4.
Colonial Office, CO537/2270, 3847, 3872, 4751.
Chiefs of Staff/MoD, DEFE2/1143, 1621, 1798. DEFE5/11, DEFE11/36, 37.
Foreign Office, FO371/48264, 48273, 58673, 58705-08, 58714, 58716, 58759, 58852, 67005, 67028, 67031, 72207, 72212-13, 72252, 72332, 78348, 78456.
Premier's Office, PREM11/47.
Treasury, T303/1, 4.

War Office, WO32/10921, 10993, 11436, 11538, 13824, 13382, 13867, 13868, 13882. WO33/2501, 2608, 2628. WO106/5884. WO166/16366, 17184. WO170/ 7558, 7654. WO202/893, 898, 908, 946-50, 952, 988. WO212/213. WO216/494. WO218/118, 223. WO231/38. WO232/10B. WO261/547, 637, 715, 759, 761, 771-72, 774. WO268/8, 10. WO350/3.

Queen's Own Hussars Regimental Museum, Warwick.
3rd. Hussars Papers, 1945-46.

Rhodes House Library, Oxford.
A.H.P. Humphrey Papers.
J.C. Litton Papers.

Suffolk Regiment Museum, Bury St. Edmunds.
Suffolk Regiment War Diaries, 1950-51.

b) Other unpublished records-
Author's collection.
Brig. J.M. Calvert, "COIN policies", 20 Mar. 1991. *Letters*: Brig. Calvert, 20 Mar. 1991; Z. Eytan, 14 Sept. 1990; E.P. Horne, 19 Aug. 1997; J. Mavrikis, 30 Apr. 1996; Lt.-Col. C.H.T. MacFetridge, 5 May 1998; Lt.-Col. D.G.C. Sutherland, - May 1996, 8 May 1996; Col. J. Waddy, 24 Sept. 1996. *Interviews*: Brig. Calvert, 10 Apr. 1991; Maj. B. Dillon, 10 May 1998; Mr. Dougan, (British Army Transport Museum), 15 Aug. 1996; E.J. Kanakakis, 2 Apr. 2001; A. Kemp, 16 May, 26 May 1996; J. Mavrikis, 16 May 1996; Maj. A. McGregor, 19 May, 2 Sept. 1996; G. Stevens, 9 July 1996; J. Thomas, 10 July 1996; Maj. M. Ward, 31 July 1996; S. Dorril, 10 July 2006.

c) Published official records.
Col. A.C. Newman *Combined operations, 1940-42* (London: HMSO, 1943).
House of Commons *Hansard, 1946-50* (5th. Series).
Special report by H.M.G. to the Council of the League of Nations on the progress of Iraq during the period 1920-31 (London: HMSO, 1931)
M.R.D. Foot *SOE in France* (London: HMSO, 1966)
P. Dennis/J. Grey *Emergency and Confrontation* (St. Leonard's, Australia: Allen & Unwin, 1996)

d) Memoirs.

C. Allen *The savage wars of peace* (London: M. Joseph, 1990) [edited collection]

H. Andrew *Who won the Malayan Emergency?* (Singapore: Graham Brash, 1995)

Capt. P. Brutton *A captain's mandate* (London: Leo Cooper, 1996)

Brig. J.M. Calvert *Fighting mad* (London: Airlife Books, 1996)

Prisoners of hope (London: Corgi, 1973)

Maj. J. Cooper *One of the Originals* (London: Pan, 1991)

Col. J.P. Cross *Jungle warfare: experience and encounters* (London: Arms & Armour Press, 1986)

Maj. R. Farran *Winged Dagger* (London: Collins, 1948)

Brig. B.E. Fergusson *The trumpet in the hall* (London: Collins, 1970)

X. Fielding *Hide and seek* (London: Secker & Warburg, 1954)

L. Large *One man's SAS* (London: W. Kimber, 1987)

Lt.-Col. D.G.C. Sutherland *He who dares* (London: Leo Cooper, 1998)

Sir R.G.K. Thompson *Make for the hills* (London: Leo Cooper, 1989)

Maj. M. Ward *Greek assignments, 1943-48* (Athens, Greece: Lycabettus Press, 1992)

Lt. R.P.P. Westerling *A challenge to terror* (London: W. Kimber, 1952)

Secondary sources:
a) Unpublished works.

D.A. Charters *Insurgency and counter-insurgency in Palestine, 1945-47* (Univ. of London, PhD, 1980)

D.J. Clark *The colonial police and anti-terrorism: Bengal, 1930-36, Palestine, 1937-47, Cyprus, 1955-59* (Univ. of Oxford, D.Phil., 1978)

G.J.L. Hall *The guerilla as mid-wife* (Univ. of Alabama, PhD, 1987)

B.R. Hoffman *Jewish terrorist activities and the British government in Palestine, 1939-47* (Univ. of Oxford, PhD, 1985)

T.L. Jones *The development of British counter-insurgency policies and doctrine, 1945-52* (Univ. of London, PhD, 1992)

P. Melshen *Pseudo-operations: the use by British and American armed forces of deception in counter-insurgencies, 1945-73* (Cambridge, PhD, 1995)

J.H. Pederson *Focal point of conflict* (Univ. of Michigan, PhD 1974)

S. Tsadka *Guerilla war in Palestine, 1944-47* (Univ. of London, PhD, 1992)

b) Published works.

Articles, chapters, etc.:

R.J. Aldrich 'Secret intelligence for a post-war world: reshaping the British intelligence community, 1944-51' in (ed.) *British intelligence, strategy and the Cold War, 1945-51* (London: Routledge, 1992)

'Unquiet in death: the post-war survival of the 'Special Operations Executive', 1945-51' in A. Gorst/L. Johnman/W.S. Lucas (eds.) *Contemporary British history, 1931-61* (London: Pinter, 1991)

/J. Zametica 'The rise and decline of a strategic concept: the Middle East, 1945-51' in Aldrich (ed.)

Anon. (P. Warner) 'Bob Bennett' *Daily Telegraph* (London: 7 Feb. 1996)

M. Bennett 'The German experience' in I.F.W. Beckett (ed.) *The roots of counter-insurgency* (London: Blandford, 1988)

D.A. Charters 'Special operations in COIN: The Farran Case, Palestine, 1947' *Journal of the RUSI* 124/2 (June 1979)

/M. Tugwell 'From Palestine to Northern Ireland' in (eds.) *Armies in low-intensity conflict* (London: Brassey's, 1989)

C. Chiclet 'The Greek Civil War' in M. Sarafis/M. Eve (eds.) *Background to contemporary Greece* (London: MacMillan, 1990)

Col. R.L. Clutterbuck 'Bertrand Stewart Prize Essay' *Army Quarterly* 66 (Apr. 1953)

Col. J. Hackett 'The employment of special forces' *Journal of the RUSI* 97 (Feb. 1952)

T.L. Jones 'The British Army, and counter-guerilla warfare in transition, 1944-52' *Small wars and insurgencies* 7/3 (Winter 1996)

'The British Army, and counter-guerilla warfare in Greece, 1945-49' *Small wars and insurgencies* 8/1 (Spring 1997)

'The SAS Regiment After World War 2' *Book Collector* (25 May 2005)

J.D Leary 'Searching for a role: the SAS in the Malayan Emergency' *Journal of the Society for Army Historical Research 73* (296) (Winter 1995)

Col. J.C. Murray 'The anti-bandit war' in T. Greene (ed.) *The guerilla and how to fight him* (New York: Praeger, 1962)

Maj. C. Newell 'SAS warfare in the jungle' *The Sphere* (11 Aug. 1956)

'The SAS' *British Army Review* 1 (Sept. 1955)

Capt. D.D. Ranft 'Parachuting in Malaya' *Army Quarterly* 67 (July 1953)

Lt.-Col. R.W. Selton 'The cradle of U.S. Cold War strategy' *Military Review* 46/8 (Aug. 1966)

C. Smith 'Communal conflict and insurrection in Palestine, 1936-48' in D.M. Anderson/D. Killingray (eds.) *Policing and decolonisation* (Manchester: Manchester Univ. Press, 1992)

'Weasal' 'Ferret Force' *Malaya* 1 (Sept. 1952)

Capt. J.M. Woodhouse 'Some personal observations on the employment of special forces in Malaya' *Army Quarterly* 66 (Apr. 1953)

Books:

J. Adams *Secret Armies* (London: Pan, 1989)

/R. Morgan/A. Bambridge *Ambush* (London: Pan, 1988)

R.J. Aldrich (ed.) *British intelligence, strategy and the Cold War, 1944-51* (London: Routledge, 1992)

G.M. Alexander *Prelude to the Truman Doctrine* (Oxford: Clarendon Press, 1982)

T.H. Anderson *The United States, Great Britain and the Cold War* (New York: Univ. of Missouri Press, 1981)

R. Asprey *War in the shadows* (London: MacDonald & Jane's, 1975)

D.D. Avant *Political institutions and military change* (London: Cornell Univ. Press, 1994)

Gen. E. Averoff-Tossizza *By fire and axe* (New York: Caratzas Brothers, 1978)

A. Baker *Battle honours of the British and Commonwealth armies* (London: Ian Allen, 1986)

R.J. Barnet *Intervention and revolution* (New York: Meridian, 1980)

N. Bethell *The Palestine triangle* (London: Futura, 1980)

S. Bidwell *The Chindit war* (London: Hodder & Stoughton, 1979)

G. Blaxland *The regiments depart* (London: W. Kimber, 1971)

J. Bloch/P. Fitzgerald *British intelligence and covert action* (London: Junction Books, 1983)

L.P. Bloomfield/A.C. Leiss *Controlling small wars* (New York: A.A. Knopf, 1969)

T. Bowden *The breakdown of public security* (London: SAGE, 1977)

R. Bradford/M. Dillon *Rogue warrior of the SAS* (London: J. Murray, 1987)

A. Brown (ed.) *Elite forces: the SAS* (London: Orbis, 1986)

S. Bull *SAS* (London: Publishing News, 2000)

D. Buxton *Sword of honour* (Solihull: Elmdon, 1986)

L.E. Cable *A conflict of myths* (New York: New York Univ. Press, 1986)

Field-Marshal Lord M. Carver *War since 1945* (London: Weidenfeld & Nicolson, 1980)

Harding of Petherton (London: Weidenfeld & Nicolson, 1984)

C. Chant *The handbook of British regiments* (London: Routledge, 1988)

D.A. Charters *The British Army and the Jewish insurgency in Palestine, 1945-47* (London: MacMillan, 1989)

/M. Tugwell (eds.) *Armies in low-intensity conflict* (London: Brassey's, 1989)

J. Cloake *Templer, tiger of Malaya* (London: Harrap, 1985)

D.H. Close *The origins of the Greek Civil War* (Harlow, Essex: Longman, 1995)

(ed.) *The Greek Civil War, 1943-50* (London: Routledge, 1993)

Col. R.L. Clutterbuck *The long, long war* (London: Cassell, 1966)

Gen. J. Coates *Suppressing insurgency* (Boulder, Colorado: Westview Press, 1992)

R.J. Compton *The Balkans* (London: Longman, 2002)

K. Connor *Ghost force* (London: Weidenfeld & Nicolson, 1998)

V. Cowles *The phantom major* (London: Crawley Features, 1958)

S. Crawford *The SAS at close quarters* (London: Brown Packaging, 1993)

The SAS encyclopedia (London: Simon & Schuster, 1996)

(ed.) *SAS- the ultimate warriors* (London: Orbis, 1996)

P. Darman *A to Z of the SAS* (London: Brown Packaging, 1993)

SAS: the world's best (London: Brown Packaging, 1994)

Weapons and equipment of the SAS (London: Brown Packaging, 1992)

B. Davies *The SAS- an illustrated history* (London: Virgin, 1996)

The complete encyclopedia of the SAS (London: Virgin, 1998)

S. Dorril *MI6* (London: Fourth Estate, 2000)

Gen. Sir P. de la Billiere *Looking for trouble* (London: Harper Collins, 1994)

Col. M. Dewar *Brushfire wars* (London: BCA, 1992)

D. Eshel *Daring to win* (London: Arms & Armour Press, 1995)

Sir R. Fiennes *Where soldiers fear to tread* (London: NEL, 1976)

M.R.D. Foot *SOE* (London: Mandarin, 1990)

/J.M. Langley *MI9* (London: Futura, 1979)

W. Fowler *SAS- behind enemy lines* (London: Harper Collins, 1997)

N. Gage *Eleni* (New York: Ballantine, 1983)

T. Geraghty *Who dares wins* (London: Fontana, 1980/1992)

This is the SAS (London: Fontana, 1982)

I.S. Hallows *Regiments and corps of the British Army* (London: New Orchard, 1994)

O. Heilbrunn *Partisan warfare* (London: George, Allen & Unwin, 1962)

Warfare in the enemy's rear (London: George, Allen & Unwin, 1963)

P. Harclerode *Para!* (London: Orion, 1996)

Fighting Dirty (London: Cassell, 2001)

R.J.T. Hills *Phantom was there* (London: E. Arnold, 1951)

A. Hoe *David Stirling* (London: Warner, 1994)

/E. Morris *Re-enter the SAS* (London: Leo Cooper, 1994)

R. Hunter *True stories of the SAS* (London: Virgin, 1985/95)

True stories of the SBS (London: Virgin, 1998)

R.R. James *Chindit* (London: J. Murray, 1980)

H. Jones *A new kind of war* (New York: Oxford Univ. Press, 1988)

T. Jones *Postwar counterinsurgency and the SAS, 1945-52: A special type of warfare* (London: Frank Cass, 2001)

SAS: Zero Hour – The Secret Origins of the SAS (Greenhill, 2006)

A. Kemp *The SAS at war, 1941-45* (London: J. Murray, 1991)

SAS- the savage wars of peace 1947 to the present (London: J. Murray, 1994)

The secret hunters (London: M. O'Mara, 1986)

Brig. F. Kitson *Low-intensity warfare* (London: Faber & Faber, 1971)

D. Kousoulas *Revolution and defeat* (London: Oxford Univ. Press, 1965)

J.D. Ladd *Commandos and Rangers of World War Two* (Newton Abbot, Devon: David & Charles, 1989)

SAS operations (London: R. Hale, 1986/99)

The SBS- invisible raiders (Newton Abbot, Devon: David & Charles, 1989)

B. Lapping *The end of Empire* (London: Granada, 1985)

J. Latimer *Deception in war* (London: J. Murray, 2001)

J.E. Lewis (ed.) *SAS and elite forces* (Avonmouth: Siena, 1996)

The handbook of the SAS and elite forces (London: Magpie, 1997)

J. Lewes *Jock Lewes* (London: Leo Cooper, 2000)

M. Lloyd *Special forces* (London: Arms & Armour Press, 1995)

J. Lodwick *The filibusters* (London: Methuen, 1947)

P. Lowe *The origins of the Korean War* (Harlow, Essex: Longman, 1995)

P. MacDonald *The SAS in action* (London: Sidgwick & Jackson, 1990)

D. Mackay *The Malaya Emergency, 1948-60* (London: Brassey's, 1997)

M. McClintock *Instruments of statecraft* (New York: Pantheon, 1992)

J. McCuen *The art of counter-revolutionary warfare* (Harrisburg, Penn.: Stackpole Books, 1966)

P. Mead Orde *Wingate and the historians* (Braunton, Devon: Merlin, 1987)

C. Messenger *The Commandos, 1940-46* (London: Granada, 1988)

T. Mockaitis *British counter-insurgency, 1919-60* (London: MacMillan, 1990)

M. Morgan *Daggers Drawn* (Thrupp, Glouc.: Sutton, 2000)

E. Morris *Guerillas in uniform* (London: Hutchinson, 1989)

Churchill's private armies (London: Hutchinson, 1986)

R. Neillands *In the combat zone* (London: Weidenfeld & Nicolson, 1997)

Maj. E. O'Ballance *The Greek Civil War* (London: Faber & Faber, 1966)

Capt. J. Paget *Counter-insurgency campaigning* (London: Faber & Faber, 1967)

J. Parker *SBS* (London: Headstone, 1997)

C. Philip/A. Taylor *Inside the SAS* (London: Bloomsbury, 1992)

B. Pitt *Special Boat Squadron* (London: Corgi, 1985)

T. Pocock *Fighting general* (London: Collins, 1973)

J. Ramsay *SAS- the soldiers' story* (London: MacMillan, 1996)

D. Rooney *Mad Mike* (London: Pen & Sword, 1997)

Wingate and the Chindits (London: Arms & Armour, 1994)

T. Rowland-Entwistle *The SAS* (Hove, E. Sussex: Wayland, 1987)

W. Seymour *British special forces* (London: Sidgwick & Jackson, 1985)

A. Short *The Communist insurrection in Malaya* (London: F. Muller, 1975)

Maj. J.G. Shortt *British special forces 1945 to the present* (London: Arms & Armour Press, 1986)

The SAS (London: Osprey, 1981)

H.J. Simson *British rule, and rebellion* (Edinburgh: W. Blackwood, 1937)

J. Simpson *The quiet operator* (London: Leo Cooper, 1993)

Brig. E.D. Smith *Battle for Burma* (London: B.T. Batsford, 1979)

Victory of a sort (London: R. Hale, 1986)

J. Smyth *Bolo Whistler* (London: F. Muller, 1967)

L. Spicer *The Suffolks in Malaya* (Peterborough: Lawton Phelps, 1998)

G. Stewart *Silent heroes: the story of the SAS* (London: M. O'Mara, 1997)

Gen. J. Strawson *A history of the SAS Regiment* (London: Grafton, 1986)

R. Stubbs *Hearts and minds in guerilla warfare* (London: Oxford Univ. Press, 1989)

C. Sykes *Orde Wingate* (London: Collins, 1959)

Gen. J. Thompson *The Imperial War Museum book of warfare behind enemy lines* (London: Sidgwick & Jackson, 1998)

The Imperial War Museum book of the war in Burma, 1942-45 (London: Sidgwick & Jackson, 2002)

L. Thompson *The SAS* (Osceola, Wis.: MotorBooks International, 1994)

Sir R.G.K. Thompson *Defeating Communist insurgency* (London: Chatto & Windus, 1966)

C.J. Townshend *Britain's civil wars* (London: Faber, 1986)

D. Tulloch *Wingate in peace and war* (London: Futura, 1972)

H. Vlavianos *Greece, 1941-49* (London: MacMillan, 1992)

P. Warner *The SAS* (London: Warner, 1971/92)

A. Weale *Secret warfare* (London: Hodder & Stoughton, 1997)

The real SAS (London: Sidgwick & Jackson, 1998)

N. West *Secret war* (London: J. Curtis, 1992)

The Friends (London: Weidenfeld & Nicolson, 1988)

T. White *The making of the SAS and the world's elite forces* (London: Brown Packaging, 1992)

The handbook of the SAS and elite forces (London: Magpie, 1997)

Fighting skills of the SAS and special forces (London: Magpie, 1997)

Swords of lightning (London: Brassey's, 1992)

L. Whittaker *Some talk of private armies* (Harpenden, Herts.: Albanium Press, 1984)

Who was who, 1951-60 (London: A. & C. Black, 1960)

P. Wilkinson/J.B. Astley *Gubbins and SOE* (London: Leo Cooper, 1993)

L.S. Wittner *United States intervention in Greece, 1943-49* (New York: Colombia Univ. Press, 1982)

E. Wood *SAS and other special forces* (London: Hodder & Stoughton, 1996)

C.M. Woodhouse *Apple of discord* (Reston, Va.: W.B. O'Neill, 1985)

The struggle for Greece (London: Granada, 1976)

S.G. Xydis *Greece and the Great Powers, 1944-47* (Thessaloniki: Institute for Balkan Studies, 1963)

B.A. Young *The Artists and the SAS* (London: 21 SAS (TA), 1960)

S. Zadka (Tsadka) *Blood in Zion* (London: Brassey's, 1995)

Videos:

SAS- Britain's secret warriors (DD Video, 1994)

SAS (W.H. Smith Exclusive, 1995)

Index